Colourful
Family
Cooking

Colourful Family Cooking

Marguerite Patten

Galley Press

Acknowledgements

The publishers would like to acknowledge the help of the following in providing photographs: **American Rice Council**: Chinese vegetable soup 40; **Argentine Beef Bureau**: Argentine beef soup 50; **British Egg Information Service**: Pastel de Tortillas 79; **Cadbury Schweppes Food Advisory Service Birmingham**: Gooseberry sparkle 103, Chocolate soufflé 108, Dauphine potatoes 39; **Chiltonian Ltd**: Composite photograph 63; **Danish Agricultural Producers**: Glazed forehock of bacon 18; **Dutch Dairy Bureau**: Cheese soufflé 84, Leeks mornay 44; **Eden Vale Ltd**: Composite photograph 95, Cottage cheese salads 58; **Fruit Producers' Council**: Jellied fruit snow 103, Chicken peach salad 57, Prawn and rice salad 59; **John West Foods Ltd**: Store cupboard omelette 79, Salmon chowder 53; **Herring Industry Board**: Prepared herrings 22, Normandy herrings 29; **National Dairy Council**: Prawn quiche 88, Haddock and mushroom scallops 28; **New Zealand Lamb Information Bureau**: Composite photograph 21, Crown roast of lamb 7, Roast lamb with apricot nut stuffing 10; **RHM Foods Ltd**: Christmas pudding 97, Fruit flan 99, Ham en croûte 18, Butterfly cakes 118, Popovers 122, Scotch Pancake 133, Shrove Tuesday pancakes 83, Old English chicken pie 86, Pizza 89, Green salad 55, Mexican macaroni 43, Stuffed peppers 47, Eskimo risotto 65; **Stork Cookery Service**: Composite photograph 119; **Tabasco sauce**: Roast pork with prune and apple stuffing 10, Corned beef plate tart 87, Creamed turkey duchesse 34; **Tate & Lyle Ltd**: Brandy snaps 117; **T. Wall & Son (Meat & Handy Foods) Ltd**: Sausage twists and sausage cheese savouries 66; **White Fish Authority**: Sole Sevilla 24, Goujons of fish 27, Fish in a jacket 30.

This edition first published 1977 by
Octopus Books Limited
59 Grosvenor Street
London W1

© 1977 Octopus Books Limited

Reprinted 1983

ISBN 0 7064 1045 9

Produced by Mandarin Publishers Limited
22a, Westlands Road, Quarry Bay, Hong Kong

Printed in Hong Kong

Contents

Metric Conversion Chart

The following table shows both an exact conversion from Imperial to metric measures and the recommended working equivalent.

weight:

imperial oz.	metric grams	working equivalent grams
1	28·35	25
2	56·7	50
4	113·4	100
8	226·8	200
12	340·2	300
1·01 lb.	453	400
1·1 lb.	$\frac{1}{2}$ kilo	
2·2 lb.	1 kilo	

liquid measures:

imperial	exact conversion	working equivalent
$\frac{1}{4}$ pint (1 gill)	142 millilitres	150 ml.
$\frac{1}{2}$ pint	284 ml.	300 ml.
1 pint	568 ml.	600 ml.
$1\frac{3}{4}$ pints	994 ml.	1 litre

linear measures:

1 inch	$2\frac{1}{2}$ cm.
2 inch	5 cm.
3 inch	$7\frac{1}{2}$ cm.
6 inch	15 cm.

It is useful to note for easy reference that: 1 kilogramme (1000 grammes) = 2·2 lb. therefore $\frac{1}{2}$ kilo (500 grammes) = roughly = 1 lb. 1 litre roughly = $1\frac{3}{4}$ imperial pints therefore $\frac{1}{2}$ litre roughly = 1 imperial pint

one
MEAT COOKERY

Meat is one of the most popular and important protein foods in most countries of the world. It is also one of the most expensive and, in order to make the best use of meat, it is worthwhile learning about the various cuts, and to recognise them in the butcher's shop or supermarket, so you may choose the best kind of meat for each and every purpose.

When one is busy the quick cooking cuts of meat for frying and grilling are an obvious choice. Because these are prime cuts they are appreciably more expensive than meat for stewing. The Blue Prints on pages 11 and 12 give information on the best way to grill and fry meats to make them as tender and appetising as possible. One of the secrets of success when frying and grilling meat is to seal the outside of the meat quickly, so the meat remains moist, which is why the Blue Prints stress the importance of this. I hope they will also give some new suggestions of the meats that may be fried and grilled. For example, the obvious choice when one wants a Wiener Schnitzel is veal, but fillets of pork are cheaper and really have more flavour than veal.

Nothing is more imposing than a really good joint of roasted meat; again this demands high quality, but if you make use of the slow roasting method on page 8 you can use the slightly cheaper cuts of meat. Stuffing and interesting accompaniments not only add flavour and help to keep the meat moist, but enable one to serve more portions from a joint, and many fruits, vegetables and herbs can be used in stuffings and sauces.

Every country has its own traditional way of cooking meat and in countries where the quality of meat is not perhaps as good as one would wish, the cooks have become experts in slow cooking to tenderise meat in casseroles, stews and cur-ries. There is a wide range of such recipes to choose from. Be adventurous in the vegetables and fruit you add to meats in stews and casseroles. Acid fruit is like wine, it gives flavour and helps to tenderise meat.

Britain has a reputation for excellent meat puddings and pies and the well-known and new recipes on pages 16 and 17 give the kind of meat dishes you will enjoy throughout the year. I have also included a selection of curries which I hope will show that spices should not obliterate but complement the flavour of meat.

Never feel that offal, or the specialist meats, are less interesting or nutritious than other cuts. The very wide variety of textures and flavours provided by these meats (liver, sweetbreads, tripe, kidneys) make them appetising and adaptable.

When one is making a fairly complicated meat dish, or buying a large quantity of meat, it is a good idea to freeze part of the dish or some of the meat to use on future occasions. On most pages in this part you will find information on home freezing of the meat or the completed dish.

There is nothing to beat the flavour of a succulent roasted joint; when you buy prime cuts there is no point in 'dressing-up' the meat, except to serve it with appropriate sauces and stuffings.

In most homes today the accepted method of roasting is in a meat tin in the oven; purists argue that this is *not* roasting, it *is* baking and that the only correct method is to cook the meat on a turning spit over open heat. If you have a rotisserie attachment on your cooker use this, for you do obtain more even browning over the *whole* joint than in a tin. If the rotisserie is under the grill then the cooking times are the same as given for fast roasting. If in the oven you can select which method you prefer—fast or slow cooking.

For top quality meat you may choose the heat at which you cook this. Personally I prefer fast roasting, for I believe the meat retains more flavour although it may shrink a little more in cooking. If the meat has been chilled, frozen or is of slightly cheaper quality then the slower cooking is better for you achieve a more tender joint.

The table that follows the Blue Print assumes the meat is fresh *not* frozen.

● **AVOID** *Trying to roast cuts of meat recommended for stewing: Using more fat than necessary, for this only hardens the outside:*

Roasting Meat

Over-cooking, this destroys flavour and texture and dries the joint.
● **TO RECTIFY** *Look at the joint during cooking, if you have been too generous with the fat pour away any excess: Dried meat is spoiled meat, so you must camouflage it with sauce or gravy.*
● **TO SLIMMERS** *A sensible way to cook meat, avoid the fatty outside, stuffings and thickened sauces or gravy.*

Blue Print Recipe

Roasting Meat

To prepare Buy meat to give a *minimum* of 8–12 oz. per person (including the weight of the bone). *Allow frozen meat to defrost.* Wash and dry the meat. Make any stuffing required, see this page and page 10. Put the meat into the roasting tin, in foil, or on the spit. Spread any fat recommended over the top of the meat. The amount of fat suggested under the meats must be increased by about 2 oz. ($\frac{1}{4}$C) if roasting potatoes round the joint.
To cook
1. IN AN OPEN ROASTING TIN Allow the times given under each meat. You can 'baste' with a little fat during cooking if wished. This means spooning some of the hot fat over the meat. The advantage of this is that it keeps the meat moist and encourages it to crisp, but it is not essential.
2. IN FOIL You need to wrap the meat and any fat in the foil and to time as under each meat, but you must allow about 20 minutes extra cooking time or set the oven 25°F or 1 Mark higher on the gas cooker. If you wish the meat to crisp and brown, open the foil for the last 20–30 minutes. There is no need to 'baste' during cooking.
3. IN A COVERED ROASTING TIN Try and use one large enough to give some space above and around the meat. This means the fat splashes the lid, drops back on to the meat and so is self-basting; it will brown well. If required, to be crisp, the lid should be removed for the last 20–30 minutes. Allow higher temperature or extra time as for foil.
4. SPIT ROASTING Time as for slow or fast roasting, but melt the fat and brush over the whole joint. 'Baste' if wished during cooking.
To serve As the suggestions on this page, and seasonal vegetables or cold with salad.

Choice and Timing for Roast Meat

Fast roasting: Set the oven to hot, this varies slightly with cookers, start at 425–450°F, Gas Mark 6–7. After 15–20 minutes lower to moderately hot, 375–400°F, Gas Mark 5–6.
Slow roasting: Set the oven at very moderate to moderate, approximately 350°F, Gas Mark 3–4. Keep at this setting.
Very small joints: accepted timing for meat has been based on larger-sized joints than many of us buy today. For a really small joint (about 2 lb.) allow an extra 10–15 minutes on the *total* cooking time.

BEEF

Cuts: *Fast or slow roasting:* Châteaubriand, sirloin, rib.
Slow roasting: topside, aitch-bone, fresh brisket.
It is a sin to over-cook prime beef, but cheaper cuts are better medium-cooked.
Fat required and timing: Use minimum of fat 1–2 oz. Sirloin needs no fat.
Fast roasting: Underdone (rare)—15 minutes per lb., 15 minutes over.
Medium to well done—20 minutes per lb. and 20 minutes over.
Slow roasting: Underdone (rare)—25 minutes per lb., 25 minutes over.
Medium to well done—35 minutes per lb. and 35 minutes over.
Serve with: Yorkshire pudding, horseradish sauce, thin gravy.
To give interest: Insert tiny strips of peeled onion into meat at regular intervals.

LAMB

Cuts: *All joints suitable for fast or slow roasting:* leg, shoulder, loin, saddle, best end of neck, breast.

Fat required and timing: Use minimum of fat 1–2 oz.
Fast roasting: Medium-cooked—20 minutes per lb., 20 minutes over. Reduce time slightly if preferred slightly 'pink'.
Slow roasting: 35 minutes per lb., 35 minutes over.
Serve with: Mint sauce, thin gravy.
To give interest: Put 1–2 sprigs fresh rosemary over lamb before roasting, or cut 1–2 cloves garlic into thin 'slivers' and insert into joint before roasting.

MUTTON OR HOGGET

Cuts: As lamb, but better slow roasted.
Fat required and timing: Mutton needs no fat. Timing as lamb.
Serve with: Onion sauce or red currant jelly.
To give interest: As lamb.

PORK

Cuts: Use open roasting tin for a crisper crackling.
I suggest fast roasting for pork but joints are suitable for fast or slow roasting: leg, fillet, bladebone, spare-rib, loin.
Fat required and timing: Use a little melted fat, lard or oil, brushed over the meat fat. Sprinkle a little salt over joint if wished. Score fat to encourage crispness.

Roast rib of beef

Blue Print Recipe

Good Gravy

Gravy can 'make or mar' a roasted joint. It should incorporate the delicious flavours from the roasting tin.

To make If you have stock from meat bones then use this as the basis of the gravy, but if no meat stock is available then use vegetable stock, obtained after straining the vegetables. This contains valuable mineral salts, so it is nutritious as well as being a source of flavour. Allow about $\frac{1}{2}$–$\frac{3}{4}$ pint ($1\frac{1}{3}$–2C) gravy for 4 people; the amount depends upon personal taste.

When the meat is cooked pour away all the fat from the roasting tin except for about 1 tablespoon. The fat poured out can be used for dripping. If convenient make the gravy in the meat tin, if not pour the fat and any 'residue' of tiny pieces of meat, etc. into a pan.
For a thin gravy Blend 1 level tablespoon flour into the fat.
To cook Heat for a few minutes or until the 'roux' turns golden brown. This is quite a risky business as it can burn, so you may like to add a little gravy browning (and flavouring) instead and just use the flour as a thickening. Gradually work in about $\frac{1}{2}$ pint stock, bring to the boil and cook until slightly thickened. Strain and use.
For a thick gravy Proceed as above but use nearly 2 level tablespoons flour to the 1 tablespoon fat.

Roasting Meat

Buy loin of lamb or 2 best end of neck joints, or loin of pork. Chine the meat, or ask the butcher to do this, and trim the bones. Tie into a circle (Crown).

Put into the roasting tin, protect the bones with foil and put the stuffing in the middle. Calculate weight of joint *and* stuffing, roast as this page.

If serving underdone beef the juices that flow from the meat may be served instead of gravy.

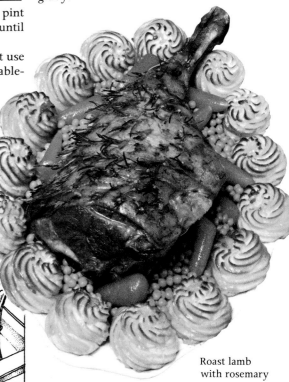

Roast lamb with rosemary

Fast roasting: 25 minutes per lb., 25 minutes over.
Slow roasting: 35 minutes per lb., 35 minutes over. Pork must be well cooked.
Serve with: Apple sauce, sage and onion or other stuffing, thick gravy.
To give interest: Put 1–2 leaves fresh sage on joint before roasting. Add whole cored, not peeled, dessert apples to the roasting tin, cook about 30–40 minutes. Pour over fresh orange juice during cooking.

VEAL

Cuts: *All joints suitable for fast or slow roasting:* leg, fillet, loin, best end of neck, breast.
Fat required and timing: Use plenty of fat, about 4 oz. ($\frac{1}{2}$C) and keep basting during cooking or wrap in foil to keep joint moist.
Fast roasting: 25 minutes per lb., 25 minutes over.
Slow roasting: 35–40 minutes per lb., 35–40 minutes over. Veal must be well cooked.
Serve with: Veal stuffing, roasted sausages, bacon rolls, thick gravy.
To give interest: Roll joint in a little seasoning to which is added finely grated lemon rind. Baste with a little fresh lemon juice during cooking.

Crown roast of lamb

Well chosen accompaniments provide extra flavour, counteract undue richness, as with pork, give a moist texture to drier meat, such as veal, and turn a *good* roasted joint into a memorable dish. Make a 'pocket' in the meat and put in the stuffing, or spread on boned meat, roll and tie firmly, then roast. *Always calculate the total weight of meat plus stuffing for cooking time.* If preferred put the stuffing into a separate dish and bake in the oven for 40–50 minutes.

● **AVOID** *Too dry stuffings.*
● **SHORT CUTS** *Use the liquidiser to make crumbs, or buy packet stuffing or bottled or canned sauces.*

TO SERVE WITH BEEF

Horseradish sauce: Whip $\frac{1}{4}$ pint ($\frac{2}{3}$C) thick cream, gradually whisk in $\frac{1}{4}$ pint ($\frac{2}{3}$C) thin cream and 2–3 teaspoons lemon juice or vinegar. Add 3–4 tablespoons grated fresh horseradish, seasoning and 3–4 teaspoons sugar. *Serves 5–6.*
New look: Blend 2–3 tablespoons shelled chopped walnuts with the sauce.

TO SERVE WITH LAMB

Apricot nut stuffing: Drain a medium-sized can of apricots, chop the fruit and blend with 3 oz. (1C) soft breadcrumbs, 2–3 tablespoons chopped peanuts or walnuts, 2 oz. ($\frac{1}{4}$C) softened margarine and the grated rind and juice of 1 orange and 1 lemon. Season well and bind with some of the juice from the can and 1 egg. *Serves 5–6.*
Pineapple nut stuffing: Use canned pineapple instead of apricots.
Mint sauce: Chop enough mint leaves to give about 5 tablespoons, add 2–3 tablespoons sugar and 3–4 tablespoons vinegar. *Serves 4–5.*
Onion sauce: Peel, chop and cook 2 large onions in about $\frac{1}{2}$ pint ($1\frac{1}{3}$C) well seasoned water. Strain the liquid and make a sauce

with $1\frac{1}{2}$ oz. butter, $1\frac{1}{2}$ oz. flour, $\frac{1}{2}$ pint ($1\frac{1}{3}$C) milk and $\frac{1}{4}$ pint ($\frac{2}{3}$C) onion stock. When thickened add the onions and season well. *Serves 5–6.*

TO SERVE WITH PORK

Apple sauce: Simmer peeled, sliced apples in a very little water until soft, sieve, beat or emulsify in the liquidiser until smooth, sweeten to taste.
New look: Add ground cinnamon, a little dried fruit or orange segments to the sauce, or serve an orange sauce (see page 19).
Sage and onion stuffing: Peel, chop and cook 2–3 large onions for 10 minutes in $\frac{1}{4}$ pint ($\frac{2}{3}$C) water. Season well, strain, then blend with 3 oz. (1C) soft breadcrumbs, 1–2 teaspoons chopped fresh sage or $\frac{1}{2}$ teaspoon dried sage and 2 oz. ($\frac{1}{3}$C) shredded suet. Bind with onion stock and/or an egg. *Serves 5–6.*
Prune and apple stuffing: Soak 8 oz. (1C) prunes overnight, drain, stone and chop. Mix with 2 oz. ($\frac{3}{4}$C) soft breadcrumbs, 2 peeled diced raw apples, grated rind and juice of 1 orange, seasoning, 1 teaspoon ground cinnamon, 1–2 tablespoons chopped parsley and 1 egg blended with $\frac{1}{2}$ teaspoon Tabasco sauce. Tabasco sauce is very hot, so reduce to $\frac{1}{4}$ teaspoon if wished. *Serves 7–8.*

TO SERVE WITH VEAL

Veal (parsley and thyme) stuffing: Blend 4 oz. ($1\frac{1}{3}$C) soft breadcrumbs, 1–2 tablespoons chopped parsley, 2 oz. ($\frac{1}{3}$C) shredded suet, 1–2 teaspoons chopped fresh thyme or good pinch dried thyme, grated rind and juice of 1 lemon and 1 egg. *Serves 5–6.*

Accompaniments to Roast Meat

Roast Potatoes

These are the favourite accompaniment with most roast joints. Peel the potatoes. If you like them to be 'floury' inside, then par-boil in salted water for about 10 minutes only and strain, otherwise use them uncooked. Roll the potatoes in the hot fat in the roasting tin (round the joint) or heat 2–3 oz. ($\frac{1}{4}$–$\frac{3}{8}$C) fat, lard or clarified dripping in a separate tin. Cook for approximately 45 minutes (for small to medium-sized potatoes) at the temperature given for fast roasting. Slow roasting is not suitable for potatoes.

A Perfect Yorkshire Pudding

Although this is the 'classic' accompaniment to roast beef, many people enjoy it with other roast joints. Sieve 4 oz. (1C) flour (preferably plain) with a good pinch salt, add 1 egg then gradually beat in $\frac{1}{2}$ pint ($1\frac{1}{3}$C) milk or milk and water.

There are two ways of producing the perfect Yorkshire pudding. The old traditional way is to lift the meat from the roasting tin and pour away all the fat, *except* about 1 tablespoon. Pour the batter into the tin and cook with the meat on a trivet, or on the shelf above. Alternatively to give a very well-risen pudding, put about $\frac{1}{2}$–1 oz. fat in a tin. Heat, then pour in the batter. Cook in the hottest part of the oven until well risen and brown.

You cannot cook a Yorkshire pudding slowly, so it is only possible if you have chosen fast roasting of the meat. Even then it is best to raise the oven temperature, it must be hot to very hot, 450–475°F, Gas Mark 7–8. Pour in the batter, cook for 10 minutes at this temperature, then lower the heat again to moderately hot. Complete the cooking, total time about 35 minutes, lift out and serve.

Roast pork with prune and apple stuffing (left)

Roast lamb with apricot nut stuffing (below)

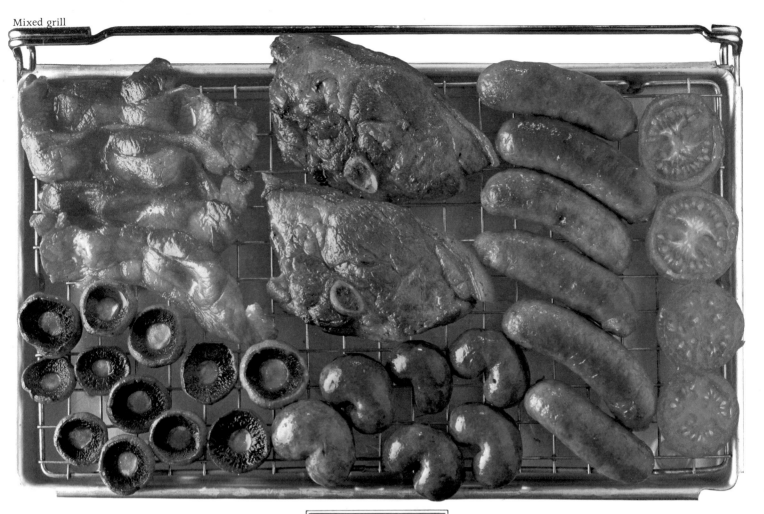

Grilling is undoubtedly one of the best methods of cooking prime quality meats, for they retain the maximum flavour and are more easily digested than when fried.

Blue Print Recipe

Grilling Meat

Switch or turn on the grill, so it is very hot before cooking commences, except for gammon.

To prepare To grill tomatoes and mushrooms put into the grill pan, top with a little melted butter or margarine or fat, season. Grill for a few minutes, then put the meat on the grid of the pan and cook with the meat; or see Mixed Grill.

Choose The same cuts of meat and time the cooking as for frying on the next page. Season the meat if wished. Brush with a little melted fat (the amount needed is about half that for shallow frying).

To cook Grill quickly for 2–3 minutes, or until the outside is sealed. Turn the meat with two knives or tongs, do not pierce with the prongs of a fork as this allows the meat juices to escape. Cook quickly for 2–3 minutes on the second side. Lower the heat slightly and/or move the grill pan further away from the heat and continue cooking until meat is tender. A Châteaubriand (very thick steak) can be grilled easily as you can move the grill pan away from the heat after sealing the outside.

To serve With grilled tomatoes, mushrooms or maître d'hôtel butter and watercress.

Grilling Meat

● **AVOID** *Grilling too slowly or putting the food under a cold grill (with the exception of gammon, where the grill is only heated when the gammon is put under to prevent the fat 'curling'): Allowing the food to dry, baste well with melted fat. Serve grilled food as soon as it is ready.*

● **TO RECTIFY** *If the grill is too cool, remove the pan, heat the grill until red and glowing, then replace the pan: If the grilled meat is dry top with a sauce or maître d'hôtel butter.*

● **TO SLIMMERS** *An ideal cooking method.*

Mexicali Lamb

1 tablespoon oil; $\frac{1}{2}$–1 tablespoon vinegar; 1 tablespoon tomato purée; 1 tablespoon made mustard; seasoning; good pinch garlic salt; 4 large or 8 small lamb chops; 4 tomatoes.

Blend the oil, vinegar, purée, mustard and seasonings. Halve the tomatoes, brush meat and tomatoes with oil mixture and grill as Blue Print. Serve with chipped potatoes and mushrooms. *Serves 4.*

Mixed Grill

4 lamb chops (in the picture are chump chops); 4–8 sausages; 4 tomatoes; about 12 mushrooms; seasoning; little fat, margarine or butter; 4 rashers bacon. *To garnish:* watercress.

Put the chops and sausages on the rack of the grill pan. Halve the tomatoes, wash and dry the mushrooms (there is no need to skin good quality mushrooms, simply cut the base of the stalks). Season lightly. Put the vegetables on to the rack, as in the picture, or into the grill pan, see Blue Print. Brush the food with melted fat, margarine or butter, cook as the Blue Print until meat is nearly tender (by this time the vegetables can be removed and kept hot if there is not much space on the grid of the grill pan). Add the bacon, cook for a further 2–3 minutes. Arrange on a hot dish with watercress. *Serves 4.*

For Special Occasions: Add halved lamb's kidneys, fingers of lamb's or calf's liver, steak and fried eggs. Serve with maître d'hôtel butter.

Maître d'Hôtel (Parsley) Butter

2 oz. ($\frac{1}{4}$C) butter; little grated lemon rind (optional); 1 tablespoon chopped parsley; 1–2 teaspoons lemon juice; seasoning.

Cream all the ingredients together, chill. Form or cut into pats. Put on the meat just before serving. *Serves 4.*

Storing and Freezing *Keep uncooked chops and steaks for 2–3 days only in the refrigerator, but store good stocks in the home freezer. Separate with squares of waxed or greaseproof paper, peel-off as required, grill or fry as pages 26 and 27 from the frozen state.*

To use any left over *Grilled or fried meats are* not *good cold or reheated.*

Frying Meat

Frying is a method of cooking that can be used for tender pieces of meat, as outlined in the table below, and some 'made-up' meat dishes, such as croquettes, rissoles and Hamburgers. Shallow frying is generally chosen for cuts of meat, also Hamburgers, but shallow *or* deep frying can be used for coated meats, such as rissoles.

Modern 'non-stick' pans enable you to fry meat with little, if any, fat, but the amount of fat given in the Blue Print pre-supposes that an ordinary pan is being used.

Blue Print Recipe

Shallow Frying of Meat

Choose a good-sized *solid* frying pan, too light a pan is inclined to over-cook the outside of the meat before it is cooked through to the centre. The amount of butter or fat suggested is enough for 3–4 portions, but this must vary according to the amount of natural fat on the meat. If frying in butter, add a few drops of olive oil, this lessens the possibility of the butter burning and discolouring.

To prepare Season the meat if wished. Coat as individual recipes. Tie fillet steaks into a round to make into tournedos if following a recipe that requires these (the butcher will do this for you). If frying mushrooms and tomatoes as an accompaniment prepare these and either fry in a separate pan or fry *before* the meat if the meat is to be very *under-done*, then keep the vegetables hot, while cooking the meat. If the meat is to be *well cooked*, then this may be fried first, lifted on to a hot dish and kept hot while the mushrooms and tomatoes are fried.

To cook Heat the butter, or butter and oil, or other fat in the pan. Add the meat and cook quickly on one side, turn with tongs or two knives (do not pierce with the prongs of a fork as this allows the meat juices to escape). Fry quickly on the second side, lower the heat and continue cooking as the timing below.

To serve Garnish with fried mushrooms and tomatoes or with watercress, parsley, lettuce or as the individual recipes.

● **AVOID** *Frying too slowly, this gives a greasy outside to the meat, which makes it less easy to digest: Keeping fried food (particularly meat) waiting before serving.*

● **TO RECTIFY** *If the meat does not begin cooking the moment it is put into the hot fat or hot pan, raise the temperature immediately.*

● **SHORT CUTS** *Have the meat cut thinly (as minute steaks) or choose very small slices of veal or pork fillet.*

● **TO SLIMMERS** *If you cannot use a 'non-stick' pan avoid frying, particularly if following a fat-free slimming diet.*

Wiener Schnitzel (or Escalopes of Veal or Pork)

Choose 4 fillets veal or pork. As Blue Print PLUS seasoning, 1 tablespoon flour, 1 egg, 3–4 tablespoons fine soft breadcrumbs, 1 lemon and a little chopped parsley.
The meat must be very thin, so flatten with a rolling pin if necessary. Coat the slices of meat in seasoned flour, then beaten egg and breadcrumbs. Cook as the Blue Print, but allow a total cooking time of about 10 minutes

Wiener Schnitzel

only. Garnish with slices of lemon and chopped parsley. If the lemon and parsley are put on the meat *in* the pan (as in the picture) and warmed for 1–2 minutes, the maximum flavour can be extracted.

For a more elaborate garnish top the lemon slices with chopped hard-boiled egg, capers and anchovy fillets. *Serves 4.*

Veal Parisienne

As above, but coat the fillets of veal in seasoned flour, beaten egg and packet sage and onion stuffing or veal (thyme and parsley) stuffing instead of crumbs. Cook as Wiener Schnitzel.

Choice and Timing for Fried Meat

BEEF

Cuts: Entrecôte, fillet, minute (very thin slices), rump, point, porterhouse, sirloin, T-bone. (Châteaubriand is very thick for frying.)
Fat required: 2–3 oz. ($\frac{1}{4}$–$\frac{3}{8}$C) fat.
Timing: *Steaks about $\frac{1}{2}$–$\frac{3}{4}$-inch thick.*
Under-done (rare): 2–3 minutes on either side.
Medium: 2–3 minutes on either side, then 5–6 minutes on lower heat.
Well done: 2–3 minutes on either side, then 8–10 minutes on lower heat.
Minute Steaks: 1–2 minutes only on either side.

LAMB

Cuts: Chops or cutlets from loin or best end of neck, chump chops, fillet from leg.
Fat required: 1 oz. fat for chops, but a little more for very lean cutlets or fillet.
Timing: *For medium-sized chops about $\frac{3}{4}$-inch*

thick: About 3 minutes on either side, then 6–8 minutes on a lower heat.

PORK

Cuts: Chops or cutlets from loin, or spare rib or chump chop or fillet (see individual recipes).
Fat required: 2–3 oz. ($\frac{1}{4}$–$\frac{3}{8}$C) fat for fillet, but grease the pan lightly for other cuts. Remove the rind from chops and snip the fat at $\frac{1}{2}$-inch intervals to encourage this to crisp.
Timing: *For medium-sized chops about $\frac{3}{4}$-inch thick:* 4–5 minutes on either side, then 8–10 minutes on lower heat.
For fillet: 3 minutes on either side, then about 4 minutes on lower heat. Never under-cook pork.

VEAL

Cuts: Chops or cutlets from loin, or fillet (see individual recipes).
Fat required: 4 oz. ($\frac{1}{2}$C) fat.
Timing: As pork.

Deep Fat Frying of Meat

Prepare the meat as the individual recipes. Heat the pan of deep fat or oil, never have this more than half filled. Heat steadily. To test if it is the correct temperature, put a cube of day-old bread into the hot fat or oil; this should turn golden brown in just over ½ minute (no quicker). Lower the basket into the pan of fat, this makes sure it is well coated and that food will not stick to it. Raise the basket from the fat, put in the food, lower gently into the fat and fry as individual recipes. Lift out and drain on absorbent paper.
● **AVOID** *Serving without draining.*

Steak au Poivre (Peppered steak)
Choose 4 fillet or rump steaks.
Version 1: As Blue Print PLUS ½–1 tablespoon crushed peppercorns.
Version 2: As Blue Print, using butter for frying, PLUS ½–1 tablespoon crushed peppercorns, 5–6 tablespoons thick cream and 1–2 tablespoons brandy.
Season the steaks with salt and press half the peppercorns into one side, then turn and repeat on the second side. Cook as the Blue Print. For the more luxurious version, prepare as above and fry as the Blue Print then add the cream and heat gently, with the meat, for 1–2 minutes. Add the brandy and ignite if wished. If preferred the cooked meat may be lifted on to a hot dish before adding first the cream and then the brandy to the pan. *Serves 4.*

Rissoles
12 oz. cooked meat (lean beef, corned beef, lean lamb or veal, or use a mixture of meats); 1 oz. butter or margarine; 1 oz. flour, ¼ pint (⅔C) brown stock or milk (see method); 2 oz. (¾C) soft breadcrumbs; seasoning; pinch mixed herbs. *To coat:* 1 tablespoon flour; 1 egg; 2–3 tablespoons crisp breadcrumbs. *To fry:* 2 oz. fat or deep fat.
Mince the meat, or chop very finely. Heat the butter or margarine in a fairly large pan, stir in the flour and cook over a low heat for several minutes, stirring carefully. Gradually add the liquid—stock naturally gives a more 'meaty' flavour; milk a creamy one. Bring to the boil and cook until thickened. Add the crumbs, minced meat, seasoning and herbs. Allow the mixture to cool then form into 8 round flat cakes. Coat in flour, then beaten egg, then in crumbs. For shallow frying heat the fat in a large pan and fry the cakes until golden brown on either side and heated through to the centre. For deep frying follow the Blue Print on this page, allow about 5 minutes only and do not turn. Drain on absorbent paper and serve with the brown or tomato sauce given below.

Sauces for Fried Meats
Brown sauce Chop a medium-sized onion and fry in 1½ oz. fat until soft. Stir in 1 oz. flour and cook gently for a few minutes. Gradually add ½ pint (1⅓C) brown stock, bring to the boil, cook until thickened and season well. Sieve or emulsify in the liquidiser if wished.
Tomato sauce Use the recipe for brown sauce but substitute 4–5 large chopped tomatoes and 4–5 tablespoons water for the brown stock.

Hamburgers
Hamburgers can be varied in many ways, but this is the basic recipe.
1 lb. minced beef (choose rump, sirloin or other prime steak for tenderness, chuck steak for economy); seasoning; 1 egg yolk (optional); pinch mixed herbs; 2–3 teaspoons oil (optional); 1 large onion (optional); 1 tablespoon seasoned flour (optional); 1–2 oz. fat for frying.
Mix the beef, seasoning, egg yolk and herbs together. If wished omit the egg yolk. If the meat is very lean add the oil. Form into 4 round flat cakes. If wishing to top the Hamburgers with onion, peel and cut into rings, then coat in seasoned flour. Fry in the fat and keep hot, then add the meat cakes and cook on both sides as the Blue Print opposite. Lower the heat and continue cooking for 2–6 minutes according to personal taste and type of meat used (chuck steak naturally takes longer). Serve with vegetables or on toasted halved Hamburger rolls.

Plus Cheese
Ingredients as above, PLUS 4 slices Cheddar or processed cheese.
Cook the onion rings and Hamburgers. Put the Hamburgers on top of halved toasted rolls, cover with the cheese and brown under the grill. Top with the onion rings. If preferred omit the fresh onion and top with rings of tomato and several small pickled onions.

Hamburger Indienne
Ingredients as above, but add 1–2 teaspoons curry powder with the seasoning, together with a little finely grated onion; OMIT onion rings.
Cook as the basic Hamburger. Top with rings of fried pineapple and a little chutney.

Nutty Hamburger
Ingredients as above, PLUS 2–3 tablespoons salted peanuts.
Cook as the basic Hamburger, top with peanuts before serving. A few chopped nuts can be added to the Hamburger mixture if liked.

Pimento Hamburger
Ingredients as above, PLUS sliced rings red and/or green pepper.
Cook as the basic Hamburger and top with the rings of fried pepper.

From the top:
Basic hamburger, Hamburger Indienne, Hamburger plus cheese, Nutty hamburger, Pimento hamburger

Never despise a joint of 'boiled meat' for some of the most appetising dishes are prepared by this method. The word 'boiling' is really incorrect, for the liquid in the pan should simmer gently, *not* boil rapidly.

Normally one chooses fairly economical joints for this purpose and it is ideal for salted meats, such as brisket, silverside and tongue although there is no reason why all joints cannot be cooked by this method if wished.

Allow minimum 8–12 oz. fresh meat with bone; less without bone. Salted meats shrink during cooking so allow minimum 8 oz. without bone.

Blue Print Recipe

Boiling Meat

Choose a large pan so that the liquid surrounds the meat. If the meat fits too tightly into the pan, the outside tends to be dry and the meat does not cook as well as it should. Make sure the lid fits well so the liquid does not evaporate too quickly.

To prepare Wash and dry then tie the meat into a neat shape if necessary and prepare any vegetables. If using salted meat then soak for about 12 hours before cooking.

To cook Put the meat with any vegetables into the saucepan. Add seasoning if required. Salted meat should have only a few peppercorns or pepper, no salt. Add herbs, other ingredients as the particular recipe and liquid, generally water. Bring to the boil, remove any grey scum that may float to the top and cover the pan tightly. Lower the heat and allow the liquid to simmer steadily for the time given in the table below.

To serve Hot or cold, according to the individual recipes. If serving hot then serve some of the unthickened liquid with the meat and vegetables.

● **AVOID** *Cooking too quickly, for this means the outside of the meat becomes over-cooked before the centre is tender: Cooking salted meats before soaking.*

● **TO RECTIFY** *Reduce the heat when the liquid in the pan boils too quickly: If you should start to cook salted meats without soaking, pour away the original cooking liquid and fill up with fresh cold water. Add plenty of vegetables to help absorb the salt.*

● **TO SLIMMERS** *A splendid way of cooking meat as no thickening is used in the liquid.*

Choice and Timing for Boiled Meat

BEEF

Cuts: Fresh or salted brisket, silverside or ox-tongue or for a very economical joint choose shin, but this is mainly used for stock. For special occasions choose rump or other prime joints, see Pot-au-feu.

Timing: 30 minutes per lb. and 30 minutes over (slightly less for prime joints).

Add: Vegetables or accompaniments such as dumplings (see recipes) or serve cold.

LAMB OR MUTTON

Cuts: Scrag or middle neck, breast, tongues or head, shank can be used but is mainly for soups. Leg could be used for special occasions.

Timing: 25 minutes per lb. and 25 minutes over for a joint. Allow 1½ hours for scrag or middle neck.

Add: Vegetables or accompaniments such as caper sauce (see recipes).

PORK

Cuts: Loin, spare rib or head, belly or trotters.

Timing: 30 minutes per lb. and 30 minutes over.

Add: Vegetables to give flavour as the meat cooks, generally served cold.

VEAL

Cuts: Boned and rolled breast, head or tongue.

Timing: 30 minutes per lb. and 30 minutes over.

Add: Mixed vegetables, and serve with parsley or brain sauce.

BACON OR HAM

See page 19.

For Family Occasions

Boiled Silverside or Brisket

Choose salted meat as it has a better flavour and colour when boiled than fresh meat. Prepare and cook as the Blue Print, adding a selection of root vegetables. Prepare dumplings and add these to the stock about 25 minutes before serving the joint. Lift the meat on to a dish, arrange the dumplings and vegetables round and serve with stock. This is excellent cold with salads.

Dumplings

4 oz. (1C) self-raising flour (or plain flour and 1 teaspoon baking powder); pinch salt, pepper and dry mustard; 2 oz. (⅓C) shredded suet; water to mix.

Sieve the flour and seasonings, add the suet and bind with water to a slightly sticky dough. Roll into 8–12 small balls with lightly floured hands. Drop into the liquid in the pan and cook for 20–25 minutes. Make sure the liquid boils when the dumplings are first put into the pan, then reduce to simmering again after about 8 minutes.

Note: Whilst dumplings are usually made with suet, other fats such as margarine or cooking fat can be used and many readers may prefer to use this.

Boiled Tongue

Although ox-tongue is cooked more often than others, the smaller lambs' tongues or calf's tongue are excellent for smaller families. Try to buy the tongues salted as this gives a better colour to the meat. Prepare and cook as the Blue Print, adding herbs, a few strips lemon rind and vegetables to flavour if wished. When the tongue or tongues are tender allow to cool sufficiently to handle. Meanwhile boil the liquid in the pan rapidly so you have just enough to cover the meat;

Boiled salt beef and tongue

this is about $\frac{3}{4}$ pint (2C) with a large ox-tongue. Remove the skin, bones and gristle from the tongue and press the meat into a round tin or pan (it needs to be a tight fit to give a good shape). Soften 2 teaspoons powdered gelatine in 2 tablespoons cold water, add to the hot liquid in the pan. Stir until the gelatine has dissolved, pour over the tongue, allow to cool, then cover with foil and a light weight and leave until firm. Turn out and serve with salad.

Boiled Lamb or Mutton
Remember the bone content of scrag or middle neck is high so buy a generous amount of meat. Put the meat into a pan with a selection of vegetables and cook as the Blue Print. Arrange on a dish and serve with the caper sauce below.

Caper Sauce
$1\frac{1}{2}$ oz. butter or margarine; $1\frac{1}{2}$ oz. flour; $\frac{1}{2}$ pint ($1\frac{1}{4}$C) milk; $\frac{1}{4}$ pint ($\frac{2}{3}$C) stock from cooking the lamb; seasoning; 2–3 teaspoons capers and a little vinegar from the jar.
Heat the butter or margarine in a pan, stir in the flour and cook the 'roux' for several minutes. Gradually add the liquid, bring to the boil and cook until thickened. Add the seasoning, capers and vinegar. Keep hot but do not boil. *Serves 4–6.*

For Special Occasions

Pot-au-Feu
Approximately 3–$3\frac{1}{2}$ lb. joint boned sirloin or rump steak; small piece salted bacon or uncooked ham; 1 small veal knuckle or 2 pig's trotters; about $1\frac{1}{2}$ lb. mixed root vegetables (carrots, turnips, celeriac, small piece parsnip); seasoning; *bouquet garni*; 6–8 small onions; 1 lb. garlic sausage; mayonnaise; tomato sauce; French mustard.
Put the meats, half the sliced vegetables, seasoning and *bouquet garni* into a pan and cook as the Blue Print for about $1\frac{1}{2}$ hours. Add the rest of the sliced vegetables, the onions and sliced sausage and cook for a further 1–$1\frac{1}{2}$ hours.
Slice the meats, arrange on a dish with the cooked vegetables round. Strain the liquid, serve in a sauce boat. Dishes of mayonnaise, tomato sauce and French mustard are generally served as well.

Storing and Freezing *Uncooked non-salted meat may be kept for several days in a refrigerator or some weeks in a home freezer. Salted meat, cooked or uncooked, keeps well in a refrigerator for some days but uncooked does not store as well in a home freezer as unsalted meat. Cooked unsalted meat freezes reasonably well but cooked salted meat, when frozen, should be used within 5–6 weeks.*
To use any left over *See above. Boiled meats may be turned into rissoles, meat pies, etc.*

Killarney hot-pot

Stews and Casseroles

Most meats can be served in a stew or casserole. The great advantage of these methods of cooking is that they 'tenderise' the cheaper cuts of meat and with imaginative use of spices, herbs, fruits and vegetables, provide both interesting and economical dishes.

Blue Print Recipe

Irish Hot-Pot

8–12 oz. belly of pork · 12 oz. leanest possible meat from a hand of pork or 4 chump chops · 1 lb. onions · 2–3 large carrots · seasoning · 1–2 teaspoons chopped fresh sage or about $\frac{1}{4}$ teaspoon dried sage · $1\frac{1}{2}$ lb. potatoes · $\frac{1}{4}$ pint ($\frac{2}{3}$C) stock or water · 1 oz. margarine.

To make Cut the belly and hand of pork into neat pieces. If using chump chops leave on the bone, or remove the meat and dice if more convenient (this means the meat takes up less space in a small casserole). Peel and cut the onions and carrots into rings. Season the meat and mix with the sage. Peel and slice the potatoes thinly, keep in water until ready to use, so they do not discolour. Put about one third of the potatoes into the casserole, season well. Add half the onions and carrots, half the meat, then another layer of potatoes (save plenty for the topping). Season each layer of vegetables. Next add the last of the meat, onions and carrots and cover with the stock or water. Arrange the last of the potato slices over the vegetables, in a neat overlapping design. Put the margarine in small pieces on the potatoes.

To cook Leave the hot-pot uncovered for about 15 minutes if possible, so the margarine melts and gives a good coating on the potatoes (this stops the lid 'sticking'). Put on the lid after 15 minutes, but remove again for the last 20 minutes to encourage the potatoes to brown and crisp. Cook for about 2 hours in the centre of a slow to very moderate oven, 300–325°F, Gas Mark 2–3.
To serve With cooked red cabbage or pickled red cabbage and apple sauce or sliced cooked beetroot. *All recipes based on this dish serve 4–5.*

● **AVOID** *Using too much stock or water, the vegetables keep the mixture moist. If you use too much liquid the potatoes on top will not crisp.*
● **SHORT CUT** *Use canned meat and canned potatoes, bake for about 45 minutes only in a moderately hot oven to crisp the potatoes.*

For Family Occasions

Welsh Hot-Pot
Method as Blue Print but choose about $1\frac{1}{2}$–2 lb. middle or scrag end of neck of mutton and substitute sliced leeks for onions.
Bake and serve as the Blue Print.

Lancashire Hot-Pot
Method as Blue Print, but MINUS the carrots and sage and use $1\frac{1}{2}$–2 lb. scrag or middle end of neck of lamb in place of pork. 1 or 2 thinly sliced lambs' kidneys may be mixed with the meat.
Bake and serve as the Blue Print.

For Special Occasions

Killarney Hot-Pot
Method as Blue Print but use 8 oz. belly of pork or fairly fat ham and 1 lb. lean fresh brisket or best quality chuck steak. Substitute $\frac{1}{4}$ pint ($\frac{2}{3}$C) brown ale for stock or water. Bake and serve as the Blue Print.

Meat Puddings

Most men (and a percentage of women) would choose a home-made steak and kidney pudding as one of the (if not *the*) ideal cold weather meat dishes. If correctly made, with a coating of not-too-thick, feather-light suet crust pastry, and a richly flavoured steak and kidney filling it is satisfying, without being 'stodgy'. The points below apply to all meat puddings.

Blue Print Recipe
Steak and Kidney Pudding

For the filling: 1½ lb. stewing steak (chuck is a good choice) · 8–12 oz. ox kidney or 6 lambs' kidneys · seasoning · 2–2½ tablespoons flour · 1 or 2 onions (optional) · water or stock · **For the pastry:** 10 oz. (2½C) flour* · pinch salt · 5 oz. (nearly 1C) shredded suet · water.

*this can be self-raising (or plain flour with 2½ level teaspoons baking powder) to give a thicker crust, or plain flour for a thin crust that does not rise.

To make Either cut the steak into neat cubes, as shown in the picture, or narrow strips. Dice the kidney, remove any gristle and skin. Either mix *with* the meat or put a small piece of kidney on each strip

Steak and kidney pudding

of steak and roll firmly. Mix the seasoning and flour on a plate or in a bag, turn or toss the meat and kidney in this until evenly coated. Chop the onions finely, if adding these, and blend with the meat. Put the liquid on one side to add later. Sieve the flour and salt together, add the suet and mix to a soft rolling consistency with cold water. Roll out and use about ¾ to line a 3-pint (8C) basin; trim the edges, put trimmings with the ¼ reserved. Put in the meat filling, add just enough water or stock to come halfway up the meat mixture. Damp the edges of the pastry. Roll out the remaining dough to form the 'lid', put on top of the meat filling, press the edges firmly. Alternatively follow instructions for lining a basin on page 96. Cover with greased greaseproof paper and foil; make a 'pleat' in the centre to allow the pudding to rise.

To cook Either put into a steamer over a pan of boiling water, or lower into a saucepan of boiling water, to stand on an upturned saucer or patty tin. Steam or boil for 4–5 hours so the meat is tender. Fill-up the pan with *boiling* water during cooking.

To serve In the basin. If this is attractive, as in the picture, there is no need to cover this. If using a less pleasing basin wrap a white or coloured table napkin round this. Top with a sprig of parsley. Either make a gravy to serve with the pudding, or when you cut out the first portion add a little good hot beef stock to the filling and use this as the gravy. *Serves 6–7.*

For Family Occasions

A smaller sized pudding for 4 people is made with about 1 lb. steak and 8 oz. (2C) flour, etc.

Steak and Vegetable Pudding
Ingredients as Blue Print MINUS the kidney and PLUS 2–3 sliced carrots, 2–3 sticks diced celery and a few mushrooms. Cook as the Blue Print.

Minced Steak Pudding
Ingredients as Blue Print but mince the steak, kidney and onions. Blend with 1–2 tablespoons rolled oats or oatmeal and 1–2 tablespoons tomato purée as well as the flour and liquid in the Blue Print. Steam for 2½–3 hours.

Mutton Pudding
Method as Blue Print, but use about 2½–3 lb. middle neck of mutton or lamb. Bone this and use instead of steak and kidney. Flavour with 1–2 teaspoons chopped parsley, little chopped mint, 12 mushrooms and 12 tiny onions *instead of* sliced onions.

For Special Occasions

Flemish Pudding
Ingredients as Blue Print (choose prime quality chuck steak) PLUS 2–3 rashers diced lean bacon and a few mushrooms. Use beer or red wine instead of water or stock in the pudding and flavour with 1 teaspoon chopped mixed herbs. Cook as the Blue Print.

Steak and Pheasant Pudding
Method as Blue Print, but omit the kidney and use the meat from a small boned pheasant instead.
Cook as the Blue Print. Serve with redcurrant jelly.

● **AVOID** *Making the suet crust pastry too dry, it needs to be a soft rolling consistency: Adding too much liquid to the filling, it boils out and spoils the appearance of the dish.*

● **SHORT CUTS** *Use ready shredded packet suet; or pastry and canned meat filling and cook for a much shorter time (about 2 hours); or cook in a pressure cooker (following the maker's instructions).*

Storing and Freezing *The cooked pudding can be stored for 2–3 days in a refrigerator and reheated. It can be frozen with great success. Cook for 2–2½ hours (to set the pastry), cool, freeze then wrap or remove from the basin and wrap.*
Allow to thaw out if using a breakable basin before completing the cooking for 2–2½ hours.
To use any left over *Cover and re-steam.*

Forfar Bridie

For Family Occasions

Thrifty Pasties

Ingredients as Blue Print, but use chuck steak instead of rump.
Put the chuck steak through a coarse mincer. Make as Blue Print, bake for 15 minutes in a hot oven, lower the heat to very moderate and cook for 40–45 minutes.

Steak and Kidney Pasties

Ingredients as Cornish Pasties PLUS 2–3 lambs' kidneys and MINUS the swede.
Skin and dice kidneys and mix with the meat. Make and bake as the Blue Print.

Forfar Bridies

Pastry ingredients as the Blue Print, using 6 oz. ($\frac{3}{4}$C) fat only to 1 lb. (4C) flour.
Cut $1\frac{1}{4}$–$1\frac{1}{2}$ lb. good quality stewing steak into thin strips about 1-inch in length and $\frac{1}{2}$-inch wide, spread with a little butter or press shredded suet on to each strip and season well. Dice about 3 large onions and mix with the meat strips, do not add stock or water. Roll out the pastry, cut into 4 large ovals or rectangles instead of rounds. Divide the filling between these. Damp pastry edges, fold one half over, seal edges and flute or crimp. Bake as the Blue Print in a hot oven for 15 minutes, then lower the heat to very moderate for just over an hour.

For Special Occasions

Gammon Pasties

Ingredients as Blue Print but substitute about $1\frac{1}{4}$ lb. lean gammon for the steak. Dice this finely and mix with the diced potatoes, onions and 1 dessert apple in place of the swede. Season well and flavour with a very little powdered sage. Blend with 1 tablespoon only white wine or stock. Make and bake as the Blue Print.

Burgundy Pasties

Ingredients as Blue Print but substitute fillet steak and Burgundy wine for stock. Omit swede and use extra onion and a crushed clove garlic. Make and bake as Blue Print.

Storing and Freezing *Uncooked pasties store for 1–2 hours only in the refrigerator as the filling makes the pastry 'soggy'. The uncooked potato and meat filling does not freeze well. Cooked pasties freeze excellently.*
To use any left over *Do not keep long. Re-heat before serving.*

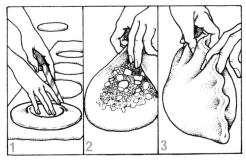

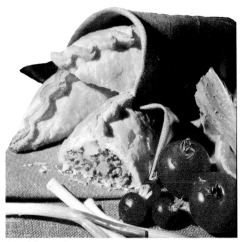
Cornish pasties

only white wine or stock. Make and bake as the Blue Print.

Meat Pasties

On this page are two of the best known meat pasties, together with variations.

Blue Print Recipe
Cornish Pasties

For the pastry: 1 lb. (4C) flour, preferably plain · pinch salt · 6–8 oz. ($\frac{3}{4}$–1C) fat (see method) · water to mix. For the filling: 1 lb. rump steak · 2 medium-sized potatoes · 2 medium-sized onions · 1 small or $\frac{1}{2}$ medium-sized swede (optional) · 2 tablespoons stock or water · seasoning. To glaze: 1 egg (optional).

To make Sieve the flour and salt and rub in the fat. Choose the smaller amount if carrying the pasties on a picnic for this ensures that the pastry is not too 'short' and fragile. Bind to a rolling consistency with the water. Cut the meat, peeled potatoes, onions and swede into neat small pieces. If omitting the swede, add a little more potato and onion to give the same amount of filling. Mix with the stock or water and seasoning. Roll out the pastry, cut round 4 teaplates, see Sketch 1. Put the filling in the centre of each round. Damp the edges of the pastry with water, bring up to form a pasty shape, see Sketch 2. Flute the edges with your fingers, as Sketch 3. Lift on to a baking tray. If wishing to give the pastry a good shine blend a beaten egg with about 2 teaspoons water and brush the pasties with this glaze.
To cook Bake for approximately 15–20 minutes in the centre of a hot oven, 425–450°F, Gas Mark 6–7, or until the pastry is golden then lower the heat to moderate, 350–375°F, Gas Mark 4–5, and cook for a further 20 minutes, or to very moderate, 325–350°F, Gas Mark 3–4 for 25–30 minutes.
To serve Hot with vegetables and a brown sauce (see page 13) or cold with salad or as part of a packed meal. *All recipes based on this serve 4.*

● **AVOID** *Making the filling too moist, add only half the stock and if you find it looks fairly liquid then omit the rest. Do not dice the potatoes, etc. too early for they discolour and become over-moist.*
● **TO RECTIFY** *If the mixture is too soft sprinkle with a little flour.*
with a little flour.
● **SHORT CUT** *Use canned steak, warm slightly then strain away surplus moisture and serve this as part of the sauce if you intend having the pasties hot.*

The spicy flavour of a good curry surely provides one of the most interesting meals. Do not imagine a good curry *must* be very hot, there are many versions of this dish and the Blue Print is for a moderately hot curry sauce only.

Blue Print Recipe
Beef Curry

2 medium-sized onions · 1–2 cloves garlic · 2 oz. ($\frac{1}{4}$C) fat, butter or ghee * · 1 small sweet apple · $\frac{1}{2}$–1 tablespoon curry powder · 1–2 teaspoons curry paste · 1 tablespoon flour · $\frac{3}{4}$ pint (2C) brown stock · 1–2 tablespoons desiccated coconut or grated fresh coconut · 1–2 tablespoons sultanas · 1–2 tablespoons chutney · 1–1$\frac{1}{4}$ lb. uncooked beef (see method) · 1 teaspoon sugar · 1 teaspoon lemon juice or vinegar · seasoning. To accompany: 6–8 oz. (1C) long grain rice · saffron powder (optional) · chutney · sliced peppers and tomatoes · Poppadums · Bombay duck · nuts · raisins · grated coconut · sliced banana · rings of raw onion or spring onions.
*ghee is clarified butter.

To make Chop the peeled onions and crush the cloves of garlic. Toss in the hot fat. Peel and slice the apple, add to the onion mixture with the curry powder, paste and flour. Fry gently for several minutes, stirring well to prevent the mixture burning. Gradually blend in the stock and bring to the boil and cook until slightly thickened. Put the coconut, sultanas and chutney into the sauce, then add the diced meat. For special occasions, choose diced topside, rump or fresh brisket; for economy choose diced chuck or flank steak.

To cook Simmer for about 1 hour in a tightly covered pan then add the sugar, lemon juice or vinegar and seasoning. Taste the sauce and add more sweetening or seasoning as desired. Cover the pan again and continue cooking for a further 1$\frac{1}{2}$–2 hours.

To cook the rice put this with about 2$\frac{1}{2}$ times the amount of cold water (i.e. to 8 oz. rice use 20 fl. oz.—1 pint water; to 1 cup use 2$\frac{1}{2}$ cups water). Add seasoning and a pinch saffron powder if desired. Bring to the boil, stir briskly, cover the pan tightly and allow to simmer for approximately 15 minutes or until the rice has absorbed the water and is tender.

To serve Arrange the curry in a border of saffron or plain rice or serve the rice in a separate dish. Arrange all the accompaniments in dishes so everyone may help themselves. The Poppadums should be fried in a very little fat until crisp. The Bombay duck (which is a dried fish) should be sprinkled over each portion of curry. *All recipes based on this dish serve 4–6.*

● **AVOID** *Cooking too quickly, one needs prolonged cooking for a true blending of flavours.*
● **TO RECTIFY** *Give yourself plenty of time to cook the sauce. If using cooked meat then allow the sauce to simmer for an hour or so before adding the meat. This prevents overcooking the meat.*
● **SHORT CUT** *Use a canned mulligatawny soup as a ready-made sauce or buy canned curry sauce and add your own flavourings.*
● **TO SLIMMERS** *Do not thicken the sauce and have very small portions of cooked rice, chutney and the fattening accompaniments.*

For Family Occasions

To vary

Very hot curry As Blue Print PLUS 2–3 sliced red chilli peppers, pinch cayenne pepper, little ground ginger or sliced stem ginger.
Mild curry As Blue Print but OMIT the curry paste and use only half the amount of curry powder.
Sweet curry As Blue Print PLUS 1–2 grated carrots and 1 medium-sized can pineapple, guavas or mangoes. Add the carrots and most of the fruit to the onion and apple mixture, and use about $\frac{1}{2}$ pint (1$\frac{1}{3}$C) only of stock and $\frac{1}{4}$ pint ($\frac{2}{3}$C) syrup from the can instead of the remainder of the stock. Garnish the curry with the remaining pieces of fruit just before serving.

Bhoona Goast

This is a very dry curry, and can be made as the Blue Print, but reduce the amount of stock to a few tablespoons only. Cook gently until the meat is tender, stirring from time to time to stop the mixture from burning. Choose diced lean mutton instead of beef and omit the apple.

For Special Occasions

Aubergine Curry

Ingredients as Blue Print, but use only 8 oz. meat, PLUS 4 thinly sliced aubergines (egg plants) and 1 or 2 lemons. The aubergines should be sprinkled with salt and left standing for about 15 minutes before adding to the curry sauce. Cook and serve as Blue Print, but garnish with thick wedges of lemon.

Lamb and Courgette Curry

Method as Blue Print but use diced lamb (from leg or shoulder) in place of beef. Cook as Blue Print. Add 3–4 thinly sliced unpeeled courgettes about 30 minutes before the end of the cooking period. Serve as Blue Print. (Illustrated on page 7.)

Storing and Freezing *Store cooked curry in the refrigerator for one or two days and reheat. Curry may be frozen but it can destroy some of the flavour.*

Sweet curry

Bacon and ham provide a wide selection of dishes for various meals, ranging from a simple breakfast dish of bacon and egg to the more elaborate Ham en Croûte and Glazed Bacon or Ham here.

Blue Print Recipe

Glazed Bacon or Ham

Choose gammon or a joint of ham for special occasions; oyster cut for medium quality; forehock or collar for family economy. Soak the bacon or ham overnight in cold water to cover, unless you have chosen 'green' or sweet-cure. This does not need soaking. Put the bacon or ham into a large pan, cover with cold water, or with cider, ginger beer or ginger ale. Add vegetables if wished. Bring the liquid to the boil, lower the heat and simmer very gently for $\frac{2}{3}$ of the total cooking time (see below). Allow the bacon or ham to cool sufficiently to remove the skin. Score (cut) the fat at regular intervals, this allows the glaze to penetrate the fat and gives more flavour to the joint. Lift into the roasting tin. Spread the glaze, as the recipes below, over the joint of bacon or ham and roast in the centre of a moderately hot oven, 400°F, Gas Mark 5–6, for the remainder of the cooking time.

Timing   Prime gammon or ham. A wide joint that is not very thick cooks more quickly, so allow 20 minutes per lb. and 20 minutes over, while a thicker joint needs 25 minutes per lb. and 25 minutes over. More economical joints need 30–35 minutes per lb. and 30–35 minutes over. Therefore a 4 lb. piece of gammon would take either 4×20 plus 20 minutes or 4×25 plus 25 minutes, i.e. either a total of 1 hour and 40 minutes or 2 hours and 5 minutes.

To serve   Hot with vegetables, cold with salad. Some of the stock may be used for a clear sauce or for parsley sauce.

Roasting Bacon or Ham

If preferred the bacon or ham can be roasted for all the cooking time. Soak as above and either fast roast (see page 9) for 20–25 minutes per lb. and 20–25 minutes over or slow roast for 35–40 minutes per lb. and 35–40 minutes over. Forehock and collar should be slow roasted, gammon, ham or oyster cut can be slow or fast roasted.

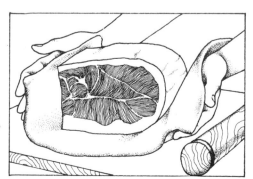

Glazed forehock of bacon

Glazes for Bacon or Ham

These are sufficient to coat the fat on a joint weighing about 4 lb. which will serve about 8.

Honey Ginger Glaze

Blend 4 tablespoons thick honey, 2 teaspoons ground ginger and 2 tablespoons finely chopped preserved ginger together. Spread over the fat and roast as the Blue Print.

Pineapple Glaze

Blend 3 tablespoons brown sugar, 3 tablespoons syrup from canned pineapple and 1 teaspoon made mustard together.

Spread over the fat and roast as the Blue Print. Put the pineapple rings from the can round the joint and cook for about 10 minutes before serving.

Sugar and Spice Glaze

Blend 3 tablespoons brown sugar, 2–3 tablespoons soft breadcrumbs (optional), 1–2 teaspoons mixed spice and 1 tablespoon golden syrup together.

Moisten to a spreading consistency with a very little stock from boiling the joint. Spread over the fat. Roast as the Blue Print, then serve hot with mixed vegetables as shown in the picture.

Ham en Croûte

Joint middle gammon or ham about $3\frac{1}{2}$–4 lb.; 1 lb. (4C) flour, preferably plain; pinch salt; 8 oz. (1C) fat; water to mix. *To glaze:* 1 egg. Soak the gammon or ham for 12 hours in cold water unless 'green' or sweet-cure. If very salt soak for 24 hours. Lift out of the water, dry thoroughly and cut away the skin. Sieve the flour and salt, rub in the fat until the mixture is like fine breadcrumbs. Mix

with cold water to a rolling consistency. Roll out to about $\frac{1}{4}$-inch in thickness and cut off $\frac{2}{3}$ of the pastry. Place the gammon or ham on this, bring up the pastry to encase the sides of the meat, see Sketch 1. Roll out the remaining pastry for the 'lid' and place over the meat. Cut away any surplus pastry, brush the edges with beaten egg and pinch together very firmly. Lift on to a baking tray. Brush with beaten egg. Cut a slit in the top to allow the steam to escape and make small 'leaves' of pastry. Press on top of the croûte and brush with beaten egg. Bake in the centre of a moderate oven, 350–375°F, Gas Mark 4–5, for 30 minutes, then reduce the heat to very moderate, 325–350°F, Gas Mark 3–4, for the remainder of the time. Allow 25 minutes per lb. and 25 minutes over, so a 4-lb. joint will take 2 hours 5 minutes. Serve hot or cold, cut into thin slices. *Serves 8–10.*

Ham and Pâté en Croûte

Ingredients as Ham en Croûte PLUS about 3–4 oz. pâté and 8 oz. mushrooms. Roll out $\frac{2}{3}$ of the pastry as Ham en Croûte. Spread with most of the pâté and finely chopped mushrooms. Wrap round the gammon. Spread the top of the gammon with pâté and mushrooms, cover with the pastry lid and proceed as Ham en Croûte.

Ham and Corn Scallops

1 oz. butter or margarine; 1 oz. flour; $\frac{1}{4}$ pint ($\frac{2}{3}$C) milk; seasoning, $\frac{1}{2}$–1 teaspoon made mustard; 8 oz. cooked ham; small can corn; 2 packets potato crisps.

Make a thick sauce with the butter or margarine, flour and milk. Add the seasoning and mustard. Add the diced ham and corn (plus any liquid from the can). Put into 4 scallop or individual dishes. Crush the potato crisps and sprinkle over the ham mixture. Heat for 15–20 minutes in the centre of a very moderate oven, 325–350°F, Gas Mark 3–4. *Serves 4.*

Ham en croûte

Offal is often called specialist or variety meats and the latter name is very appropriate, for there are many kinds of meat grouped under this heading and they can be cooked in an unlimited number of ways. The most popular offal are:

LIVER

Liver is an excellent source of iron as well as protein, but can be spoiled by over-cooking. Choose calf's liver for the best quality, lambs' or pig's liver for tender, but less delicately flavoured liver. The simplest way to cook tender liver is to slice it fairly thinly, coat lightly in seasoned flour and fry for about 6–7 minutes in butter, dripping or bacon fat until tender. Serve with fried or grilled bacon. Ox-liver needs longer, slower cooking, as in the Ragoût Sicilienne below.

Liver Ragoût Sicilienne

$1\frac{1}{4}$ lb. ox-liver; 1 oz. flour; seasoning; 3 medium-sized onions; 1–2 cloves garlic; 2 oz. ($\frac{1}{4}$C) dripping or fat; $\frac{1}{2}$ pint ($1\frac{1}{3}$C) stock; $\frac{1}{2}$ pint ($1\frac{1}{3}$C) cider or inexpensive red wine; a generous tablespoon red currant jelly; $\frac{1}{2}$ teaspoon grated lemon rind; 2–3 tablespoons green olives.

Cut the liver into narrow strips. Mix the flour with seasoning, coat the liver in this. Cut the peeled onions into rings and crush the cloves of garlic. Heat the dripping or fat in a pan, toss the liver in this, lift out and fry the onion rings and garlic for a few minutes. Gradually blend in the stock and cider or wine, bring to the boil and cook until slightly thickened. Add the jelly and lemon rind. Replace the strips of liver, put a lid on the pan and simmer very slowly for about 2 hours. Add the olives just before serving. Serve with creamed potatoes, boiled rice or noodles. *Serves 4–5.*

Kidney Ragoût Sicilienne

Use sliced ox-kidney in place of liver.

Liver Kebabs with Orange Sauce

For the sauce: 2 oranges; $\frac{1}{2}$ pint ($1\frac{1}{3}$C) brown stock; 1 oz. cornflour; 1 oz. butter; seasoning; $\frac{1}{2}$–1 teaspoon sugar. *For the kebabs:* 1 lb. calf's liver (cut in one piece about 1-inch thick); seasoning; pinch mixed dried herbs; about 12 mushrooms; 12 small cocktail onions; 4 rashers bacon; 2 oz. ($\frac{1}{4}$C) melted butter. *To serve:* boiled rice.

Pare the rind very thinly from the oranges and simmer this in half the stock for about 5 minutes. Strain, return to the pan. Blend the cornflour with the rest of the stock, add to the liquid in the pan with the juice of the oranges, the butter, seasoning and sugar. Bring to the boil, cook gently and stir until smooth and thickened. Meanwhile cut the liver into cubes, roll in seasoning and herbs, put on to 4 metal skewers with the mushrooms, onions and halved bacon rashers, in neat rolls. Brush with the melted butter and cook under a hot grill for about 8 minutes. Turn several times during cooking, so the

food cooks evenly. Serve on a bed of boiled rice with the orange sauce. *Serves 4.*
Note Extra orange segments can be added to the sauce, if liked.

Kidney Kebabs

Use 8–12 skinned whole or halved lambs' kidneys in place of the calf's liver.

KIDNEY

Kidney adds flavour to many dishes such as the steak and kidney pudding on page 16 and the less expensive, but less tender ox-kidney can be used for this purpose. Lambs' kidneys can be grilled or fried and form an important part of a mixed grill. They make a delicious dish for special occasions when cooked in red wine, as in the recipe below. Smaller quantities can be used as a filling for pancakes and omelettes or to serve on toast as a light snack.

Kidneys Bordelaise

About 20 lambs' kidneys; $1\frac{1}{2}$ oz. flour; seasoning; good pinch grated nutmeg; 2 medium-sized onions; 2 rashers bacon; 2–3 oz. ($\frac{1}{4}$–$\frac{3}{8}$C) good dripping or butter; 1 tablespoon chopped parsley; $\frac{1}{2}$ pint ($1\frac{1}{3}$C) brown stock; $\frac{1}{4}$ pint ($\frac{2}{3}$C) red wine. *To serve:* about $1\frac{1}{2}$ lb. creamed potatoes. *To garnish:* parsley.

Skin the kidneys, halve for quicker cooking if wished. Mix the flour, seasoning and nutmeg and coat the kidneys in the flour mixture. Peel and cut the onions into thin rings, cut the bacon into narrow strips. Heat the dripping or butter in a pan, fry the onion rings and bacon gently for a few minutes, then add the kidneys and cook gently for 5 minutes, stirring well. Add the parsley, mix thoroughly, then gradually blend in the stock and wine. Bring the sauce to the boil, stir and

cook until thickened. Cover the pan and simmer for about 15 minutes. Meanwhile pipe the creamed potatoes on to a heat-proof serving dish, brown under the grill. Spoon the kidney mixture into the centre of the potatoes and garnish with parsley. Sliced pigs' kidneys may be used instead.
Serves 5–6.

Kidneys Marengo

Recipe as above, but omit the potatoes. Top the kidney mixture with 5–6 fried or poached eggs and garnish with fried croûtons of bread.

Boiled Calf's Head

1 calf's head; 1 lb. diced shin of beef; small piece of diced lean ham or gammon; 1 lemon; 1–2 bay leaves; 1–2 onions; *bouquet garni*; seasoning.

Wash the head in cold water. Place all ingredients except ham or gammon in a large pan. Cover with cold water and bring to the boil. Skim and simmer, covered, for $2\frac{1}{4}$ hours. Add ham or gammon and cook further 45 minutes. Remove meat from bones and return to pan to keep hot. Use brains to make sauce below. *Serves 6–8 according to the size of the head.*

Brain Sauce

$1\frac{1}{2}$ oz. butter or margarine; $1\frac{1}{2}$ oz. flour; $\frac{1}{2}$ pint ($1\frac{1}{3}$C) stock from cooking the head; $\frac{1}{4}$ pint ($\frac{2}{3}$C) milk; the brains from the head; seasoning.

Heat the butter or margarine in a pan, stir in the flour and cook the 'roux' for several minutes. Gradually add the liquid, bring to the boil and cook until thickened. Add the chopped brains and season to taste.

If preferred, parsley sauce can be served instead of brain sauce. Add 1–2 tablespoons chopped parsley to the sauce in place of the brains.

Kidney kebabs with orange sauce (above)

This part covers two very important groups of food, fish of all kinds and poultry, together with the basic methods of cooking these and some new recipes and ideas.

Fish is not only an important protein food but a very adaptable one. There are so many different kinds of fish from which to choose and such a variety of ways in which fish may be cooked, that it should never be monotonous. If you are following a slimming diet, fish, if served without rich sauces or high calorie garnishes, is relatively low in calories, particularly if you choose the white or shell variety. White fish is very easily digested, shell fish and oily fish are more indigestible.

Fish is a highly perishable food, so choose it wisely. Fresh white fish is firm in texture, with bright eyes and a pleasant smell. If it has a strong smell of ammonia, it is *stale*. Shell fish is of good quality when it has a firm-looking shell. The tails of lobster or prawns should 'spring back' again after being pulled out and both crab and lobster should feel heavy for their size. If they are surprisingly light it is because they are 'watery' and are, therefore,

two
FISH AND POULTRY

not a good buy. Oily fish, such as mackerel and herrings, should have bright silver scales and bright eyes. If the scales and eyes look dull, then be critical about buying the fish. Store fish carefully, put it as near the freezing compartment in the refrigerator as possible and use quickly. Most fish freezes well and you can substitute frozen fish for fresh in many recipes.

From page 31 onwards are methods of cooking all kinds of assorted poultry, with particular emphasis on chicken. Young chickens have become both plentiful and comparatively inexpensive.

Chicken can be cooked in many different ways, but choose the right kind of

chicken for each cooking process. A large roasting chicken, when jointed, would take too long to fry so could be overcooked on the outside before being cooked through to the centre. Very young chickens are better cooked in a simple manner, such as frying and grilling, or poached and served in a cream sauce. This ensures that the delicate flavour is not lost and the young flesh does not become dry. Young chickens (often called 'broilers') have firm legs and plump breasts. The skin should be dry and firm looking.

Roasting chickens should have a flexible 'wish-bone', firm, but not 'sinewy' looking legs and a really firm plump breast. If untrussed, the eyes should be bright and the comb firm and bright in colour. A boiling fowl should have a reasonable amount of fat, but do not buy if there is an excessive amount of pale creamy-yellow fat, for the bird will be wasteful.

A good turkey is broad-breasted with firm legs. Avoid turkeys where the legs seem deficient in flesh. Duck and goose rarely have very plump breasts, but check that there is a fairly generous amount of meat and not too much fat.

Fish dishes are often very under-rated. They can be quite outstanding. It is, of course, very important to choose fresh fish and the points to look for are given on page 21. Careful cooking is essential if the fish is not to be spoiled.

Sometimes you will wish to bone the fish, unless the fishmonger has done this for you. The pictures on this page show how to bone herrings, but other fish, of a similar shape, can be dealt with in the same way. If you wish to fillet and skin flat fish, see the sketches on page 24.

Blue Print

To Cook Fish

The following points apply whichever method of cooking the fish is chosen.

1. Wash and dry the fish.
2. Season it lightly.
3. Choose any other flavouring desired. Remember most fish has a delicate flavour and this is easily lost if very strong tasting ingredients are added. The most successful flavourings with fish are:

Fresh or dried herbs   lemon thyme, dill, chervil, parsley, chives.

Fruits   lemon, orange, apple (particularly with herrings and mackerel), gooseberries (make a purée to serve with mackerel).

Vegetables   tomatoes, mushrooms, peas and other green vegetables, onions (use sparingly), garlic (use sparingly).

Other flavourings   horseradish (particularly with smoked fish), spices (particularly with oily fish), nutmeg, tomato ketchup or concentrated tomato purée, mustard (particularly with herrings).

Liquids   milk, cream, wines of all kinds (but white are better), cider, vinegar.

Stuffings   many stuffings blend well with fish and you will find a number of suggestions opposite.

4. Choose your method of cooking and prepare as the particular Blue Print or recipe.
5. Cook for the recommended time, but always test before serving since the thickness of fish fillets, steaks, etc., varies so much. The fish is cooked if it *just* flakes from the skin or bone when tested with the tip of a knife.
6. Have any sauces all ready by the time the fish is cooked, unless you need the stock in which the fish has been cooked. Fish spoils if kept waiting for too long.
7. In order to enjoy a fish dish, choose the rest of your menu carefully. Do not precede a delicately flavoured sole dish with a very strong flavoured pâté or soup which would make the fish seem tasteless by comparison.

● **AVOID**   *Handling the fish carelessly, support it with a fish slice, for fish breaks easily and this can spoil the appearance: Either under or over-cooking the fish: Serving fish that may not appear 100% fresh.*

● **TO RECTIFY**   *If the fish does break, arrange neatly on the serving dish or plate and garnish or coat carefully with sauce to 'mask' the broken pieces.*

● **SHORT CUTS**   *Use frozen fish for quick dishes or make use of canned fish: Choose the quick cooking methods, i.e. grilling and frying.*

● **TO SLIMMERS**   *You are fortunate in that fish is low in calories; choose the methods that do not add extra calories to the dish—grilling, baking (without fattening garnishes or sauces), poaching or steaming.*

Quantities

Allow per person:

1 medium-sized sole or similar fish, 1 medium-sized to large trout or similar fish.

4–6 oz. fish fillet, without bone or thick skin, rather more if there are large bones and heavy skin, as on cutlets of fish (often called steaks).

½ medium-sized, or 1 small lobster or crab (if served in a sauce the fish can be used more economically).

1 pint mussels.

Minimum about 2 oz. shelled prawns or ½ pint with shells.

1 large or a pair of smaller kippers.

2–3 oz. roe for a savoury, up to 6 oz. for a main dish.

Storing and Freezing   *In order to avoid continual repetition the points here apply to most fish, but where there is a particular point of importance you will find this given on the relevant page.*

Store fresh fish with the greatest care. Even in a refrigerator it should be kept for the minimum period. Read your manufacturer's instructions about freezing fish and use within the suggested period.

Put the fish as near the freezing compartment as possible in the refrigerator. Often one can use ready-frozen fish to take the place of fresh fish in a recipe. The general recommendations about defrosting are as follows, you can cook from the frozen state if the pieces of fish are small, but when cooking large fish I find it better to let them defrost before cooking, otherwise the outside tends to become over-cooked before the centre is tender.

To use any left over   *Cooked fish must be used quickly, unless you wish to freeze this. It can be put into fish pies, fish cakes, etc. There are certain methods of cooking which enable you to make better use of cooked fish, i.e. poached and baked are better than fried or grilled fish.*

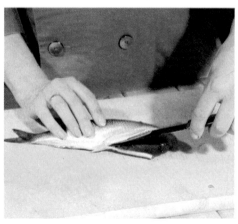

1. Cut the head off the fish, remove the intestines and wash well. Save the roe to use with the fish. Wash in cold water.
2. Split the fish along the belly.
3. Open out and lay on a wooden surface with the cut side downwards, run your fingers firmly along the back bone.
4. Turn the fish over and you will find you can remove the bones very easily.

This is one of the most adaptable ways of cooking fish, for the fish can be placed into a suitable dish in the oven with a little margarine or butter, with milk, with vegetables or with a sauce, and cooked until tender.

The fish may be stuffed before baking and recipes for stuffings, suitable for most fish, are given on this page.

Blue Print

To Bake Fish

This method is suitable for all white, oily, smoked and fresh water fish, but is less successful with shell fish, except in a sauce.

If Baking With No Additional Ingredients

Set the oven to moderate to moderately hot, 375–400°F, Gas Mark 5–6. Rub the bottom of an oven-proof dish with a little butter or margarine. Put the prepared fish on this, top with a little more butter or margarine and seasoning to taste or any other flavouring, i.e. a little chopped parsley, squeeze lemon juice, etc.

If you wish to have a slightly golden coloured look to the fish *do not cover*. If you wish the fish to remain very moist, *cover* the dish with a lid, foil or transparent cooking wrap.

Put, unless stated to the contrary, fillets of fish towards the top of the oven, but thicker steaks (cutlets) or whole fish should be put in or near the centre of the oven. This makes certain the outside of the fish is not over-cooked before the centre is tender.

Timing

Thin fillets take about 12 minutes, or about 15 minutes if covered.

Folded fillets take about 16 minutes, or about 20 minutes if covered.

Whole flat fish, e.g. sole, thick steaks (cutlets) or very thick fillets take about 25 minutes, or about 30 minutes if covered.

Thick whole fish, e.g. trout, take about 30–35 minutes, or about 40 minutes if stuffed *or* covered, or a little longer if both stuffed and covered.

Baking with Additional Ingredients

Baking with liquid You can omit the butter or margarine, although this can be added. The cooking times are the same as above.

Baking with vegetables i.e. sliced tomatoes, mushrooms and onions. Always slice onions *very thinly* or chop finely, since they take longer to cook than most fish. The cooking times will be a little longer than those given above.

Wrapping in foil Allow an extra 5–10 minutes cooking time.

Baking Fish

Quick Ways to Give Flavour to Baked Fish

Add a little cider or wine to the fish.

Put the fish on a bed of sliced tomatoes, season and top with sliced tomatoes, season well.

Blend a little paprika (sweet pepper) with thin cream, pour over the fish and bake.

Add tiny pieces of lemon flesh, chopped parsley and plenty of melted butter to the fish.

Sole and Lemon

4 small to medium-sized sole or other white fish; seasoning; 2 oz. ($\frac{1}{4}$C) butter or margarine; 2 small onions; 2 lemons. *To garnish:* parsley.

The fish may be cooked whole or divided into fillets for this dish. Season lightly. Cut 4 large pieces of aluminium foil, sufficient to wrap round the fish. Grease with half the butter or margarine and place the fish in the centre. Peel the onions and cut into thin rings. Put over the fish. Slice the lemons thinly, remove any pips (which would give a bitter flavour to the fish). Put over the onions and top with the remaining butter. Wrap the foil round the fish, put on flat baking trays and bake as the Blue Print. Open the foil and tip on to the hot serving dish or plates. Garnish with parsley. *Serves 4.*

Note Cooked lemons have a delicious but unusual flavour, obviously you may not like this, in which case add the lemons as garnish afterwards.

Some Stuffings for Fish

While you can use most stuffing recipes the following are particularly suitable. The amounts below give enough stuffing for 4 generous portions.

Asparagus and onion Chop the stalks from a small can of asparagus or a small bunch of cooked asparagus (save the tips for garnishing the finished dish). Blend with 2 oz. ($\frac{2}{3}$C) soft breadcrumbs, 1 small grated onion, seasoning and 2 oz. ($\frac{1}{4}$C) melted butter or margarine. This is suitable for most fish, but particularly fish with a delicate flavour.

Celery and apple Chop several sticks celery, blend with 2 peeled chopped dessert apples, 2 teaspoons chopped onion, seasoning, 1 teaspoon sugar (optional) and 1 tablespoon raisins. This is a difficult stuffing to handle as it has no crumbs, etc., so is suitable for baking separately and serving with the fish, or putting into whole fish. It can be varied by adding chopped parsley. This is suitable for mackerel and fairly strongly flavoured fish.

Mushroom and tomato Chop 4 oz. (1C) mushrooms, mix with 2 large skinned chopped tomatoes, a little chopped parsley, 1 oz. melted butter or margarine, and plenty of seasoning. This is suitable for all fish.

Sage and onion This is suitable only for fish with a strong flavour.

Parsley and thyme (veal) stuffing This is suitable for most fish.

Sole and lemon

The following fish dishes, although entirely different in flavour and appearance, are based on the process of baking fish described on page 23.

Somerset Fish

This is suitable for fish with a fairly good texture and flavour, such as trout, herring and mackerel.

4 portions or whole fish; 2–3 small onions; seasoning; 2 dessert apples; about ½ pint (1⅓C) cider; 2–3 bay leaves. *To garnish:* 1 lemon.

Wash and dry the fish. Peel and cut the onions into thin rings. Season the fish and put into an oven-proof dish with most of the onions, separated into rings, the peeled, finely chopped apples and the cider. Put the bay leaves into the liquid (the flavour of this herb is very strong, so add 1 leaf only if you are not fond of it). Top with the few remaining onion rings. Bake as the Blue Print on page 23. Garnish with the lemon and serve in the baking dish.

For Special Occasions

Sole with White Wine Sauce

4 large or 8 smaller fillets of sole (or use other white fish, whiting is excellent for this dish); seasoning; about 2 oz. (¼C) butter; about ⅔ pint (nearly 2C) white wine; 1 oz. flour; ¼ pint (⅔C) milk; 2–3 tablespoons thick or thin cream. *To garnish:* paprika; 1 lemon.

Roll or fold the fillets of fish, put into a baking dish and season lightly. Top with nearly half the butter and the white wine. Cover the dish and bake in a moderate oven, 350–375°F, Gas

Sole Sevilla (above)
Somerset trout (below)

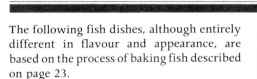

Dishes Based on Baked Fish

Mark 4–5, for about 20 minutes or a little less, since the fish has to be kept waiting while finishing the sauce. Meanwhile heat the remainder of the butter in a saucepan, stir in the flour and continue stirring over a low heat for a few minutes. Gradually blend in the milk and bring to the boil, stir until a very thick sauce. Lift the fish on to a very hot serving dish, strain the liquid from cooking the fish gradually into the thick sauce, then stir gently until smooth. Stir in the cream, heat without boiling. Pour over the baked fish, top with paprika and garnish with sliced lemon.

To vary

Sole Véronique Add a few de-seeded grapes (peel if wished) to the wine and fish. Garnish with more grapes and lemon.

Sole Sevilla Place slices of orange under each rolled fillet when cooked and proceed as the recipe above. Garnish with de-seeded grapes; peel if wished.

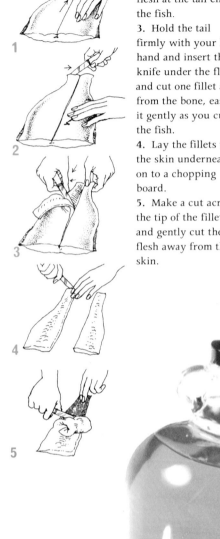

1. Cut the fish down the centre and round the edges.
2. Make a cut in the flesh at the tail end of the fish.
3. Hold the tail firmly with your left hand and insert the knife under the flesh and cut one fillet away from the bone, easing it gently as you cut the fish.
4. Lay the fillets with the skin underneath on to a chopping board.
5. Make a cut across the tip of the fillet and gently cut the flesh away from the skin.

Grilling Fish

Grilling is not only a quick method of cooking fish, but a very wise one too. Fish that is grilled is more easily digested and certainly less fattening than fried fish.

Blue Print

To Grill Fish

This method is suitable for most fish except some smoked fish.

Heat the grill before placing the fish under the heat, for it is important the fish is cooked quickly. Thin fillets do not need turning over, but thicker pieces of fish should be turned. Lift the fish carefully, for it can easily be broken.

Always brush the fish with melted butter or other fat before cooking, so it does not become dry and 'baste' with a little more butter or fat during cooking or when turning the fish; if cooking the fish on the grid cover this with buttered foil or grease the grid so the fish does not stick.

Vegetables such as mushrooms or tomatoes may be cooked on the grid of the grill pan or in the grill pan itself. Season the vegetables lightly and brush or coat these with a little butter or fat.

Timing

Thin fillets take about 5 minutes.
Thicker fillets take about 8–9 minutes.
Thick steaks (cutlets) or whole fish take about 10 minutes.

Lift the fish from the grill pan or grid with a fish slice and put on to a serving dish. There is no need to drain grilled fish on absorbent paper. Garnish with parsley and lemon or cooked tomatoes and mushrooms. Tartare sauce or other sauces may be served with the fish if desired.

● **AVOID** *Over-cooking and cooking too slowly: Allowing the fish to dry.*
● **TO RECTIFY** *The grill should be pre-heated and the heat may be lowered after browning the outside of the fish: Keep well basted with melted butter.*

Storing and Freezing *See page 22. Fish can be grilled from the frozen state.*
To use any left over *Any grilled fish can be used in salads, or in fish cakes or fish pies, see page 30.*

Quick Ways to Give Flavour to Grilled Fish

The following flavourings can be added to the melted butter, or other fat, used to brush the fish before grilling.
Grated lemon rind and lemon juice.
A little tomato ketchup or fresh or canned tomato purée.
A crushed clove garlic and seasoning.
A little curry powder and a few drops Worcestershire and/or chilli sauce.

The following toppings can be put on to the fish when it is nearly tender.
Fine soft breadcrumbs, blended with melted butter and seasoning.
Grated cheese, blended with breadcrumbs.
Slices of Cheddar cheese.
Cottage cheese, mixed with chopped parsley and chopped chives.

For Special Occasions

Savoury Grilled Turbot

3 oz. ($\frac{3}{8}$C) butter; 1 tablespoon lemon juice; $\frac{1}{2}$–1 teaspoon paprika; seasoning; 4 steaks (cutlets) turbot or other white fish. *To garnish:* parsley; lemon.
Heat the butter in a pan until it turns golden brown, this gives a delicious flavour to the fish, but it is essential the butter does not become too dark. Add the lemon juice, paprika and seasoning. Brush one side of the fish with some of the butter mixture and put on the greased grid or on buttered foil. Cook as the Blue Print, turning once. Serve topped with any hot butter and garnish with parsley and lemon. Serve with new potatoes. *Serves 4.*

Chablis Halibut

About 2 wineglasses Chablis or other dry white wine; 4 steaks (cutlets) halibut or other white fish; seasoning; 2 oz. ($\frac{1}{4}$C) butter. *To*

garnish: cooked or canned sweetcorn; red pepper; parsley.
Put the wine in a shallow dish and leave the fish soaking in this for 1 hour. Turn the fish after 30 minutes. Lift the fish out of the wine, season lightly. Melt the butter, brush the fish with this and grill as the Blue Print, turning once. Serve with the hot sweet corn, topped with red pepper and garnish with parsley. Heat any wine left in the dish and spoon over the fish before serving. *Serves 4.*

Grilled Lobster

Split a cooked lobster, remove the intestinal vein, crack the large claws and remove the flesh. Lay this on top of the flesh in the body of the fish. Brush with well seasoned butter and grill steadily until warmed through and the top is golden coloured. This can be done over a barbecue fire for a luxury dish. Serve with green salad. *1 medium-sized lobster serves 2.*

Grilled Prawns

Do not shell the prawns. Naturally for this dish they need to be the very large type. Lay the prawns on foil on the grid of the grill pan, brush with a little oil, then grill until the shells are brown. Live prawns may be grilled this way instead of boiling them. They also may be cooked over a barbecue fire. Serve with lemon and cayenne pepper.

Pacific Cutlets

Grill 4 portions of white fish as the Blue Print. Top with grated or sliced cheese and melt under the grill. Meanwhile toss 2–4 oz. ($\frac{1}{4}$–$\frac{1}{2}$C) chopped shelled large Pacific prawns or smaller prawns in a little butter for 2–3 minutes, add 2 teaspoons lemon juice and a good shake of pepper. Spoon on top of the fish and serve at once. Garnish with wedges of lemon or whole unshelled prawns. *Serves 4.*

Frying Fish

Frying is undoubtedly one of the, if not the, most popular forms of fish cookery. It is an excellent method, for the coating ensures that the moisture and flavour are 'sealed in' the fish.

Blue Prints

1. To Fry Fish

Fish can be fried in two ways.
In shallow fat, this can be butter or margarine, cooking fat or oil.
In deep fat or oil.
Although fish can, and often is fried without coating, see Fish Meunière, it is frequently coated before frying. The coating gives a pleasant crispness to the outside as well as keeping the fish moist.
There are several ways of coating fish.
1. With seasoned flour. Allow about ½ tablespoon flour to each portion of fish.
2. With seasoned flour and then with beaten egg and fine crisp breadcrumbs (you can use fine soft crumbs if preferred). It is a good idea to coat the fish with a very thin layer of flour (about ¼ tablespoon per portion) before the egg, as this helps the final coating to adhere to the fish. 1 egg plus about 2 oz. (1C) crisp breadcrumbs should coat 4 portions.
3. With a batter, this is described opposite.
4. With more unusual coatings, such as oatmeal.

2. To Fry Fish in Shallow Fat

This method is suitable for all white and oily fish and some shell fish (such as shrimps and prawns), but is unsuitable for smoked fish and most shell fish.
It is excellent for fillets of fish, but deep frying is preferable for thick portions of fish for you have better overall browning, although they *can* be cooked in a small amount of fat.
Heat enough oil or cooking fat in a frying pan to give a depth of about ¼ inch, or preferably ½ inch. Put in the prepared fish and fry quickly until crisp and brown on the under side, turn and fry on the second side, lower the heat and continue cooking until tender.

Timing

Thin fillets take about 4 minutes.
Thicker fillets take about 5–6 minutes.
Thick steaks (cutlets) or whole fish take about 10 minutes.
Lift the fish from the fat with a fish slice and drain on absorbent paper before serving. Fried fish can be served without a sauce, just garnished with lemon and parsley, but tartare sauce is the usual accompaniment, see opposite.

● **AVOID** *Too cool fat which would make the fish greasy or too hot fat which would over-cook the outside before the centre is cooked.*

Quick Ways to Give Flavour to Fried Fish

Mix the juice of a small lemon with each egg used for coating the fish and blend the finely grated lemon rind with the crumbs. Add a small quantity of grated cheese to the crumbs used in coating the fish. *It is important that this cheese coating is used only on thin fillets.* Cheese is spoiled if over-cooked and thicker portions of fish take too long to cook.
Add a little chopped parsley or chives to the crumbs used in coating the fish.

Herrings in Oatmeal

Cut off the heads from fresh herrings, remove the intestines and clean. Remove the back bone (see pictures page 22). Fillet if wished. Wash and dry the fish. Mix fine or medium oatmeal with a little seasoning and coat the fish in this. Fry as Blue Print 2 on this page.

For Special Occasions

Fish Meunière

Choose fillets of white fish, small whole white fish, trout or shelled prawns.
4 portions fish or the equivalent in prawns; seasoning; 3 oz. (⅜C) butter (even a little more if you like rather rich food); 1–2 tablespoons lemon juice; little chopped parsley; few capers (optional). *To garnish:* lemon.
Wash and dry the fish and season lightly. Heat the butter in a large pan and fry the fish until just tender. Lift the fish on to a very hot dish. If there is very little butter left in the pan you will need to add more. Heat the butter until it turns golden brown, add the lemon juice, parsley and capers and pour over the fish. Garnish with sliced lemon and serve at once. *Serves 4.*

Fish Belle Meunière

Cook the fish as above, but omit the parsley and capers. Instead fry a few soft roes and prawns in the browned butter.

Trout Woolpack

Although trout is shown in the picture, this recipe is suitable for most other fish. You will need about 5 oz. (⅝C) butter for 4 portions fish or whole fish. Fry the fish, remove from the pan, but do not allow the butter to turn too brown. Fry 4 oz. (1C) sliced button mushrooms and a generous amount of small prawns or shrimps in the butter, add 1–2 tablespoons lemon juice as the recipe above, together with extra seasoning. Spoon over the fish and garnish with parsley and lemon. *Serves 4.*

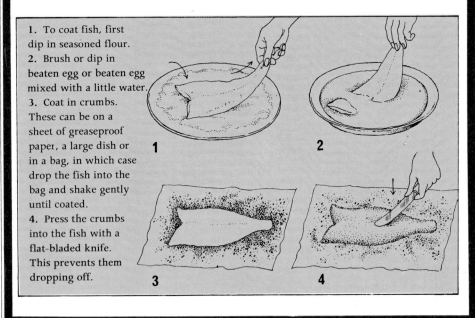

1. To coat fish, first dip in seasoned flour.
2. Brush or dip in beaten egg or beaten egg mixed with a little water.
3. Coat in crumbs. These can be on a sheet of greaseproof paper, a large dish or in a bag, in which case drop the fish into the bag and shake gently until coated.
4. Press the crumbs into the fish with a flat-bladed knife. This prevents them dropping off.

Trout woolpack

Rolled Fillets of Fish

Roll fillets of skinned white fish and secure with wooden cocktail sticks. Dip in the coating, remove sticks before frying. Use an egg and breadcrumb or batter coating, fry as the Blue Print on this page. If the fillets are rolled they take slightly longer to cook.

Stuffed Rolled Fillets of Fish

Spread the fillets with a fairly firm stuffing, such as parsley and thyme or mushroom and tomato (pae 23). Roll, then coat and fry.

Goujons (Ribbons) of Fish

This is a way of making the more expensive white fish, such as sole, 'go further'. Divide the fish (sole, plaice, whiting or small pieces of pilchard can be used) into neat strips, coat in egg and crumbs or batter and fry as the Blue Print. Small sprigs of raw or lightly cooked cauliflower can also be coated with batter and fried with the fish as in the picture. Garnish with lemon.

   This is another advantage of deep frying, the flavours do not intermingle or impart flavour to the fat or oil. Potato chips or other vegetables, such as onion rings, can be fried immediately before the fish and kept hot. Traditional fish and chips are illustrated on page 21.

Tartare Sauce

$\frac{1}{4}$ pint ($\frac{2}{3}$C) mayonnaise or Hollandaise sauce; 2 teaspoons each chopped parsley, chopped gherkins and capers; few drops tarragon vinegar (optional).

Mix all the ingredients together. If using mayonnaise as a basis for this sauce you can make a large quantity and store the remainder in a screw-topped bottle in the refrigerator.

Storing and Freezing   *Ready frozen fish may be used, without waiting for it to thaw out, although it is difficult to coat frozen fish. Remember though you can buy ready-coated portions of frozen fish for shallow or deep frying. The cooking time is only a few minutes longer.*

To use any left over   *Fried fish is not very suitable for using in other ways. It could be frozen, ready to reheat, but take care it is not over-cooked.*

Do not imagine that frying fish in deep fat (or oil) is more extravagant than shallow frying. If the temperature of the fat or oil is correct it is surprising just how *little* is absorbed by the fish coating.

Blue Print

To Fry Fish in Deep Fat

This method is suitable for white fish and for large prawns. It is rarely used for oily fish and other shell fish and never for smoked fish. It is better to coat the fish when using this method of cooking. Choose either egg and crumbs, i.e. **2** on the Blue Print opposite or the batter coating below.

To make a batter to coat 4 portions of fish (or equivalent in large prawns—scampi), sieve 4 oz. (1C) flour, plain or self-raising, with a pinch salt. Add 1 egg and about 12 tablespoons (1C) milk or milk and water. When coating in batter, dip the fish in seasoned flour first (allow about $\frac{1}{4}$ tablespoon per portion), this encourages the batter to adhere to the fish. Dip in the batter, allow any surplus batter to drop back into the basin so you do not have too thick a coating.

Make sure the pan of fat or oil is not overfilled, for naturally the level will rise when the fish is placed into the pan. *Test the temperature of the fat or oil*, it should be 365°F, or a cube of day-old bread should turn golden brown within under 1 minute. Place the frying basket into the hot fat or oil so this becomes coated, which prevents the fish sticking to the mesh. Lift the warmed basket from the fat or oil, lower the coated fish into this.

Timing

Thin fillets take about 3 minutes.
Thicker fillets take about 4 minutes.
Thick steaks (cutlets) or whole fish take about 5–6 minutes.

Lift the fish from the fat or oil, allow the basket to remain over the top of the pan for a few seconds for any surplus fat to drop back into the pan. Drain on absorbent paper and serve. Deep fried fish can be served without a sauce, but a tartare sauce is the usual accompaniment.

● **AVOID** *Too hot fat or oil which will scorch the outside: Too cool fat or oil which will cause the coating to become greasy or even 'drop off' the fish.*
● **TO RECTIFY** *Test the temperature of the fat before frying (see Blue Print).*

AVOID ANY DANGER OF FIRE—NEVER LEAVE A PAN OF FAT OR OIL UNATTENDED AND ALWAYS TURN THE HANDLE TOWARDS THE CENTRE OF THE COOKER SO IT CANNOT BE KNOCKED AGAINST.

Goujons of fish (above left). Rolled fillets of fish (above).

Poaching Fish

I have used the term 'poach', rather than 'boil', for it describes the method that should be used for cooking fish. If fish really is boiled in liquid, it is cooked too rapidly and the outer flesh can, and probably will, break badly and become 'watery'. Poaching means cooking gently in simmering liquid.

Blue Print

To Poach Fish

This is suitable for all kinds of fish including shell fish.

The liquid in which the fish is poached can be:

1. Seasoned water or when 'boiling' crab, lobster, etc. many people like to use sea water.
2. Wine, cider or wine and water.
3. Milk or milk and thin cream.
4. A court bouillon. This is made by using either fish stock (made by boiling the head, skins and bones of fish) or fish stock blended with white wine, a *bouquet garni* and seasoning.

The amount of liquid varies according to the thickness of the fish. Some people like to put the fish into cold liquid, bring the liquid to simmering point and continue, others like to put the fish into the simmering liquid. If putting into warmed liquid shorten the cooking times below by about 2 minutes.

Timing

Thin fillets take about 7–8 minutes.
Thicker fillets, steaks (cutlets) or small whole fish take about 10–12 minutes.
Whole fish—allow 7–8 minutes per lb. or up to 10 minutes per lb. for solid type fish, i.e. salmon.

Lift the fish out of the liquid with a fish slice, drain for a moment over the pan, then put on to a heated serving dish. If serving cold, allow to cool in the liquid; the cooking time should therefore be reduced by about 5 minutes. Poached fish is generally served with a sauce and the easiest and most simple sauces are on this page.

● **AVOID** *Over-cooking: Failing to season the liquid which produces rather tasteless fish.*
● **TO SLIMMERS** *An ideal method of cooking.*

SAUCES TO SERVE WITH POACHED FISH

White Sauce

1 oz. butter or margarine; 1 oz. flour; ½ pint (1⅓C) milk or use half milk and half liquid from cooking the fish; seasoning.

Heat the butter or margarine in a saucepan. Stir in the flour and continue stirring over a low heat until the 'roux' forms a dry mixture. Gradually add the milk or milk and other liquid, bring to the boil, cook until thickened, stirring all the time. Add seasoning to taste.

Anchovy sauce   Use no salt in the sauce, add a few drops of anchovy essence.

Cheese sauce   Add 3–4 tablespoons grated cheese to the thickened sauce, stir over a low heat, do not boil again. A little mustard can be added, if liked.

Cream sauce   Add 2–3 tablespoons thick cream to the thickened sauce, heat gently.

Lemon sauce   Add the grated rind of 1 lemon to the flour. Add 1–2 tablespoons lemon juice to the thickened sauce, do not boil again and heat very gently.

Parsley sauce   Add 1–2 tablespoons chopped parsley to the thickened sauce. Allow the parsley to cook for 2–3 minutes in the sauce for a milder flavour.

Shrimp or prawn sauce   Add a few tablespoons whole shrimps or chopped prawns to the sauce, heat gently so the shell fish is not toughened.

More Fish Dishes

On this page are a variety of fish dishes, including two other Blue Prints for simple methods of cooking fish.

Haddock and Mushroom Scallops

Little butter and cream; 1 lb. (2C) cooked potatoes; about 8 oz. fresh haddock; about 8 oz. smoked haddock; 1 pint (2⅔C) milk; 1½ oz. butter; 1 oz. flour; 4 oz. (1C) mushrooms; seasoning; 1 small can sweet corn. *To garnish:* 4 tomatoes; parsley.

Blend a little butter and cream into the mashed potatoes. Put into a piping bag with a ½-inch rose and pipe a border round the edge of 6 scallop shells or individual heat-proof dishes. Brown gently under a very low grill or in a very moderate to moderate oven while making the fish mixture. Put the fish into the milk with about one third of the butter. Simmer steadily until tender, i.e. about 10–12 minutes. Lift the fish out of the milk on to a flat dish, allow to cool slightly, then skin and flake. Meanwhile heat the remaining butter in a pan, stir in the flour and cook for several minutes, stirring all the time. Strain the milk, used in cooking the fish, into the 'roux'. Bring gradually to the boil and cook until thickened, stirring all the time. Put in the whole mushrooms and simmer for about 5 minutes, then add the flaked fish. Season to taste, add some of the sweet corn. Put the sauce mixture into the border of potato and top with hot sweet corn. Garnish with wedges of tomato and parsley. *Serves 6.*

Note   Other white and smoked fish can be used in this recipe.

Blue Prints

1. To Roast Fish

This method is suitable for white and oily fish.

It is similar to baking fish, as the instructions on page 23, but a more generous amount of butter or other fat is used. The fish is basted in the hot butter or fat as it cooks in a moderately hot to hot oven, 375–400°F, Gas Mark 5–6, so the outside skin becomes crisp and brown. The cooking time is similar to that given for baking. It is very suitable for whole fish or thick pieces of cod, fresh haddock, etc.

2. To Steam Fish

This method is suitable for white fish, preferably whiting, sole, plaice and similar fish. It is an excellent way of cooking fish for small children, older people or invalids as it is the

Haddock and mushroom scallops

most easily digested form of cooked fish. The easiest method of steaming fish is to put the lightly seasoned fish on a buttered plate and top with a little butter. Sometimes this must be omitted if people are on a fat-free diet, but obviously it makes the fish more interesting. Top with a small quantity of milk. Put the plate over a pan of boiling water and cover with another plate, foil or a saucepan lid. Keep the water boiling and allow the following times.

Timing

Thin fillets take about 8–10 minutes.
Thicker fillets or thin steaks take about 12–15 minutes.
The liquid left on the plate can be added to a white, cheese or anchovy sauce (see opposite) to serve with the fish.

Fish Milanaise

4 portions white fish (preferably large fillets sole, whiting, plaice, etc.); seasoning; 2–3 tablespoons white wine; 2 oz. ($\frac{1}{4}$C) butter; about 6 oz. ribbon noodles; 2–4 oz. ($\frac{1}{2}$–1C) button mushrooms; few cooked peas. *To garnish*: paprika; lemon.
Put the fish on to a large plate, add the seasoning, wine and about $\frac{1}{2}$ oz. only of butter. Steam as the Blue Print. Meanwhile boil the noodles in plenty of well seasoned water and fry the mushrooms in the remaining butter. Drain the noodles, return to the saucepan with the peas and mushrooms. Heat gently for a few minutes, then put on a hot dish. Lift the fish on top of the noodles and garnish with paprika and lemon. This can be served with any of the sauces opposite. *Serves 4.*

Normandy Herrings

4 large herrings; seasoning; 1 oz. flour; 3 oz. ($\frac{3}{8}$C) butter or margarine; 1 large onion; 2–3 dessert apples; 1 tablespoon lemon juice. *To garnish*: parsley.
Remove the heads from the fish, clean and remove the back bone, if wished, as instructions on page 22. Season the flour and roll

Normandy herrings

Fish Milanaise

the fish in this. Heat about 2 oz. ($\frac{1}{4}$C) of the butter or margarine in a large pan. Peel and chop the onion. Core the apples, slice 1 apple for garnish, as in the picture, and chop the remainder. Fry the apples and onions in the pan until the apples are soft and the onion is transparent. Add the lemon juice. Put the chopped onions and apples into a hot serving dish and keep warm; keep the apple slices separate. Heat the remaining butter or margarine in the frying pan and cook the fish until tender. Put on top of the mixture in the serving dish and garnish with the apple slices and parsley. *Serves 4.*

To vary Use shelled prawns in place of the apples and onion. Fry the fish first, remove and keep warm, then fry the prawns in the cleaned pan in a little extra butter. Add 1–2 tablespoons Chablis or Calvados and spoon over the fish.

Fish Pies and Patties

Although ready-cooked fish can be used in fish pies and patties, it is obviously better to choose the right fish and cook or prepare it specially for these economical and interesting dishes.

Seafood Pie

1½ lb. white fish (inexpensive kind); about ½ pint (1⅓C) fish stock or water; seasoning; 1 pint (2⅔C) white or other sauce (see page 168); few prawns; about 1 lb. (2C) creamed potato; little butter or margarine.

Bake or poach the fish as the Blue Prints on pages 23 and 28, using the fish stock or water and seasoning. Drain and flake the fish, use the liquid as part of the sauce if wished. Mix the sauce and fish, add the prawns. Put into a pie dish and top with the creamed potato and a little butter or margarine. Bake for approximately 30 minutes just above the centre of a moderate to moderately hot oven, 375–400°F, Gas Mark 5–6. *Serves 4–5.*

Salmon Pie

Use cooked fresh or canned salmon in place of white fish in the recipe above. Mix with the sauce, then add a few sliced cooked carrots, 2 chopped hard boiled eggs and about 3–4 tablespoons grated cheese. Top with the creamed potato or a puff pastry crust (made with 5–6 oz. (1¼–1½C) flour, etc.). If using potato, bake as the recipe above. If using puff pastry, bake as the recipe below for Fish in a Jacket.

Fish Pie Americaine

Fry 2–3 rashers chopped bacon with 1–2 chopped onions, then add about 3 chopped and skinned tomatoes. Stir in 1 oz. flour and cook for several minutes, stirring all the time. Gradually blend in ¾ pint (2C) chicken or fish stock. Bring to the boil, cook until a thickened mixture. Stir well as the mixture thickens. Add about 1–1½ lb. flaked cooked white fish, season well. Put into a pie dish, top with creamed potato and bake as the Seafood Pie.

Fish in a Jacket

1 lb. frozen puff pastry or puff pastry made with 8 oz. (2C) flour, etc.; 4 very large or 6 smaller fillets white fish; seasoning; 1 oz. butter; 1 oz. flour; ¼ pint (⅔C) milk; about 4 oz. (1C) mushrooms. *To glaze:* 1 egg; 1 tablespoon water. *To garnish:* sliced lemon and parsley.

Prepare the pastry and roll out thinly, then cut into 4 or 6 squares, large enough to cover the fish. Lay the fillets flat on a board, season lightly. Make a thick sauce with the butter, flour and milk as the method on page 28. Add the chopped uncooked mushrooms and season well. Spread over half of each fillet, see Sketch 1. Fold the other half of the fish over the sauce, see Sketch 2. Lay on the squares of pastry, moisten the edges, fold over in triangles and seal the edges, see Sketches 3 and 4. Lift on to a baking sheet, brush with a little beaten egg, blended with water. Bake for 10 minutes just above the centre of a very hot oven, 475°F, Gas Mark 8, then lower the heat to moderate and cook for a further 20–25 minutes until golden brown and well risen. Garnish with lemon and parsley and serve hot. *Serves 4–6.*

To vary If preferred, blend flaked cooked fish with a thick sauce and chopped mushrooms and use as a filling for the pastry.

Fish Cakes

8 oz. cooked fish*; 8 oz. (1C) creamed potatoes; 1 egg; seasoning. *To coat:* ½ oz. flour; 1 egg; approximately 2 oz. (1C) crisp breadcrumbs. *To fry:* about 2 oz. (¼C) fat or 2 tablespoons oil.

*white fish, herrings, kippers, tuna (canned or fresh) or salmon (canned or fresh) may be used.

Flake the cooked fish finely, blend with the potatoes, the egg and seasoning. Form into 8 flat cakes. Coat in the flour, blended with a little seasoning, then the egg and breadcrumbs. Pat into a good shape with a flat-bladed knife. Heat the fat or oil in a frying pan and fry the fish cakes until crisp and brown on both sides. Drain on absorbent paper and serve hot with lemon or with a sauce (see page 28). *Serves 4.*

To vary Bind with a thick white sauce (as the recipe for Fish in a Jacket) instead of the egg.

Add 1–2 tablespoons chopped parsley to the fish mixture.

Bind the fish cakes with about 4 tablespoons fresh, well seasoned tomato puree instead of egg.

Flavour with 2–3 teaspoons chopped chives.

Storing and Freezing *Fish cakes freeze splendidly and can be cooked from the frozen state.*

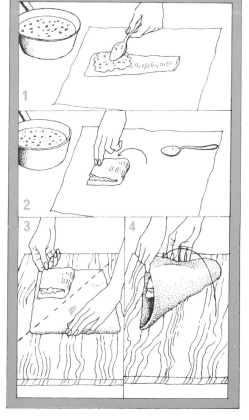

Fish in a jacket

In most families the traditional bird at Christmas time is a turkey, and indeed roasted poultry or game is an ideal choice for a celebration meal. The points about selecting poultry will be found on page 21. Choose quick roasting for prime birds and slower roasting for poorer quality, or when the bird has been frozen. *Always allow frozen poultry to thaw out before cooking, this takes up to 48 hours with a very large turkey.*

Blue Print Recipes

1. To Roast Chicken and Turkey

A large roasting fowl or capon serves 6–8. A medium-sized chicken can be cut into 4 portions and small spring chickens halved, or if very small, left whole as a portion for one. Guinea fowl is cooked and served as chicken. When buying turkey, remember there is a considerable weight of bone, so allow at least 12 oz. per person, i.e. a 12 lb. bird (weight when trussed) would provide portions for 14–16 people.

These are dry-fleshed birds and must be kept moist during cooking, so cover the bird, particularly the breast, with a generous amount of fat bacon or fat. Put stuffing inside the bird as it helps to keep it moist. Always weigh the bird after stuffing to calculate the cooking time. Baste the bird from time to time to keep it moist.

Timing

For quick roasting Set the oven to hot,

425–450°F, Gas Mark 7–8, the heat may be reduced to moderately hot after 15 minutes if roasting a small chicken and 30 minutes for a larger bird.

Chicken 15 minutes per lb. and 15 minutes over.

Turkey 15 minutes per lb. and 15 minutes over for a bird up to 12 lb. in weight. After this add an additional 12 minutes per lb. up to 21 lb., after this allow only 10 minutes for each additional 1 lb. If the bird is exceptionally broad breasted be a little generous with the cooking time.

For slower roasting Set the oven to moderate, 350–375°F, Gas Mark 4–5, only.

Chicken 25 minutes per lb. and 25 minutes over.

Turkey 25 minutes per lb. and 25 minutes over for a bird up to 12 lb. in weight. After this add an additional 20 minutes per lb. up to 21 lb. then allow 15 minutes for each additional 1 lb. If the bird is exceptionally broad breasted then allow an extra 5 minutes per lb.

If using a covered roasting tin or foil allow an extra 15–20 minutes cooking time. Lift the lid of the tin or open the foil for about 30 minutes before the end of the cooking period so the skin may brown and crisp. Extra cooking time is *not* necessary when using cooking film or roasting bags.

Accompaniments

The traditional accompaniments with both these birds are: bread sauce (or cranberry sauce with turkey); parsley and thyme (veal) stuffing and/or chestnut stuffing· roasted sausages and bacon rolls; thickened gravy. There are however more unusual accompaniments which may be served such as orange or wine sauce.

When roasting a chicken or turkey, prepare the bird, i.e. put in stuffing, see the sketches. Heat the oven, cover the bird with fat or fat bacon. Cook for the time calculated. Add the sausages about 30 minutes before the end of the cooking time and the bacon rolls about 10–15 minutes before 'dishing-up'. Lift the bird on to the hot serving dish and use a little of the fat in the tin to add to the gravy. Hints on making gravy will be found on page 9.

1. Insert the stuffing under the skin of the neck.
2. Pull the skin right over the stuffing and

secure with a skewer.
3. Put any remaining stuffing (or if using two kinds, the second one) inside the bird.

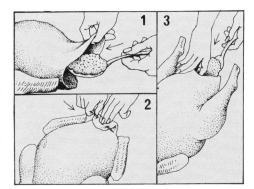

2. To Roast Duck and Goose

Duck and goose are birds that contain a high percentage of fat. I find I obtain a really 'fat free' bird, with deliciously crisp skin if I cook the bird for about 30 minutes then take the roasting tin out of the oven. Prick the skin carefully, do not prick too deeply, with a fine skewer and the excess fat 'spurts out'. Do this once or twice for duck but at least twice more for a goose. Do not add extra fat when cooking duck or goose. The cooking times are the same as for chicken and turkey.

Quantities

A large duck can be cut into 4 joints, but a small duckling should be halved.

Goose is a very extravagant bird, for it has very large bones and relatively little meat, so you should allow at least 1 lb. weight per person (after the bird is trussed).

Accompaniments

The traditional accompaniments with both these birds are apple sauce; sage and onion stuffing and thickened gravy. Less usual accompaniments are orange sauce and wine sauce. Duckling always looks more interesting if garnished with slices of orange.

Roast turkey

Frying and Grilling Chicken

I have headed this page as two methods of cooking chicken, for young chickens are very plentiful and inexpensive. Neither duck nor goose are suitable for frying or grilling and joints of turkey are too large. Certain recipes on these pages can be used with very young game.

Blue Print

1. To Fry Chicken

Choose young frying (broiler) chickens. If not ready-jointed, then cut the chicken into neat joints, with a very sharp knife.

If the chickens are frozen, they can be cooked without defrosting, but I find I get a better coating if I allow the chickens to defrost, dry the joints, then coat them.

Coat the chicken joints with seasoned flour, or egg and crumbs, or batter, in exactly the same way as described under frying fish on pages 26 and 27; the coating clings better if the skin is removed from the joints.

The chicken joints may be cooked in shallow or deep fat.

Timing

The cooking times will be about 15 minutes in shallow fat, turning the joints regularly or about 10–12 minutes in deep fat or oil.

Drain on absorbent paper and serve with salad, or with cooked rice, as shown in the pictures, or with mixed vegetables.

● **AVOID** *Having the fat too hot or too cold. See the Blue Print on page 27.*

2. To Grill Chicken

Choose young chickens (broilers). Joint as described under Blue Print 1. They may be grilled from the frozen state or defrosted, dried well then grilled.

Make sure the grill is very hot before putting the chickens under the heat. Brush the grid of the grill pan with melted butter, margarine or fat, to prevent the joints sticking.

Brush the joints of chicken with melted fat of some kind, season if wished. Cook for approximately 15 minutes, turning several times and basting with the fat. When the outside of the chicken joints are brown and crisp, the heat may be reduced so the chicken is cooked through to the centre. Mushrooms and tomatoes may be cooked on the grid of the grill pan, or in the grill pan itself at the same time. Season the vegetables, brush with melted butter, margarine or oil before cooking, so they do not dry.

● **AVOID** *Cooking the chicken too slowly: Cooking the chicken without fat (unless counting calories), for it will become very dry.*

● **TO SLIMMERS** *Grilling is an excellent method of cooking any food and young chicken is relatively low in calories. You can try 'basting' the chicken with fruit juice, rather than fat.*

Storing and Freezing *Young chickens keep relatively well in a cool place or refrigerator. Frozen joints may be stored in the freezing compartment of the refrigerator for the time stated on the package. You can freeze your own young chicken joints.*

To use any left over *Use in salads or sandwiches. Do not cook again as the delicate flavour and texture is easily spoiled.*

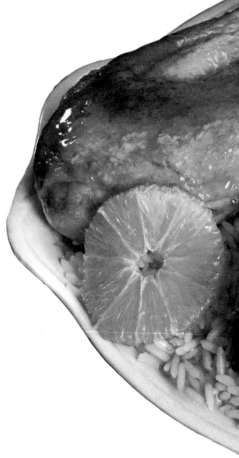

Fried chicken and oranges

For Family Occasions

Fried Chicken and Oranges

4 portions chicken; 1 oz. flour; seasoning; 2 oz. ($\frac{1}{4}$C) butter; $\frac{1}{2}$ tablespoon oil; 3 large oranges.

Dry the portions of chicken and coat in seasoned flour. Heat the butter and oil in a pan. Fry the chicken as Blue Print 1 until nearly tender. Squeeze the juice from 2 oranges, pour over the chicken and finish cooking. Serve the chicken joints on a bed of boiled rice and garnish with the remaining orange, peeled and cut into rings. *Serves 4.*

To vary This is even more delicious if 2–3 tablespoons halved walnuts are added to the pan with the orange juice. The combination of crisp nuts and orange juice is very pleasant.

Fried Chicken Italienne

8 drumsticks of young chicken; 1 level tablespoon flour; seasoning; 1 or 2 eggs (depending upon the size); 2–3 oz. (1–1$\frac{1}{2}$C) crisp breadcrumbs; 2 tablespoons grated Parmesan cheese. *To fry:* deep fat or oil. *For the rice*

Fried chicken Italienne

mixture: 2 oz. ($\frac{1}{4}$C) butter or margarine; 1 green and 1 red pepper; 8 oz. (1C) long grain rice; 1 pint (2$\frac{2}{3}$C) chicken stock or water and 1 or 2 stock cubes; seasoning; few cooked peas; little cooked or canned sweet corn. *To garnish:* watercress or cooked spinach or other green vegetable.

Coat the drumsticks with the flour mixed with seasoning, the beaten egg, then the crumbs, blended with the cheese. If possible chill for a while so the coating sets well. Meanwhile heat the butter or margarine in a pan. Dice the peppers, removing the cores and seeds and toss in the butter for a few minutes. Add the rice and mix with the butter and peppers. Put the stock or water and stock cubes into the pan, bring to the boil, stir, season well and cook until the rice is nearly tender. Add the peas and sweet corn and finish cooking until the rice is tender and the liquid absorbed. Meanwhile deep fry the drumsticks as Blue Print 1; take particular care that the fat or oil is not too hot, otherwise the cheese will scorch. Drain on absorbent paper. Pile the rice mixture on to a very hot dish. Arrange the drumsticks around and garnish with the watercress or alternative. *Serves 4.*

Stuffed Chicken Cutlets

4 joints chicken, preferably breast joints; 8 oz. pork sausagemeat; 1 tablespoon chopped parsley; 2 oz. ($\frac{1}{2}$C) mushrooms; butter or chicken fat for frying or grilling. *To garnish:* cooked tomatoes.

Remove the bones from the chicken joints. Blend the sausagemeat, parsley and finely chopped mushrooms together. Divide this mixture into 4 portions and press each portion against the joints of chicken. Do this on the underside where the bones were removed. Fry or grill the joints as Blue Prints 1 or 2, frying in or basting with the butter or chicken fat. Serve with fried or grilled tomatoes. *Serves 4.*

For Special Occasions

Spatchcock of Chicken

4 very small young chickens or 2 larger ones; seasoning; 2 oz. ($\frac{1}{4}$C) butter; grated rind 1 lemon. *To garnish:* watercress; lemon.
Split the chickens right down the backbone, so they open out quite flat, see the sketches. Mix the seasoning with the melted butter, add the lemon rind. Grill the chickens as

described under Blue Print 2, basting with the butter as they cook. Garnish with watercress and sliced lemon. *Serves 4.*
To vary Very young pigeons or partridges may be cooked in the same way. Omit the lemon if wished and flavour the butter with a few drops Worcestershire sauce and a pinch curry powder.

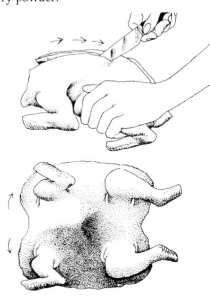

The recipes on this page make good use of cooked poultry and game. Read the points outlined in the Blue Print before preparing the recipes.

Blue Print

Using Cooked Poultry and Game

Never waste the carcass of a bird, simmer in water to give a good stock, flavour the liquid with herbs and vegetables and season well.

Choose recipes where the meats are given the minimum heating time. Both poultry and game (with the exception of duck and goose) tend to have a dry flesh which will be spoiled by a second long cooking. Remember a certain amount of flavour is lost when food is cooked a second time, so compensate for this by adding herbs, cooking fresh vegetables in the sauce or using spices. Serve the dish as soon as possible after cooking and make sure the accompaniments are interesting and freshly cooked; crisp salads are splendid with any of these dishes.

Creamed Turkey Duchesse

1–1¼ lb. (2–2½C) mashed potatoes; 2 eggs or 2 egg yolks; 2 oz. (¼C) butter or margarine; seasoning; 4 oz. (1C) button mushrooms; 1 green pepper; ½ pint (1⅓C) turkey stock (made by simmering the carcass or giblets); 1 oz. flour; ¼ pint (⅔C) milk; few drops Tabasco sauce; about 1 lb. diced cooked turkey plus any small pieces of stuffing (optional); 2–3 tablespoons top of the milk or thin cream. *To garnish:* parsley.

Blend the mashed potatoes with 1 egg or egg yolk and half the butter or margarine, season well. Form into a border round the edge of an oven-proof dish. Brush with the second egg or egg yolk, diluted with a few drops of water and brown in a moderate oven, 350–375°F, Gas Mark 4–5. Meanwhile simmer the mushrooms and diced green pepper (discard the core and seeds) in the stock for 10 minutes. Strain the liquid from the mushrooms and pepper, put this on one side for the sauce. Heat the remainder of the butter or margarine in a saucepan, stir in the flour, cook for several minutes, stirring all the time, add the milk gradually, then the stock. Bring to the boil, and cook until thickened, stirring briskly, season well. Flavour with the Tabasco. Taste and add a little more Tabasco, if desired. Put the vegetables and turkey into the sauce and heat gently for a few minutes. Add the stuffing and cream towards the end of the heating period. Bring the dish out of the oven. Pile the turkey mixture into the centre and garnish with parsley. *Serves 4–6.*

To vary Cooked pheasant or chicken may be used instead of turkey. If using pheasant simmer 1–2 diced onions in the stock to give more flavour.

Chicken Pilau

2 onions; 1 clove garlic (optional); 2 tablespoons chicken fat or oil; 8 oz. (1C) long grain rice; 1 pint (2⅔C) chicken stock (made by simmering chicken carcass or giblets); 1–2 oz. sultanas; few pine or other nuts (optional); 12 oz. diced chicken; seasoning. *To garnish:* few nuts or crisp breadcrumbs.

Peel and chop the onions, crush the garlic. Fry in the hot fat or oil for a few minutes, then add the rice, turn in the fat or oil. Add the stock, bring to the boil, stir, then simmer in an open pan for about 10 minutes. Add the rest of the ingredients and cook for a further 10–15 minutes until the liquid has just been absorbed. Pile on to a hot dish and top with the nuts or crumbs. *Serves 4–5.*

Duck and Chestnuts

8 oz.–1 lb. chestnuts; about 12 small onions or shallots; 2 oz. (¼C) duck fat or margarine; 1 oz. flour; ½ pint (1⅓C) duck stock (made by simmering the carcass or giblets); ¼ pint (⅔C) red wine; seasoning; 1 small dessert apple; 8–12 oz. diced cooked duck plus any skin; little fat to fry the skin. *To garnish:* 1 dessert apple; little lemon juice.

Slit the chestnuts, boil for 5–10 minutes, remove the skins while warm. Peel the onions. Toss the onions in the hot duck fat or margarine until golden. Lift out of the pan, stir in the flour and cook the 'roux' for several minutes. Add the duck stock gradually, bring to the boil, cook until thickened, stirring all the time. Add the wine. Put the chestnuts and onions into the sauce, season well. Cover the pan, simmer for 20–25 minutes. Peel, core and dice the apple, put into the sauce with the duck and heat for a few minutes. To many people the skin of a duck is almost the most delicious part, so cut any pieces of skin left into neat dice. Put a little fat in a small frying pan, heat and fry the diced skin until very crisp. Put the duck mixture into a hot serving dish. Garnish with rings of apple, dipped in lemon juice and top these with the very hot crisp skin. *Serves 4–5.*

Creamed turkey duchesse

three
VEGETABLES AND MEALS WITHOUT MEAT

In this section you will find a great number of dishes using vegetables. Some of the recipes treat them as an accompaniment to the main dish, in others the vegetables themselves are the basis of the meal.

With modern freezing, canning and drying, it is now possible to obtain almost every vegetable at any time during the year. Frozen vegetables are always very young and tender, so do not over-cook them, follow the directions carefully on the package.

Canned vegetables have been cooked in the process of canning, so should be heated only. Prolonged cooking spoils much of their flavour and texture. Dehydrated vegetables are of two types, firstly the modern Accelerated Freeze Dried variety (i.e. the type that are first frozen and then dried), these need very little soaking and a short cooking time. Secondly there are the more traditional dried vegetables which should be soaked well and/or given a long cooking period.

It is surprising how often beautifully fresh vegetables are spoiled by over-cooking and this applies particularly to green vegetables. They contain essential mineral salts and Vitamin C (the vitamin that helps to build up resistance to colds, and give a clear healthy skin). Unfortunately this vitamin is lost if the vegetables are stale (so shop critically), or if the vegetables are over-cooked. Page 36 gives the correct *modern* method of cooking green vegetables, known as the Conserved Method. Please do not consider this only as a method of cooking to pre- serve food values. It also ensures you have vegetables that are full of flavour, a good colour and an interesting texture.

Onions, leeks and garlic are bulb vegetables (although garlic is often classed as a herb). Although these are used frequently to provide additional flavour to other dishes, both onions and leeks can be the basis of interesting meals.

Most people, young and old, are fond of fried potatoes—but how often are these disappointing? The perfect fried potato should be dry, not greasy, crisp, not 'soggy' and an even golden brown in colour. Page 38 deals with the '8 secrets' of successful fried potatoes and gives some new ways of shaping and presenting fried potatoes too.

The usual protein foods, meat, fish and poultry are expensive and there may be times when you wish to serve a sustaining meal without using them. You will find a great number of the dishes, especially in the latter part of this section, give a really good meal, based upon vegetables.

Although the list of green vegetables is very long and cooking times vary, the basic principles of cooking practically every variety are covered in the Blue Print. This page deals with the 'homely' green vegetables and the methods of dealing with the more luxurious ones are given on page 48.

Buying Green Vegetables

In order to ensure you have the very *best* green vegetables available, check on the following points when buying.

Broccoli—green or purple—should have very green leaves (if they have the slightest yellow tinge, they are stale); the flower should be firm.

Avoid cabbage or greens with slightly yellow leaves, these indicate a stale vegetable. Feel the vegetables, they should be heavy for their size, if surprisingly light this indicates there is little heart to the cabbage.

The outer leaves of cauliflower should be green and firm looking and the flower firm and white.

If spinach or greens look limp do not buy if possible—they could 'revive' when put into cold water, but they may be too stale to be good.

Storing Green Vegetables

Unpack as soon as possible. If you have a very large refrigerator you can pack the vegetables into covered containers, but as this is unlikely for most people, this is the way to store:

Keep as much air circulation as possible around the vegetables.
Store away from bright light if possible.
Keep in the coolest place possible.
If storing cabbage, sprouts and firm greens for more than a day, sprinkle lightly with cold water.
If storing spinach, greens or broccoli for more than a day (which is not advisable) then keep dry, if sprinkled with water they are inclined to become 'slimy'.

Preparing Green Vegetables

Do not wash, soak, cut or shred the vegetables until ready to cook. Mineral salts are soluble in water and will be 'lost' by soaking. Vitamin C is destroyed by leaving cut surfaces exposed to the air.
Wash the vegetables in cold water, leave in the water for the shortest time possible.
If you add a little salt to the water it makes sure that tiny insects, that often are found in green vegetables, will be 'drawn out'.

Cabbage and Similar Green Vegetables Shred as finely as possible, with a sharp knife, to shorten cooking time.

Sprouts Remove only the very outer leaves, all too often much of each sprout is wasted by excess removal of leaves. Make a cross at the base of each sprout, this helps to shorten cooking time.

Cauliflower The stems and green leaves are delicious, so remove these and trim ready for cooking. Discard only the imperfect outer stems and leaves. You can trim the thick part of the stems, but if these are placed into the boiling water a few minutes *before* the flower, they become tender when ready to 'dish up' the vegetable.

Spinach There are two types, the small leafed (New Zealand) and the large leafed (Beet) spinach. When preparing the small leafed spinach just break away any surplus stalks at the base. When preparing the large leafed spinach I pull the green leaves away from the stems, then trim the stems and cook as a separate vegetable. These are delicious when cooked in boiling salted water, strained and topped with melted butter and chopped chives or parsley.

Broccoli Remove the very outer leaves. Keep the flower heads and the small leaves surrounding these intact. Choose a large saucepan, so the flowers and stalks may be laid flat in the boiling salted water in the pan.

Blue Print
The Conserved Method of Cooking

1. Prepare the vegetables as this page.
2. Put only enough water into the pan to give a depth of 1–1½ inches—except for cauliflower and spinach, see below. Add a good pinch salt.
3. Make sure the saucepan has a tightly fitting lid.
4. Bring the water to the boil.
5. Remove the vegetables from the water in which they were washed, drain—except for spinach, see below.
6. Take the prepared vegetables over to the cooker in a colander or bowl.
7. Add the vegetables *gradually to the boiling water*. This is important for the water should continue to boil and it will do this if the vegetables are added steadily, rather than all at once.
8. When all the vegetables have been added to the water, put on the lid and time the cooking.

Shredded Cabbage can be ready in 2–3 minutes, tougher types of cabbage take a minute or so longer.
Sprouts, if small, will take only 5–6 minutes.
Broccoli about 8–10 minutes.
Cauliflower As this vegetable does take longer to cook than cabbage, allow about 3 inches of water. Follow points 1–7 above, place the flower or flower sprigs downwards in the boiling salted water.
Allow about 15–20 minutes for a whole cauliflower but 10–15 minutes for sprigged cauliflower, until the stems are just tender but the flower unbroken.

Cauliflower with brown sauce topping

Cabbage pancakes

Spinach This contains a high percentage of water, so wash well (often spinach has a lot of sand and soil sticking to the leaves, so may need washing in 2–3 changes of cold water), do not drain. Simply put into the pan with *no extra water*, just the water adhering to the leaves. Add a little salt. Cook steadily for 2–3 minutes, so the water runs off the leaves, then raise the heat slightly and continue cooking until tender.

The very young small leafed spinach takes only about 7–8 minutes. The larger leafed spinach rather more. If you are worried about the spinach sticking to the pan, put in $\frac{1}{2}$ inch water, bring to the boil, then add the damp vegetable.

9. Strain the vegetables *as soon as they are cooked*, top with a little butter or margarine and serve as quickly as possible.

Use the vegetable water if possible to add to gravy, soups and stews. Some people like to drink it, but that, I must confess, is an acquired taste.

Toppings for Green Vegetables
Sprinkle the vegetables with freshly chopped herbs.

Top broccoli, cauliflower or cooked spinach with Hollandaise sauce (page 94), white or cheese sauce (this will make Cauliflower Cheese). Always incorporate some of the vegetable liquid into the sauce.

Make a tomato sauce (see page 48—Artichokes Barigoule) or a brown sauce (see page 72 for recipe). Spoon over cooked cauliflower and top with chopped parsley.

● **AVOID** *Over-cooking green vegetables, or keeping them for any length of time before serving.*

● **TO RECTIFY** *Although you cannot 'revive' over-cooked vegetables, some of the toppings on this page give additional flavour.*

● **SHORT CUT** *The smaller the pieces of vegetable, the quicker the cooking time.*

● **TO SLIMMERS** *All green vegetables are low in calories, so when you are planning slimming meals serve as great a variety of green vegetables as possible.*

Storing and Freezing *Details of storing are given opposite. Raw spinach, cauliflower and broccoli freeze very well, cabbage is less successful.*

New Ways with Green Vegetables

Remember that firm Dutch white cabbage (excellent as the basis for Coleslaw) or red cabbage (often considered only for pickling) can be used instead of green cabbage or cabbage greens in any of the recipes. As the leaves of these are firmer than those of a tender green cabbage, allow 3–4 minutes longer cooking time than that given in the Blue Print. It is usual to cook red cabbage until quite tender and this can take a minimum of 30 minutes. You may, however, prefer its very firm (rather than crisp) texture if cooked for a shorter time.

Cabbage Pancakes
1 very small green cabbage, or use the *tender* outer leaves of a large cabbage and save the heart for another occasion; seasoning. *For the batter:* 4 oz. (1C) plain flour; pinch salt; 1 egg; $\frac{1}{2}$ pint (1$\frac{1}{3}$C) milk and water. *For frying:* oil or fat.
Shred the cabbage and cook *very lightly* as in the Blue Print opposite, season well. Meanwhile make a pancake batter with the flour, salt, egg and milk and water. Strain the cabbage and mix with the batter. Heat a little oil or fat in a pan, pour enough of the mixture into the pan to give a thin coating. Cook until golden brown on the under side, turn and cook on the second side. Continue to make the rest of the pancakes. Serve topped with grilled or fried mushrooms. *Serves 4–6.*

Vichy Cabbage
1 small cabbage; 1–2 onions; at least 1 tablespoon chopped parsley; about 1 oz. margarine; $\frac{1}{4}$ pint ($\frac{2}{3}$C) beef or chicken stock; seasoning.
Shred the cabbage and chop the onion. Mix the onion and parsley together. Heat the margarine in a pan, toss the onion and parsley in this. Add the stock, bring to the boil, put in the cabbage gradually, as described in the Blue Print opposite. Cover the pan and cook for 2–3 minutes, lift the lid of the pan, add seasoning to taste, turn the cabbage round in the stock and allow this to boil for another 1–2 minutes until the mixture is still crisp and the liquid evaporated. This makes a pleasant alternative to the more usual way of cooking. (Illustrated on page 35.) *Serves 4–6.*

Viennese Cabbage
1 small red, green or white cabbage; seasoning; 2–4 teaspoons sugar (preferably brown); 2 oz. ($\frac{1}{4}$C) butter; 1 small apple; $\frac{1}{2}$ pint (1$\frac{1}{3}$C) chicken stock or water and $\frac{1}{2}$ stock cube; 1 tablespoon vinegar; 1 level tablespoon flour.
Shred the cabbage finely, season lightly. Put the sugar and butter into a large saucepan and stir over a low heat. Continue cooking until the mixture turns golden brown, taking care it does not burn, stir once or twice. Add

the peeled chopped apple and nearly all the stock or water and $\frac{1}{2}$ stock cube. Bring to the boil. Add the cabbage gradually, so the liquid continues to boil, then stir in the vinegar. Cook for about 5–6 minutes with green cabbage, 10–15 minutes with white cabbage and 30 minutes with red cabbage. The vegetable should just be slightly crisp. Blend the flour with the rest of the liquid, stir into the cabbage, stir very well and continue stirring until the mixture thickens slightly. Test the cabbage and if sufficiently cooked serve, otherwise continue cooking for a few more minutes, adding a little extra stock or water if necessary. *Serves 4–6.*

Cauliflower Fritters
1 medium-sized cauliflower; salt. *For the batter:* 4 oz. (1C) flour, plain or self-raising; pinch salt; 2 eggs; $\frac{1}{4}$ pint ($\frac{2}{3}$C) water; 4 tablespoons milk. *For frying:* oil or fat.
Sprig the cauliflower and cook in boiling salted water as the Blue Print opposite; take particular care that the vegetable *is not overcooked*. Sieve the flour and salt, add the egg yolks, water and milk, then fold in the stiffly whisked egg whites. Strain the cauliflower carefully, so the sprigs are not broken. Heat the oil or fat. While you can fry these fritters in shallow fat it is easier and better to use deep fat. Dip the sprigs into the batter and fry for 1–2 minutes only in the hot fat. Drain on absorbent paper.
To make a light supper dish, toss in grated Cheddar, Gruyère or Parmesan cheese. *Serves 4–8.*

To vary Brussels sprouts or broccoli can be used instead of cauliflower.
Yoghourt fritters Use yoghourt or soured cream instead of water and milk.
Tomato and cauliflower fritters Use tomato juice instead of water and milk.

Cauliflower Pancake Gâteau
Pancake batter (see Cabbage Pancakes). *For frying:* oil or fat. *For the filling:* 1 cauliflower; salt; little butter and thick cream; chopped chives and chopped parsley (optional). *To serve:* melted butter.
Make a pancake batter as the recipe for Cabbage Pancakes. Cook the pancakes in hot oil or fat. Keep hot while the sprigged cauliflower is cooked in salted water, as the Blue Print. Strain the cauliflower, tip into a hot basin and mash roughly with a fork. Blend with a little melted butter and cream. Spread each pancake with this mixture, pile one on top of the other. Top the pile with the chopped chives and parsley, if liked. Pour a little melted butter on top and serve at once. Serve with poached or baked eggs. *Serves 4–6.*

To vary Cooked creamed spinach or even creamed broccoli can be used instead of cauliflower, or spinach and cauliflower can be used alternately. (Illustrated on page 35.)

Cooking Potatoes

Potatoes may be cooked and served in dozens of different ways, but however interesting and unusual the recipe, it is based on the methods outlined here.

Blue Print

To Fry Potatoes

Although it is possible to fry raw potatoes in shallow fat, a better result is obtained by cooking in a deep pan of oil or fat.

To make Peel the potatoes, cut into the required shape, i.e. fingers (chips), slices, etc. Keep in cold water until ready to cook, then dry thoroughly in a cloth.

To cook Heat the oil or fat to 365°F. To test this, drop in one chip or slice; it should start to cook at once. If it drops to the bottom of the oil or fat, this is not sufficiently hot. Put the basket into the hot oil or fat (this makes sure the potatoes do not stick). Lift the basket from the oil. Put some of the prepared potatoes into this, lower into the hot oil or fat and cook until tender. Lift out of the pan. Continue cooking all the potatoes until tender. Reheat the oil or fat then fry the potatoes very quickly until golden brown, this takes approximately 2 minutes for each batch.

To serve Drain on absorbent paper and serve as soon as possible. The potatoes may be sprinkled with salt just before serving.

For perfect fried potatoes remember:

1. Dry the potatoes well.
2. Test the temperature of the oil or fat.
3. Heat the frying basket so they do not stick.
4. Do not cook too many potatoes at one time.
5. Cook until tender only.
6. Reheat the oil or fat.
7. Fry very quickly for the second time.
8. Drain on absorbent paper and serve.

To vary New potatoes may be washed, but not peeled, dried then fried as the Blue Print.

Ribbon potatoes Cut ribbons from the potatoes and fry as the Blue Print.

Allumette potatoes (match-sticks) Cut very thin fingers and fry as the Blue Print.

Potato balls Make balls with a vegetable scoop and fry as the Blue Print.

To Boil Potatoes

If you have never boiled potatoes with the skins left on, you are missing much of their good flavour. The skins may be removed after cooking and they pull off quite easily. This is an excellent method of cooking potatoes that tend to break in boiling.

If you wish to peel before cooking, cut away the peel from old potatoes, scrape away the skin from new potatoes. Keep in cold water until ready to cook, so the potatoes do not discolour. Put the potatoes into boiling salted water, lower the heat, so the potatoes cook steadily, rather than rapidly. Allow from 20–30 minutes according to size. Flavour new potatoes with a sprig of fresh mint during cooking, remove this before serving. Strain the potatoes and return to the pan with melted butter and chopped parsley.

To Roast Potatoes

I think nothing is more delicious than new potatoes, washed, dried then roasted in their skins. If roasting old potatoes, peel and divide large potatoes into convenient-sized pieces. Keep in cold water until ready to cook. Dry thoroughly.

Make sure the fat round the meat or in a separate roasting tin is *really* hot. There is no need to use more than 2 oz. ($\frac{1}{4}$C) fat to each 1–1$\frac{1}{2}$ lb. potatoes. Cooking fat, clarified dripping or lard are ideal. Roll the potatoes in the hot fat and roast in a hot oven, 425–450°F, Gas Mark 7–8. Allow 45–55 minutes for medium-sized potatoes. The potatoes may be turned once during cooking, but this is not essential.

To Steam Potatoes

Put well washed or peeled potatoes into a steamer over a pan of boiling water. Sprinkle with a little salt and cook as boiled potatoes but allow an extra 5–10 minutes cooking time.

To Bake Potatoes

Old potatoes bake better than new potatoes for they have a delicious 'floury' texture, but I have baked new potatoes. Wash and dry large potatoes. If you like a crisp skin, brush this with a little melted butter or margarine. Prick the potatoes with a fork so the skins will not burst. Put on to a baking tray.

For large potatoes, allow 1 hour in the centre of a moderate to moderately hot oven, 375–400°F, Gas Mark 5–6, or 1$\frac{1}{4}$–1$\frac{1}{2}$ hours in a very moderate oven. Lift the potatoes from the oven. Mark a cross on top and serve with butter.

Mashed or Creamed Potatoes

Boil old potatoes as the method above. Strain, return to the pan and break with a fork or masher until quite smooth. If you need *perfectly* smooth mashed potatoes, then sieve and return to the pan. To give a white fluffy texture add *hot* milk plus a knob of butter or margarine. Beat hard with a wooden spoon until very white. Pile into a hot dish and fork into shape.

Duchesse Potatoes

Sieve cooked and strained boiled potatoes. Add about 2 oz. ($\frac{1}{4}$C) butter or margarine and 1–2 egg yolks to each 1 lb. potatoes. As you wish the potatoes to hold a shape, omit the milk used in creamed potatoes. Duchesse potatoes are used for forming a border round a dish or to make a nest shape. Put the potatoes into a cloth piping bag with a $\frac{1}{2}$–1-inch potato rose. Pipe into the required shape and brown in a moderately hot oven, 400°F, Gas Mark 6.

Cheese and potato ring

New Ways of Cooking Potatoes

On this page are some of the classic methods of cooking and serving potatoes, together with original ideas for you to try, including suggestions for sweet potatoes and yams.

Potatoes Dauphine

8 oz. (1C) sieved potatoes and seasoning (or use dehydrated (instant) potatoes, prepared as instructions on the packet). *For the choux pastry:* 2 oz. ($\frac{1}{4}$C) butter; $\frac{1}{4}$ pint ($\frac{2}{3}$C) water; 3 oz. ($\frac{3}{4}$C) flour, preferably plain; 2 eggs plus 1 egg yolk; seasoning. *For frying:* deep oil or fat.

Beat the sieved potatoes with seasoning until very smooth (or make up the dehydrated potatoes). Put the butter and water into a pan and heat until the butter has melted. Remove the pan from the heat, add the flour and stir over a low heat until the flour mixture forms a dry ball. Gradually beat the eggs and egg yolk into the choux pastry then blend in the potato purée. Taste, add more seasoning if required. Heat the oil or fat, to test see fried potatoes opposite. Either pipe or spoon small balls of the mixture into the oil or fat and fry for a few minutes until golden brown. Drain on absorbent paper and serve at once. *Serves 4–6.*

To vary The above recipe gives a particularly light version. You can use up to 1 lb. (2C) sieved potatoes to the amount of choux pastry given.

Add 2–3 tablespoons finely grated cheese (Parmesan, Gruyère, Cheddar) to the mixture, with or after adding the potatoes.

Flavour with chopped parsley and/or nutmeg.

Potato Cakes

Cream the potatoes as the recipe opposite, but to each 1 lb. potatoes add 1 tablespoon flour. Form into flat cakes, roll in seasoned flour and fry in shallow fat until crisp and golden brown. Drain on absorbent paper and serve at once.

Potatoes Almondine

Cream the potatoes or make Duchesse potatoes as the recipes opposite. Form into small balls. Roll in finely chopped almonds and fry for 2–3 minutes in deep fat or oil. Drain on absorbent paper and serve at once.

Cheese and Potato Ring

1 lb. old potatoes (weight when peeled); 12 oz. onions (weight when peeled); 2 oz. ($\frac{1}{4}$C) margarine; 6 oz. (nearly 2C) *coarsely* grated cheese; seasoning; paprika. *To garnish:* parsley.

Either grate the potatoes and onions very coarsely or cut into small narrow and thin strips. Melt the margarine and toss the vegetables in this with half the cheese and plenty of seasoning and paprika. Put a well greased 8-inch ring tin into the oven to become very hot (this makes sure the mixture does not stick). Put the potato mixture into the tin, press down well. Cover with greased foil. Bake for approximately 45 minutes in the centre of a moderate oven, 350–375°F, Gas Mark 4–5. Turn out carefully on to a heated oven-proof dish. Spoon the rest of the cheese over the ring at intervals, return to the oven for 5–10 minutes until melted. Top with sprigs of parsley and serve. This makes a light main dish by itself or an accompaniment to a meal. *Serves 4–6.*

To vary To give the rather 'rough' look in the picture, use the recipe above, turn out on to the dish then gently 'pull out' the vegetables from their neat round.

Dauphine potatoes

Sweet Potatoes

These may be cooked in any of the ways suggested for ordinary potatoes. I think they are particularly good roasted. Be careful they do not burn in the hot fat, for they *are* sweeter than an ordinary potato. Sweet potatoes are often used as an ingredient in puddings. Yams are similar in flavour, but not appearance. Sweet potatoes are pink in colour and yams brown.

Potato Pancakes

2 large old potatoes; seasoning; 1 egg; 1 oz. flour, plain or self-raising; milk; 2–3 oz. ($\frac{1}{4}$–$\frac{3}{8}$C) fat. *To serve:* chopped parsley.

Peel and grate the potatoes into a basin, add seasoning, the egg and flour and enough milk to make the consistency of a thick batter. Allow to stand for about 15 minutes. Heat the fat in a large pan. Drop in spoonfuls of the mixture and fry until golden brown on one side. Turn and cook on the second side, then lower the heat and allow a little extra cooking time. Serve topped with chopped parsley. *Makes about 8–10.*

Storing and Freezing *The recipes on this page, with the exception of Potatoes Dauphine and Cheese and Potato Ring, store well for 1–2 days and can be reheated or they can be frozen. Fried Potato Chips, opposite, freeze well if fried for the first time, drained well and separated on flat trays during freezing. They may then be packed in the usual way.*

To use any left over *Cooked boiled potatoes may be used in salads, or made into Sauté potatoes. Fry in a little hot fat until brown on both sides.*

Cooking Root Vegetables

Root vegetables are not only an excellent addition to soups and stews and a splendid basis for Russian salad, but they are well worth cooking in various ways to serve with fish and meat, or as a dish by themselves. Leeks and onions are not included here, but will be found on page 44. Potatoes are covered on pages 38–39.

Blue Print

To Cook Root Vegetables by Boiling

1. Prepare the vegetables as this page.
2. Since most root vegetables take longer to cook than green vegetables, put about 3 inches of water into the pan.
3. Bring the water to the boil, add salt to taste.
4. Add the vegetables steadily (see the Blue Print on page 36) and cook until tender. This will vary according to the size but an indication is given below.
Artichokes—Jerusalem 25 minutes, add 2 teaspoons lemon juice to the water.

Chinese style vegetable soup

Beetroot Allow 1½–2 hours, according to size. Do not add salt.
Carrots Young whole baby carrots, 15 minutes. Sliced older carrots, 20–30 minutes. Whole old carrots, 45 minutes.
Celeriac (celery root) As turnips, add 2 teaspoons lemon juice to the water.
Celery, Fennel and Seakale (oyster plant) Diced will take 10–15 minutes.
Chicory As celery, add 2 teaspoons lemon juice to the water.
Parsnips, Swedes and Turnips If young and sliced, about 15 minutes. If old and diced into ½–¾-inch cubes, 20 minutes, if sliced about 30 minutes.
5. Cook the vegetables until tender, boil steadily *not* too rapidly otherwise the vegetables often break on the outside.
6. Strain then return to the pan with a little butter or margarine and toss in the pan as the fat melts.
7. Add chopped fresh herbs if desired, then serve.

● **AVOID** *Over-cooking these vegetables, naturally they must be tender when served hot, but they must retain a little of their firm texture to be interesting.*
● **TO RECTIFY** *If over-cooked, mash the vegetables as potatoes (see page 38).*
● **TO SLIMMERS** *Although some of the vegetables in this group are higher in calories than green vegetables, i.e. swedes and turnips, small portions will be allowed in most slimming diets. Celery and chicory are very low in calories.*

Preparing Root Vegetables

These vary in character a great deal.
Artichokes Scrape or peel. Keep in cold water with a little lemon juice until ready to cook as they darken in colour.
Beetroot Remove stalks and leaves. Wash, do not cut otherwise the vegetable bleeds.
Carrots, Turnips, Swedes, Parsnips Remove stalks and leaves. If very young, scrub well or scrape gently. If old, peel thinly.
Celeriac (celery root) Peel and slice or dice. Treat as artichokes before cooking.
Celery and Seakale (oyster plant) Wash in cold water and divide into neat piéces.
Chicory Needs just the outer leaves removing.
Fennel Remove the leaves, these can be chopped and added to white or other sauces instead of parsley. Wash and slice the root.

Buying Root Vegetables

Check to see they are unblemished. If you buy ready washed root vegetables use fairly quickly as the soil adhering to vegetables acts as a protection.

New Ways to Cook and Flavour Root Vegetables

Cook in chicken stock instead of water. Use only enough stock to keep the vegetables from burning. Lift the lid of the pan for the last few minutes so the excess liquid evaporates. This method is excellent with *all* root vegetables.
Cook the vegetables as the Blue Print, then toss in butter or margarine, mixed with a very *little sugar*; excellent with carrots, turnips, parsnips and swedes.
Mash some root vegetables as potatoes, see page 38.
Roast or fry some root vegetables as potatoes, see page 38. The most successful to roast are parsnips and swedes. Parsnips should be parboiled for 10–15 minutes before roasting. The most successful to fry are artichokes, carrots, parsnips and swedes.

Chinese Style Vegetable Soup

1 tablespoon corn or olive oil; 3 tablespoons long grain rice; 2 pints (5⅓C) chicken stock or water and 2–3 chicken stock cubes; seasoning; 1 small carrot; 1 small turnip; small piece swede; 1–2 sticks celery. *To garnish*: chopped parsley.
Heat the oil in a saucepan. Add the rice and turn in the oil for several minutes. Pour the stock into the pan, or the water and stock cubes, bring to the boil. Stir briskly, add seasoning. Lower the heat and cover the pan. Simmer gently for 20 minutes, until the rice is *just* tender. Grate the vegetables finely or coarsely according to personal taste, add to the soup and heat for a few minutes only so the vegetables retain their firm texture. Add extra seasoning if required. Serve topped with parsley. *Serves 4–6.*
To vary Add yoghourt to the soup just before serving.

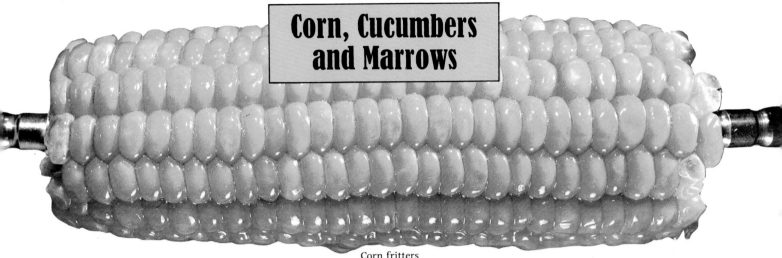

Corn fritters

Corn on the cob makes an excellent hot hors d'oeuvre. The younger generation in particular seem to enjoy the golden corn, dripping with melted butter.

Cucumber is surprisingly good as a cooked vegetable. Naturally it loses the firm crisp taste that is apparent when served in a salad.

To Cook Corn on the Cob

Choose corn with fresh looking pale green leaves and golden coloured kernels. If too pale the corn is under-ripe and will be lacking in flavour. Pull away the leaves before cooking and put the whole cob into boiling water. Cook for about 12 minutes until nearly tender, add a little salt and give an extra few minutes cooking. If the corn is salted at the beginning of the cooking period I find it tends to toughen it. Test the corn early, for over-cooking also toughens the vegetable.

Lift from the boiling water, drain well and serve with plenty of melted butter. If you wish to serve the corn off the cob pull the kernels away with the prongs of a fork, when it is just tender.

Frozen corn on the cob is cooked in the same way as fresh. The frozen corn kernels are not pre-cooked so need cooking until tender, see the directions on the packet. Canned corn is available as kernels off the cob. It is often mixed with diced red pepper (capsicum), or canned with a creamed sauce. It just needs heating. Do not over-cook for this causes the corn to darken in colour.

Corn Fritters

Corn fritters are an excellent accompaniment to chicken, meat or fish, they can be served topped with cheese to make a light main dish, or served with salad, as in the picture. Use cooked or canned sweet corn for the fritters and drain well before using.

8 oz. (2C) sweet corn; fritter batter as Cauliflower Fritters (page 37). *For frying:* oil or fat.

Mix the sweet corn with the batter. Blend thoroughly, then drop spoonfuls into hot deep or shallow oil or fat. Fry until crisp and golden brown on both sides. Drain on absorbent paper and serve. *Serves 4–6.*

To vary Mix a little finely chopped ham, corned beef, fried bacon or cooked chicken with the batter and use only 4–6 oz. (1–1½C) sweet corn.

Add 2–3 oz. (½–¾C) grated Cheddar cheese to the batter, add the corn and cook as above.

Corn Risotto

1 medium-sized onion; 1 small green pepper; 1 small red pepper; 2 tablespoons corn or olive oil; 6 oz. (generous ¾C) long grain rice; 1 pint (2⅔C) water; *bouquet garni*; seasoning; 8 oz. (2C) canned or cooked sweet corn.

Chop the onion and dice the peppers, removing cores and seeds. Heat the oil in a pan. Toss the vegetables, with the rice, in this making sure the onion does not discolour. Add the water. Bring to the boil, stir well, add the herbs and seasoning. Cover the pan and simmer steadily for nearly 15 minutes. Lift the lid, stir the rice mixture, add the corn and heat for a few minutes, until the rice has absorbed all the liquid. Remove the *bouquet garni*. Serve as an accompaniment to main dishes or turn into a light dish by serving with big bowls of grated cheese. *Serves 4–6.*

To Cook Cucumber

If the cucumbers are forced they can be cooked *with* the skin, but the outdoor type tend to develop a rather tough, strongly flavoured skin and generally it is advisable to remove this.

To boil cucumber Cut into slices about ½-inch in thickness and boil as green vegetables on page 36 for 6–8 minutes. Drain and toss in butter and parsley or chopped chives or serve with a white or cheese sauce, see page 44—Leeks Mornay.

To fry cucumber Cut into slices about ½-inch in thickness, then dip each slice in well seasoned flour. Fry in deep or shallow fat for about 4–5 minutes until golden brown. Drain on absorbent paper and serve. This is an excellent vegetable with cooked fish.

To Cook Marrow

The small marrows (courgettes or zucchini as they often are called) are described on page 48. The larger marrows may be cooked in the same way. When the marrows are young do not peel, simply slice or cut into segments. There may be no seeds to remove. When the marrow becomes older, remove both the skin and the seeds. Remember the big mature marrows, that look so impressive, are not very good for cooking. They are, however, excellent to use for jam and pickles.

To boil marrow Cook as the Blue Print on page 182; allow 7–10 minutes. Drain well and top with melted butter and chopped parsley or a white or cheese sauce, see page 44—Leeks Mornay. Do not over-cook. Marrow can be steamed over boiling water for approximately the same time.

To roast marrow Put fairly large pieces into very hot fat and roast as potatoes, page 38. Allow approximately 40 minutes, turning once or twice. The marrow never becomes crisp and brown, but this method retains the maximum of flavour.

Stuffed marrow is one of the best ways of serving this vegetable. A recipe is given on page 45, and the stuffing used on page 47 is equally as good for marrow as for green peppers.

Storing and Freezing *All these vegetables store well. Keep cucumbers in a cool place. Corn freezes well but neither marrows nor cucumbers can be frozen in a raw state. Marrow can be frozen as part of a dish like Ratatouille.*

To use any left over *Corn can be added to soups and stews. Cucumber and marrow should be reheated for a few minutes.*

These vegetables are called 'pulses' and they
have the great value of adding protein to our
meals; they can be served in place of meat or
fish. Once these vegetables were called
'second class proteins', but today that is considered incorrect. There is nothing 'second
class' about them, they are simply vegetable
rather than animal proteins.

Peas and beans of various kinds can be
cooked as fresh vegetables. Lentils, of course,
are dried and these need longer cooking. The
modern Accelerated Freeze Dried peas and
green beans can be cooked quite quickly.
Remember you can obtain ordinary dried
peas and beans and these do need longer
cooking and preferably soaking. Frozen and
canned peas and beans may be used in
recipes when fresh vegetables are out of
season.

To Cook Fresh Peas

All peas, with the exception of the mange-
tout type, need removing from the pods. If
you are fortunate enough to be able to buy
the rather flat-looking mange-tout peas,
simply wash, cut away the ends and cook the
whole pods with the tiny peas inside. Peas
are cooked in boiling salted water, as the
Blue Print on page 36. Most people like a
pinch of sugar and sprig of fresh mint added
to the water. Cook for 10–15 minutes only
when the peas are young. Over-cooking
toughens them. Drain and toss in a little
melted butter or margarine. Mange-tout peas
cook in a few minutes only.

To Cook Fresh Beans

Beans vary in type a great deal.
Haricots verts Very thin green beans,
which need just the ends removing.
French beans Medium-sized green beans,
remove either end and string (cut away the
very edges). Do not slice.
Runner beans Larger green beans, string
the sides, remove either end, cut into thin
slices. Put the beans into boiling salted water
and cook for approximately 15 minutes, or
until tender. Drain and toss in melted butter
or margarine.
Broad beans A green bean, but it is the
inside that is normally cooked. I find when
these are very young that you can remove
the beans from the pods, prepare, slice and
cook the pods as runner beans. Cook the
broad beans themselves in boiling salted
water for about 15 minutes, drain, toss in
melted butter or margarine.
Flageolets These are fresh haricot beans—
cook as broad beans.

To Flavour Fresh Peas and Beans

Toss the cooked peas or beans in freshly
chopped herbs or chopped or crushed garlic.
Mix the cooked peas or beans with tiny fried
onions.
Mix the cooked peas or beans with a well
seasoned fresh tomato purée or with sliced
fried onions and/or fried mushrooms.

To Cook Dried Peas and Beans

Dried peas and dried haricot or butter beans
are better if soaked overnight in cold water
or pour boiling water over them and soak.
Put into a pan with the same water and

Key
1. French beans
2. Red kidney
   beans
3. Dried haricot
   beans
4. Flageolets
5. Butter beans
6. Lentils
7. AFD peas
8. AFD beans
9. Split peas

seasoning. Simmer steadily until tender. This takes about 2 hours or a little longer with butter beans. Drain, toss in melted butter or margarine and chopped parsley, or serve in a white or cheese sauce, see page 44—Leeks Mornay.

Pressure cooking saves a great deal of time. Soak the dried vegetables as above. Put into the pressure cooker. Bring up to 15 lb. pressure and allow 15 minutes for peas and 30 minutes for haricot and butter beans. Allow the pressure to drop at room temperature.

Boston Baked Beans

1 lb. dried haricot beans; water to cover; 2 large tomatoes; 1–2 tablespoons black treacle; 1–2 teaspoons made mustard; seasoning; 12 oz. fat salt pork; 1–2 onions. *To garnish:* parsley.

Soak the beans overnight as described above. Simmer without seasoning in the water for 10–15 minutes. Strain the beans, but save a generous $\frac{1}{2}$ pint ($1\frac{1}{3}$C) of the liquid. Simmer this with the tomatoes to make a thin sauce. Sieve. Add the treacle and mustard and a generous amount of seasoning. Dice the pork, slice the onions very thinly. Put the beans, pork and onions into a deep casserole. Pour over the tomato sauce and mix well. Allow plenty of space for the beans to swell during cooking. Put on the lid. Cover very tightly. If the lid does not fit well put foil round the dish. Cook in the centre of a very slow oven, 250–275°F, Gas Mark $\frac{1}{2}$–1, for about 5 hours. Check the progress of the cooking after $2\frac{1}{2}$ hours. If the beans are still very hard, raise the temperature slightly. If they are becoming a little dry, add boiling water to moisten, but do not make them too wet. Top with

parsley before serving. These can be served as a dish by themselves or an accompaniment. *Serves about 8.*

To vary Omit the pork and add 1–2 crushed cloves of garlic with the tomato mixture. The tomatoes can be omitted and a little more treacle and mustard used for flavouring.

Lentil Vegetable Roast

12 oz. ($1\frac{1}{2}$C) lentils; water; seasoning; *bouquet garni*; 2 large onions; 1 clove garlic; 3 oz. ($\frac{3}{8}$C) margarine; 1 small dessert apple; few sticks celery; 1 small green pepper.

Put the lentils into a pan with only enough cold water to cover. Add the seasoning and herbs. Leave for 1–2 hours if possible, for this shortens the cooking time slightly. Simmer steadily for $1\frac{1}{4}$ hours until the water has evaporated and the lentils are tender. Remove the *bouquet garni*. Meanwhile chop the onions and crush the clove of garlic. Fry in 2 oz. ($\frac{1}{4}$C) margarine until tender. Add to the warm lentil mixture in the pan, with the peeled diced apple, chopped celery and pepper (discard the core and seeds). Season well. Grease a 2-lb. baking dish or tin with half the remaining margarine. Put in the lentil mixture. Top with the remaining margarine. Do not cover if you want a crisp topping. Bake for 1 hour in the centre of a moderate oven, 350–375°F, Gas Mark 4–5. Turn out and serve with roast potatoes. (Illustrated on page 35.) *Serves 4–6.*

To vary

Crisp-coated roast Coat the sides of the greased dish or tin with a thick layer of crumbs and top the lentil mixture with crumbs and margarine before baking.

Add a little curry powder and chopped herbs to flavour or 2–3 skinned tomatoes plus a

Mexican macaroni

pinch chilli powder. Add the tomatoes to the onions then blend with the cooked lentils.
Use sieved cooked butter beans in place of lentils.

Mexican Macaroni

For the cheese sauce: 1 oz. margarine; 1 oz. flour; $\frac{1}{2}$ pint ($1\frac{1}{3}$C) milk; 4 oz. (1C) grated Cheddar cheese; seasoning; pinch cayenne pepper (or use a packet cheese sauce mix with $\frac{1}{2}$ pint ($1\frac{1}{3}$C) milk); 4 oz. macaroni; 1–2 teaspoons made mustard; 8 Frankfurter sausages; 4–6 oz. ($1–1\frac{1}{2}$C) cooked fresh peas.

Make the cheese sauce with the margarine, flour, milk and cheese. Season well and add the cayenne pepper (or make up the packet of cheese sauce mix). Meanwhile boil the macaroni in salted water, drain, add to the sauce. Stir in enough made mustard to give a fairly hot taste. Chop the Frankfurter sausages, add to the sauce with the peas. Heat for a few minutes then serve.

To vary To make a meatless meal, increase the amount of sauce to $\frac{3}{4}$ pint (2C). Use twice the amount of peas or mix peas and cooked or canned haricot beans.

Country Style Beans

2 onions; 2 carrots; 2 oz. ($\frac{1}{4}$C) margarine; $\frac{3}{4}$ pint (2C) water; seasoning; $1\frac{1}{2}$ lb. French beans. *To garnish:* chopped chives.

Peel and grate both the onions and carrots. Toss in the hot margarine. Add the water. Bring to the boil and season well. Prepare the French beans, put into the flavoured liquid. Cook until tender in an open pan, so the liquid evaporates. Top with chopped chives. *Serves 4–6.*

To vary Flavour the water with a little Worcestershire sauce.

This is an excellent way to serve ready cooked butter or haricot beans, or cooked dried peas. Reduce the amount of water to $\frac{1}{2}$ pint ($1\frac{1}{3}$C) only for the beans or peas need heating only.

Storing and Freezing *Peas and green beans should be eaten when fresh, they can be frozen with great success. Cut runner beans into fairly thick slices for freezing.*
To use any left over *Add to salads, soups and stews.*

Boston baked beans

Both leeks and onions can be cooked in a variety of ways and can form the basis of main meals.

To Prepare

Leeks Trim the green end and the root of the leeks. Wash thoroughly between the folds of the vegetables; these often are very dirty. Either cut into convenient lengths or thin slices, leave whole or halve lengthways.
Onions Remove the outer skin and trim the vegetable at both ends. Wash in cold water. Slice and separate the rings of onion, this is the method used for frying, or chop.

To Boil

Put the prepared vegetables into boiling salted water, see the Blue Print on page 40. Allow approximately 10–20 minutes for leeks (according to size).
Allow about 30 minutes for small whole onions, but up to 50–60 minutes for really large whole onions. It is important to boil the water steadily, rather than rapidly, so the whole onion becomes tender, not just the outside. Chopped onions will take about 5–10 minutes cooking time.

To Bake

Prepare the vegetables, then cut into thin slices. Put into a dish with a little milk, seasoning and margarine. Cover with greased foil or a lid. Bake in the centre of a very moderate to moderate oven, 325–350°F, Gas Mark 3–4, for approximately 45 minutes to 1 hour. Top with chopped parsley.

To Roast

Although leeks can be roasted in hot fat, they are less successful than onions. For 4 medium-sized onions or large leeks allow 2 oz. (¼C) fat. Heat the fat in a roasting tin. Prepare the vegetables, dry thoroughly and turn in the hot fat. Roast towards the top of a moderately hot to hot oven, 375–400°F, Gas Mark 5–6. Allow about 45 minutes for medium-sized onions or leeks and a generous 1 hour for large onions or leeks.

To Fry

Fried leeks are served less often than fried onions, but they are very pleasant, if a trifle 'leathery' compared to the texture of an onion. Prepare the vegetables and cut into slices. You can separate the rings of leek, but I find it easier to fry them in lengths of about ¼–½ inch. Onion slices should be separated into rings.
For shallow frying, simply dry the vegetables, coat in a little seasoned flour if wished, then fry in hot fat or oil in a frying pan for approximately 5–6 minutes. Drain on absorbent paper.
If you want really crisply fried leeks, coat in seasoned flour then in batter (see the batter under Cauliflower Fritters on page 37) and deep fry.

Cooking Leeks and Onions

If you want really crisp onion rings, dip in milk then in seasoned flour. Put into a heated frying basket and lower into hot fat or oil and fry until crisp and golden brown. For a very crisp result fry as potatoes, i.e. cook steadily in the fat or oil until tender, but not quite brown. Remove from the pan. Reheat the fat or oil then fry for a second time for about 2 minutes. Drain on absorbent paper.

Leeks Mornay

8 good-sized leeks; seasoning; 1 oz. butter; 1 oz. flour; pinch dry mustard; ½ pint (1⅓C) milk or use half milk and half stock from cooking the leeks; 4 oz. (1C) grated cheese; paprika.
*Dutch Gouda cheese gives a pleasantly mild flavour.

Prepare and boil the leeks as the instructions on this page. Season the cooking liquid well. Drain, put on to a heated serving dish and save ¼ pint (⅔C) of the stock unless using all milk. Heat the butter in a pan, stir in the flour and mustard and cook for several minutes. Gradually blend in the milk or milk and leek stock. Bring to the boil and stir as the sauce thickens. Stir in the cheese, add seasoning and heat for 1–2 minutes only. Pour over the leeks and top with paprika. This makes a light main dish by itself or an accompaniment to a meal. *Serves 4.*

Know Your Onions

The information on this page has assumed you are using large type onions (naturally these vary considerably in size). In addition there are the very small onions (often called pickling onions), that can be used in cooking and a similar vegetable known as a shallot. Shallots are used a great deal in Continental recipes, for they have a somewhat more defined flavour than an onion. They are sometimes slightly pink in colour.
Spring onions are used mainly in salads, but are excellent in cooking.

● **AVOID** *The strong smell of leeks or onions cooking by keeping the pan well covered.*
● **TO RECTIFY** *You can put in a slice of bread to absorb the smell, but this is not practical if you wish to use the leek or onion stock as it disintegrates in the liquid.*
● **SHORT CUT** *There are very useful dehydrated chopped onions which may be used for flavouring, but cannot be served as a main dish.*
● **TO SLIMMERS** *Both leeks and onions are low in calories.*

Storing and Freezing *Both leeks and onions store well, the latter will keep for some weeks in a cool dry place if mature. Young immature onions do not keep well. Both cooked leeks and onions can be frozen, but the raw vegetable when frozen, loses texture and taste.*

Leeks mornay

Mushrooms, like so many other vegetables, are invaluable for giving flavour to savoury dishes. They also make excellent light snacks and meals.

To Cook Mushrooms

To prepare mushrooms The cultivated mushrooms need not be skinned, in fact it is a mistake to do so, for the skin enhances the flavour. All that is required is to wash the mushrooms well and trim the base of the stalks. Wild, or less perfect mushrooms should be skinned before use.

To boil mushrooms If the mushrooms are put into boiling stock and simmered for about 5 minutes they are tender and you have added no fattening ingredients to these low calorie vegetables. If you have no stock, use water plus a little yeast extract and seasoning.

To fry mushrooms While mushrooms can be coated in seasoned flour or egg and crumbs or batter and fried in deep oil or fat, they are better if shallow fried. Heat enough margarine, butter, cooking fat, oil or, best of all, well clarified beef dripping in a frying pan to give a depth of about $\frac{1}{4}$ inch. Put in the mushrooms and turn in the fat until tender. This takes about 5 minutes.

To bake mushrooms Put the prepared mushrooms with plenty of margarine or butter or a little stock or milk into an oven-proof dish. Season well and cover with a lid or foil. Bake in the centre of a moderate to moderately hot oven, 375–400°F, Gas Mark 5–6, for 15–20 minutes.

Mushrooms

To grill mushrooms Put the prepared mushrooms in a generous amount of melted fat (see under frying) in the grill pan. Cook under the grill, spooning the hot fat over the vegetables once or twice.

Raw Mushrooms

Many people never try one of the best ways of serving mushrooms, i.e. raw. Mushrooms and tomatoes, thinly sliced and served raw in a vinaigrette sauce are delicious.

Tomatoes and mushrooms vinaigrette Skin and slice 4–6 really firm, but ripe tomatoes. Wash, dry and slice 4 oz. (1C) perfect button mushrooms. Blend $\frac{1}{2}$ teaspoon made mustard, a good pinch salt, sugar and shake of pepper with 3 tablespoons olive oil and $1\frac{1}{2}$ tablespoons lemon juice or white wine vinegar. Add a crushed clove of garlic or a little chopped onion if wished. Arrange the tomatoes in 4 individual dishes. Spoon the dressing over the top. Add the sliced mushrooms and top with chopped parsley. Mix well before eating. *Serves 4.*

Spinach and Mushroom Cream

1 lb. cooked spinach; 12 oz. (3C) button mushrooms; 1 medium-sized onion; 2 oz. ($\frac{1}{4}$C) butter or margarine; 2 eggs; $\frac{1}{2}$ pint ($1\frac{1}{3}$C) milk or use half milk and half single cream; seasoning; 2 tablespoons soft breadcrumbs; 2 tablespoons grated Parmesan cheese.

Chop or sieve the spinach to give a smooth purée. Slice the mushrooms and onion, toss in the hot butter or margarine. Arrange alternate layers of spinach and mushroom mixture in a pie or oven-proof dish. Beat the eggs with the warmed milk or milk and cream, season well. Pour over the vegetables. Top with crumbs and cheese. Cover the dish with buttered foil and bake for 30 minutes in the centre of a very moderate to moderate oven, 325–350°F, Gas Mark 3–4, remove the foil and cook for a further 10 minutes. *Serves 4–6.*

Quick Dishes Using Mushrooms

Grill or fry mushrooms, top with cream cheese and grill for a few more minutes.

Grill or fry mushrooms, top with lightly scrambled eggs, blended with chopped parsley and chives.

Grill or fry mushrooms, top with soured cream, blended with chopped raw or fried onions and paprika.

Storing and Freezing *Mushrooms keep well in a covered container in the refrigerator for several days, but are best when eaten very fresh. They can be frozen after blanching or after frying or grilling.*

It would be difficult to visualise cooking without tomatoes, for they not only add flavour they give so much colour to dishes.

To Cook Tomatoes

To prepare tomatoes Skin the tomatoes, if wished, before cooking. Either put into boiling water for a very short time, then lift into cold water to cool rapidly and skin, or insert a fine skewer into the tomatoes and hold over a gas burner or electric hotplate until the skin 'pops'. Pull away the skin.

To boil tomatoes Put the tomatoes into a pan with a little liquid if wished. Season well and add a pinch of sugar if you like a fairly sweet flavour. Chopped herbs, chopped or grated onion or garlic may be added. Cook until hot or until a smooth purée.

To fry tomatoes Skin if wished and halve. Season lightly and cook in a little hot fat (see mushrooms above). They take about 4–5 minutes to become tender.

To grill tomatoes Put the halved or whole tomatoes in the grill pan or on the grid of the grill pan. Season lightly and top with a little hot margarine or butter. Cook for about 4 minutes under a hot grill.

To bake tomatoes Put the whole or halved well seasoned tomatoes into a greased dish. Top with a little margarine or butter and a lid if you wish them to be rather soft. Bake for approximately 15–20 minutes, depending upon size, towards the top of a moderate

Tomatoes

to moderately hot oven, 375–400°F, Gas Mark 5–6.

Cheddar Tomatoes

4 very large firm tomatoes; $\frac{1}{4}$ medium-sized cucumber; 4–6 oz. (1–1$\frac{1}{2}$C) grated Cheddar cheese; seasoning; mayonnaise; portion cooked cauliflower; paprika. *To garnish:* watercress.

Cut a slice off one end of the tomatoes. Scoop out the centre pulp, put into a basin and chop finely. Dice half the cucumber, slice the remainder. Mix the tomato pulp with half the diced cucumber, the cheese, seasoning and a little mayonnaise. Spoon into the tomato cases. Blend the rest of the diced cucumber with mayonnaise, put on top of each tomato with small sprigs of cauliflower topped with paprika. Serve in individual dishes with sliced cucumber and watercress. *Serves 4.*

Cheddar tomatoes

Tomato Stuffed Marrow

1 medium-sized marrow; seasoning; 2 medium-sized onions; 2–3 oz. ($\frac{1}{4}$–$\frac{3}{8}$C) margarine or fat; 1 lb. tomatoes; 3 oz. (1C) soft breadcrumbs; 2 tablespoons chopped parsley or use a mixture of herbs.

Peel the marrow and slice lengthways. Remove the seeds. Sprinkle the marrow very lightly with seasoning and leave for about 30 minutes; the salt 'draws out' some of the water and makes it easier to brown the vegetable in the oven. Chop the onions and fry in half the margarine or fat. Add the skinned chopped tomatoes, crumbs and herbs. Season well. Put the stuffing into both halves of the marrow, then press together. Either tie or skewer the vegetable. Heat the rest of the margarine or fat. Pour over the marrow. Bake in the centre of a moderate oven, 350–375°F, Gas Mark 4–5, for 1 hour. Baste once or twice during cooking. *Serves 4–6.*

To vary To turn this into a more sustaining main dish add cooked lentils or haricot beans to the tomato mixture in place of crumbs.

Add 3–4 beaten eggs to the stuffing. This makes it rather soft when it first goes into the marrow, so handle carefully.

Add about 4 oz. (1C) chopped nuts to the stuffing.

Storing and Freezing *Store tomatoes in a cool place. If put in the refrigerator cover well. Tomato purée freezes excellently.*

Nothing turns an ordinary meal into a special one more easily than an interesting selection of vegetable dishes. Some of the vegetables on these two pages can be served as a separate course.

Ratatouille

1 medium-sized to large aubergine (egg plant); about 8 oz. courgettes; seasoning; 1 lb. ripe tomatoes; 4 medium-sized onions; 1–2 cloves garlic; 1 green pepper; 1 red pepper; 3–4 tablespoons olive oil. *To garnish:* chopped or sprigged parsley (optional).

If you dislike the taste of the peel on an aubergine remove this, otherwise dice the vegetable neatly with the peel on. Slice the courgettes. These two vegetables can be put into a bowl, sprinkled lightly with salt and pepper and left for 30 minutes. This minimises the bitter taste from the aubergine peel and 'draws out' the water from the courgettes. Skin and slice or chop the tomatoes and onions; chop or crush the cloves of garlic. Dice the flesh from the green and red peppers, discard the cores and seeds. Heat the olive oil in a pan, add the tomatoes and onions and cook gently in the oil for a few minutes, for the juice to flow from the tomatoes. This makes sure the mixture will not stick to the pan. Add the rest of the vegetables, stir well. Season and cover the pan with a tightly fitting lid. Simmer gently until as tender as you would wish (about 30 minutes in all). The picture shows the vegetables clearly defined and retaining their individual textures. I

Special Occasion Vegetable Dishes

think this is delicious if serving hot, but if you wish this to be a cold hors d'oeuvre then I suggest cooking them a little longer. Top with parsley if wished before serving. *Serves 6–8.*

To vary   The recipe above uses the minimum of oil, many people prefer to use rather more than this.

Add 3–4 tablespoons chopped parsley or parsley and chives to the vegetables before cooking. This gives a very pleasant flavour. Cook the mixture in a tightly covered casserole for about 45 minutes in a very moderate oven, or at least 1 hour in a slow oven.

The proportions of vegetables are entirely a matter of personal taste. You can add sliced mushrooms if wished, omit the peppers or increase these. The recipe above though gives the generally accepted amounts of vegetables for a well balanced flavour.

Stuffed Aubergines

Aubergines, or 'little slippers' as I have heard them called, can be stuffed in a variety of ways. The method of preparing the aubergines is as follows:

Wash and dry the vegetables. If you wish to minimise the slightly bitter flavour, score the skins lightly, see sketch opposite, sprinkle with salt and leave for at least 15 minutes.

Cut the aubergines lengthways at the end of this time. Remove the centre strip of the vegetable. Chop this very finely. Brush the top of the halved aubergine with a generous amount of oil and cook under a low grill or in a moderate oven for about 15–20 minutes, until the pulp is softened. Remove the softened pulp, mix with the chopped core part and the selected stuffing. Put the halved aubergines in a well oiled dish in the oven to cook the stuffing. Allow approximately 30 minutes in a moderate oven, 350–375°F, Gas Mark 4–5. Do not cover the dish, unless stated in the recipe. The stuffing quantities below are enough to fill 8 halves, i.e. 4 medium-sized aubergines. *This would serve 4 as a light main dish.*

To vary

The aubergines may be boiled in salted water for 10–15 minutes then halved and filled. This gives a softer texture to the skin than cooking in the manner suggested above.

Espagnole Stuffing   Chop 2 medium-sized onions finely, crush 1 clove garlic. Fry in 2 tablespoons oil until very soft. Add 3 skinned chopped tomatoes, 4 oz. (1C) chopped mushrooms and the aubergine pulp. Season well. Press into the aubergines, top with soft breadcrumbs and a little oil. Cook as above.

Cheese Filling   Blend 4 oz. (1C tightly packed) cream cheese, 2–3 tablespoons grated Parmesan cheese, the aubergine pulp, 1 tablespoon chopped parsley, 1 egg and 2 oz. ($\frac{2}{3}$C) soft breadcrumbs. Press into the aubergine halves, top with more breadcrumbs and a little grated Parmesan cheese. Cook as above.

Ham Stuffing   Fry 1 chopped onion in 1 oz. margarine or butter, add 2–3 tablespoons finely chopped celery, 8 oz. cooked diced lean ham and the aubergine pulp. Mix well, then stir in 1 egg, 1–2 tablespoons chopped parsley and seasoning. Press into the aubergine halves. Cover the dish to prevent the filling becoming too brown.

Nut Stuffing   Follow the directions for the ham stuffing but substitute chopped nuts or nutmeat for the ham.

Stuffed Peppers

Although red peppers can be stuffed, the green (which are the under-ripe capsicums) have more flavour when cooked in this way. Cut the stalk end from the peppers, remove

Stuffed peppers (top)
Ratatouille (below)

the core and seeds carefully, so you do not break the flesh. Put the slices removed and the shells into boiling salted water and cook for approximately 10 minutes if you like the peppers firm, but over 15 minutes if you prefer them softer. Dice the slices removed, so these may be added to the selected stuffing or keep intact and use as 'lids' for the stuffing. Choose any of the stuffings suggested for aubergines or try the stuffing shown in the picture. Put the filled peppers into a well oiled dish in the oven and cook for approximately 30 minutes in a moderate oven, 350–375°F, Gas Mark 4–5. Do not cover the dish, unless stated in the recipe.

In addition to the fillings given opposite for aubergines try:

Speedy Herb Stuffing Empty the contents of a packet of parsley and thyme stuffing, add 2–3 chopped mushrooms, a grated onion and about 12 oz. chopped corned beef or minced cooked meat. Bind with an egg and 2 oz. ($\frac{1}{4}$C) melted margarine. Season lightly. Mix the diced pepper slices with this. Press into 4 pepper cases and cook as above. This is excellent served with lightly cooked sliced carrots. *Serves 4.*

Vegetable Herb Stuffing Omit the meat and add cooked haricot beans and 2 skinned chopped tomatoes to the ingredients in the Speedy Herb Stuffing.

Baked Avocado Pears

Although avocado pears are a fruit and not a vegetable I think they are delicious if baked round the joint. Halve the pears, remove the stones, sprinkle with lemon juice then season and brush with plenty of oil. Do not skin. Put round the joint and cook for approximately 30 minutes, until softened. They are particularly good with pork. If you want a meatless hot dish then try the following curry stuffed pears.

Avocado Pears Indienne

2 large ripe avocado pears; lemon juice; seasoning; 1$\frac{1}{2}$ tablespoons olive oil; 1 onion; 1 teaspoon curry powder; 4–6 oz. (1–1$\frac{1}{2}$C tightly packed) soft cream cheese; 3 oz. (1C) soft breadcrumbs; 2 tablespoons grated Parmesan cheese.
Halve the avocado pears, remove the stones. Sprinkle with lemon juice and seasoning. Brush with a little oil. Heat the remainder of the oil and fry the very finely chopped or grated onion until soft. Add the curry powder and mix well. Blend in the cream cheese and half the crumbs. Press into the centre of the pears, top with the rest of the crumbs and grated cheese. Bake for about 30 minutes in the centre of a moderate oven, 350–375°F, Gas Mark 4–5. *Serves 4.*

French Fried Fennel

1 fennel root; 2 oz. ($\frac{1}{2}$C) flour; 1 egg; 6 tablespoons milk; seasoning. *For frying:* oil or fat. Wash the fennel and slice the white root. Save the green leaves for garnish. Separate

French fried fennel

into rings. Mix the flour, egg and milk into a smooth batter. Season well. Dip the rings of fennel into the batter. Heat the oil or fat (deep oil or fat is better for frying this particular dish). Put in the coated rings and fry for 2–3 minutes only. This gives a cooked crisp outside without losing the natural firmness of the vegetable. *Serves 4 as an accompaniment to a main course.*

Red Cabbage with Apples

1 red cabbage; 2 oz. ($\frac{1}{4}$C) margarine; 2 dess t apples; 1 small onion; seasoning; 12 tablespoons (1C) red wine; little grated nutmeg. Shred the cabbage finely. Melt the margarine in a large pan, add the cabbage, the peeled chopped apples and onion and seasoning. Heat for a few minutes, turning the cabbage once or twice. Add the wine and nutmeg. Cover the pan tightly and cook steadily until the liquid has just evaporated and the cabbage is tender. This takes about 35 minutes. Naturally in this particular recipe the cab-

bage is softer than when using the Blue Print method on page 36. This is excellent with pork or goose. *Serves 4–6.*

Storing and Freezing *Ratatouille stores well for several days, and freezes perfectly. The other vegetable dishes are better eaten fresh, but can be stored for 1–2 days or can be frozen, but the texture of the peppers and aubergines and stuffed avocado pears is not improved by freezing.*
To use any left over *Ratatouille seems just as good when any left is reheated as when it is first made.*

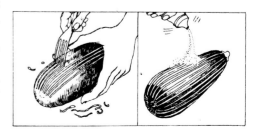

A Touch of Luxury

Some green vegetables are frankly a luxury and deserve to be served as a separate course. Three of the most interesting are globe artichokes, asparagus and courgettes (often called zucchini).

Globe Artichokes

The green globe artichokes make an excellent hors d'oeuvre; Jerusalem artichokes are described on page 40.

To prepare artichokes Wash in cold salted water. Cut away any stalk and pull off any rather tough outer leaves. You can cut the leaves in a straight line with scissors, if wished.

To cook artichokes Cook the whole artichokes in boiling salted water until tender. The time varies, small very young artichokes take about 25 minutes, very large ones take about 40 minutes. Test to see if you can pull away a leaf. Drain, remove the 'choke' with the centre leaves and serve with melted butter.

To eat artichokes, pull away each leaf, dip the base in the butter and eat the tender part. The base of the artichoke, often called the heart, is eaten with a knife and fork.

Artichokes Vinaigrette

Prepare and cook the artichokes as above. Allow to cool. Remove the centre 'choke' as above, if wished. Make an oil and vinegar dressing, season well and either spoon into the centre of each artichoke or serve separately.

Artichokes Barigoule

4 large globe artichokes; salt. *For the stuffing:* 6 oz. (1½C) button mushrooms; 2 medium-sized onions; 2 oz. (¼C) margarine or butter; 2 oz. (½C) soft breadcrumbs; 1 teaspoon chopped parsley; 1 teaspoon chopped chives; seasoning. *For the tomato sauce:* 2 oz. (¼C) margarine or butter; 1 onion; 4 large tomatoes; ¼ pint (⅔C) white stock; 1 tablespoon flour; 1 tablespoon tomato purée.
Prepare and cook the artichokes as above in boiling salted water. While the vegetables are cooking, wash and chop the mushrooms, peel and chop the onions finely. Toss in the hot margarine or butter. Add the crumbs, herbs and seasoning. Drain the artichokes, remove the 'chokes' and centre leaves, pack the filling in the centres and put into an oven-proof dish. Pour the thick tomato sauce round the vegetables. To make the sauce, heat the margarine or butter in a pan, add the peeled and chopped onion and tomatoes, cook for a few minutes. Blend the stock with the flour, pour into the pan. Add the tomato purée and seasoning. Stir over a moderate heat until the

sauce thickens. Cover the dish with a lid or foil and bake for 25 minutes in the centre of a moderate oven, 350–375°F, Gas Mark 4–5. *Serves 4.*

Asparagus

To prepare asparagus Scrape the base of the stems gently with a knife. Cut the ends off the asparagus. Tie in bundles with raffia or thin string.
To cook asparagus Stand upright in a deep pan of boiling salted water; it is possible to buy special asparagus pans.
Cover the pan with a lid, or if the asparagus is too long and protrudes above the level of the pan, put foil over this. You must keep the steam in, so that the whole stem cooks evenly. Allow 15–20 minutes for fairly thin stems but up to 25 minutes for thicker ones. Lift out of the pan, drain and serve hot with plenty of melted butter.

Eat asparagus with your fingers. Asparagus can be served cold with oil and vinegar as the globe artichokes above or hot or cold with Hollandaise sauce (see page 94).

Courgettes

To prepare courgettes Wash well, do not peel. Remove the rather hard stalk end. Either cut each courgette in half lengthways or cut into thin slices.
To cook courgettes Cook in boiling salted water as the Blue Print on page 36 for about 5–8 minutes, drain and top with melted butter. Alternatively season the courgettes and steam for approximately the same time.

Courgettes in Butter

4 courgettes; 2–3 oz. (¼–⅜C) butter; seasoning; 2–3 tablespoons water or white stock.
Prepare the courgettes as above. Heat the butter with a little seasoning and the liquid in a large pan. Put in the vegetables and cook for 8–10 minutes, until the liquid has evaporated. *Serves 4.*
To vary Cook the courgettes in boiling salted water for 2–3 minutes. Drain thoroughly. Heat 2–3 oz. (¼–⅜C) butter or margarine in a pan. Put in the courgettes and cook in a covered pan for another 8–10 minutes, turning or shaking the pan to prevent them from sticking.

Fried Courgettes

Prepare and slice the courgettes as above. Coat with well seasoned flour or with flour then beaten egg and crisp breadcrumbs or with batter (see the batter under Cauliflower Fritters, page 37). Fy in hot fat or oil until crisp and golden brown on either side and quite tender. Either shallow or deep fat or oil may be used. Drain on absorbent paper before serving.

Storing and Freezing *Globe artichokes and courgettes keep well for 2–3 days if stored in a cool place. Asparagus should be used within 1–2 days, otherwise it becomes dry. Asparagus freezes excellently. Courgettes only freeze as part of a cooked dish, for example in Rataouille, page 46. Globe artichokes do not freeze well.*

Four
SOUPS, SALADS AND SNACKS

At the beginning of this chapter of this cookbook you will find a selection of soups. I am a great lover of home-made soups. I find that if I am tired that a bowl of interesting hot soup is a wonderful light meal. The soup is easy to digest and gives one a feeling of warmth and well being. Because so many of us are 'calorie-conscious' these days I have also included some soups for slimmers. Many soups can provide a 'meal in a bowl'; others are more suitable for the start of a meal. Do not forget that soups are excellent in hot weather, when they can be served cold, iced or jellied.

Making soups today need not be a long and tiresome job. If you have a pressure cooker, use this for making stocks and soups and reduce the cooking time to a matter of minutes. If you possess a liquidiser (blender), then emulsify the soup in this to give it a smooth texture. It takes almost no time at all to produce a smooth purée, and saves the tiresome chore of sieving.

If you possess a freezer, soups are also a useful way of using up surplus vegetables from the garden, or making use of cheap vegetables in season, when you have more than you can eat fresh. Provided that you do not add either single cream or eggs to the soup, prior to freezing, (these can be stirred in at the last minute when the soup has been thawed, reheated and is almost ready to serve), most soups will respond well to this method of preservation.

It is a mistake to think that salads are just for hot weather. With the wide variety of ingredients available from which to create good salads, they can be served throughout the year. Often one can serve a crisp green or mixed salad with a hot dish as a change from cooked vegetables. You will find old favourite recipes and lots of new ideas.

Salads are also highly nutritious. Most vegetables lose a little of their goodness in cooking, so to eat them raw is to gain the most advantage from them both in terms of vitamin content and often of flavour too. Crunchy carrots, crisp endives, celery and cabbage provide a mouthwatering contrast of colour, flavour and texture that not only taskes and looks good but does you good. As well as varying the choice of salad by experimenting with new ingredients and getting away from the traditional lettuce and tomato, another way is by serving the salad tossed in different sauces. Salads are extremely versatile and may be served as a first course, a main course or as a side dish, so it is well worth the while to experiment a little and add a few more dishes to your repertoire.

Making Soups

Meat soups, some of which are covered on this page, are among the easiest to make. Meat has such a pronounced flavour, that it not only gives an excellent stock, but makes a complete soup with few additional ingredients, see Blue Print 2, Consommé. Of course there are many meat soups where other ingredients are added to give a more filling dish.

Blue Print Recipes

1. To Make Stock

The term 'stock' is used when making many soups, also in stews and other savoury dishes.

A **brown stock** is made from beef or game bones. A marrow bone gives the finest stock of all.

A **white stock** is made from veal, chicken or turkey bones. If you add the giblets of the poultry you darken the stock, although you do give additional flavour.

To make Cover the washed bones with cold water.

To cook Bring the water to the boil, remove any grey 'scum' if this has formed. Add seasoning, a *bouquet garni* of herbs and simmer in a tightly covered pan for 2–3 hours, or allow at least 40 minutes, at 15 lb. in a pressure cooker.

Various vegetables can be added to give flavour, but remember that a stock that has had vegetables in it does not keep as well as one without.

● **AVOID** *Adding too much liquid, other-*

wise the stock has little flavour.
● **TO RECTIFY** *If the stock is lacking in flavour, remove the saucepan lid and let the liquid evaporate and become more concentrated.*
● **SHORT CUT** *Use stock cubes instead of making stock.*
● **TO SLIMMERS** *Good clear, unthickened stocks are ideal for low calorie soups.*

2. Consommé

1 lb. shin of beef · 2½ pints (6⅔C) beef stock (see Blue Print 1) · 1 carrot (optional) · 1 onion (optional) · bay leaf · seasoning · 2 egg whites plus shells · sherry to taste · To garnish: as individual recipes.

To make Cut the meat into neat pieces. Put into the pan with the stock.
To cook Bring to the boil. Add the whole vegetables (if the stock is well flavoured these should not be necessary). Put in the bay leaf and a little seasoning. Simmer steadily for about 1½ hours. Strain the consommé, return to the pan, add the egg whites and shells and simmer very gently for about 10 minutes. The egg whites and shells 'gather-up' any tiny particles of meat etc., and give a perfectly clear soup. Strain and add a little sherry before serving.
To serve Hot, lightly frozen or jellied. The consommé may set lightly without gelatine, but if it will not, then dissolve about 1 teaspoon softened gelatine in each 1 pint (2⅔C) warm consommé. Allow to set lightly, whisk and serve in chilled soup cups. *All recipes based on this serve 4–6.*

Making stock

Garnishes for Consommé
The garnish gives the name to the particular consommé. Add tiny cubes of cooked vegetables, the soup is then **Consommé Jardinière**; add match-stick shapes of cooked vegetables for **Consommé Julienne.**

Here are some more versions of consommé. **Consommé à l'Africaine** Garnish with cooked rice; flavour with curry powder and sliced canned or cooked artichoke hearts. **Consommé Epicurien** Garnish with shredded blanched almonds and chopped chervil. **Consommé Nouilles** Garnish with noodles. This may be made more interesting by adding clear, very well sieved, tomato pulp or a little concentrated tomato purée.

Argentine Beef Soup
2 tablespoons olive or other oil; 2 large onions; 2–3 rashers streaky bacon; 1 oz. flour; about 4 large skinned tomatoes plus 2–3 tablespoons water or medium-sized can tomatoes; 1½ pints (4C) beef stock (see Blue Print 1); 8 oz. chuck steak; 4 oz. (nearly ¾C)

Argentine beef soup

fresh or frozen peas; 2–3 large carrots; *bouquet garni*; seasoning.
Heat the oil in a large pan, fry the peeled chopped onions for several minutes, add the chopped bacon and cook for a further few minutes. Stir in the flour, cook until a thickened 'roux'. Stir well. Add the chopped fresh tomatoes and water, or the canned tomatoes, and the stock. Bring to the boil, put in the diced beef, peas, peeled diced carrots, *bouquet garni* and a little seasoning. Cover the pan and simmer gently for about 2 hours. Serve with hot toast. *Serves 6.*
A little pasta can be added to the soup 30 minutes before the end of the cooking time.
Storing and Freezing *Stock is a highly perishable liquid so store in a cool place or in the refrigerator. Even so it will need boiling every 2–3 days. You can freeze stock. Remember the container should not be too full as the stock will expand in freezing. Leave about ¾-inch 'head-room'. Treat consommé in the same way, but try to freeze without the sherry and add this when defrosted. The reason is that alcohol loses flavour in freezing.*
To use any left over *Never waste good stock, add it to a gravy, stew or casserole.*

Poultry and Game Soups

These soups can be extremely economical, for the basis of many poultry or game soups is the carcass. Do not discard poultry or game bones. There is a great deal of flavour to be obtained by simmering these. The giblets should be used for this purpose also, although you may like to omit the liver, as it tends to give a bitter flavour. Naturally part of a chicken or a less tender game bird could be used instead of the carcass. This produces a stock with more flavour and the flesh of the poultry may be sieved or chopped and added to the soup.

Blue Print Recipe

Chicken Soup

The carcass of a chicken · about 2½–3 pints (7–8½C) water to cover · seasoning · 1–2 onions · 1–2 carrots · *bouquet garni* · 1 oz. flour. To garnish: fried croûtons (see page 117).

To make Put the chicken carcass, plus the giblets (less the liver) if available, into a saucepan. Cover with water, add seasoning, vegetables and herbs.
To cook Bring the liquid to the boil, cover the pan and simmer for at least 2 hours or allow about 40 minutes at 15 lb. pressure. Strain the stock. Any small pieces of chicken can be chopped or sieved and added to the stock. Blend the flour with a little stock, put into the pan with the remainder of the stock and cook until slightly thickened, stirring well.
To serve Hot topped with croûtons.
All recipes based on this serve 5–6.

● **AVOID** *Using too much liquid, otherwise the soup lacks flavour.*
● **TO RECTIFY** *If too much liquid has been added, lift the lid of the pan so the liquid evaporates.*
● **SHORT CUT** *Shorten the cooking time and add 1–2 chicken stock cubes to flavour.*
● **TO SLIMMERS** *Do not thicken.*
Storing and Freezing *Keep for 2–3 days only in the refrigerator. All these soups freeze well, with the exception of the noodle variety; pasta in a soup is over-softened and is spoiled by freezing.*
To use any left over *Heat as the recipe. Avoid boiling the soup when cream and egg yolks are already added.*

Tomato Chicken Soup

Ingredients as Blue Print PLUS 2–3 tablespoons concentrated tomato purée.
Make the soup as the Blue Print, add the tomato purée gradually. Taste after adding some of the purée to check that the flavour is not too strong.

Chicken Noodle Soup

Ingredients as Blue Print PLUS 3–4 tablespoons shell noodles.
Make the soup as the Blue Print, add the noodles and cook steadily for about 15 minutes until tender.

To vary Add about 2 tablespoons concentrated tomato purée to the soup, blend thoroughly, *then* add the noodles. If desired diced carrots, chopped onions and peas may be added to the soup *with* the noodles.

Cream of Chicken Soup

Ingredients as Blue Print PLUS ¼–½ pint (⅔–1⅓C) thin or thick cream and 1–2 egg yolks.
Make the soup as the Blue Print, when thickened draw the pan on one side so the soup is no longer boiling. Blend the cream

and egg yolks and whisk into the soup. A little dry sherry or white wine can be added for extra flavour.
Garnishes Top the soup with lightly browned almonds, asparagus tips, parsley, paprika and/or croûtons (see page 53).

Game Soup

Method as Blue Print but use the carcass of a small hare or 1–2 pheasants or other game birds, such as partridge, grouse, quail or wild duck in place of chicken.
Flavour the completed soup with a little red wine and 1 tablespoon red currant jelly.

Chicken Broth

Ingredients as Blue Print PLUS about 12 oz. (1½–2C) diced vegetables.
Make the soup as the Blue Print. Add the vegetables to the strained stock *before* thickening and cook for about 15 minutes. Thicken as the Blue Print or thicken and *then* add a little cream or cream and egg yolks, as the Cream of Chicken Soup.
To vary Add 1 oz. rice or pearl barley. Add a few cooked prunes.

Fish Soups

It is surprising just how rarely one is given fish soup in a private home, although many restaurants specialise in this. Fish soups are so varied, ranging from delicate creamy flavours to highly spiced soups and the luxurious shell fish bisques. In many cases you need fish stock for the soup and the Blue Print deals with making this.

Blue Print Recipe

Fish Stock

To make Use the skins and bones from fish or, if insufficient to give a good flavoured stock, buy a fish head too. When using lobster or similar shell fish, simmer the shells in liquid. This produces a very delicate pale pink stock, which enhances the colour of the soup.

To cook Put the bones, skin, head or shells into a pan. Cover with cold water, or use partially water and partially white wine. Add seasoning and a *bouquet garni*. Bring the liquid to the boil, remove any grey scum, simmer steadily for about 30–40 minutes in a covered pan, or allow about 10–15 minutes at 15 lb. in a pressure cooker. Sliced onions, carrots and celery may be added. Strain the stock carefully.

● **AVOID** *Over-cooking fish stock, it does not improve the flavour.*
● **SHORT CUT** *It may sound unusual, but chicken stock, or water and a chicken stock cube can be used in fish soups, or use water and a little anchovy essence.*
● **TO SLIMMERS** *Fish is a low calorie food and some of the unthickened fish soups would be a very wise choice.*

Creamed Fish Soup

About 8–12 oz. white fish; 1½ pints (4C) fish stock (see Blue Print); 1 oz. cornflour; 1–2 oz. butter; seasoning; grated rind 1 lemon; ¼ pint (⅔C) milk; ¼ pint (⅔C) thick cream. *To garnish:* chopped parsley or dill and/or cooked peas; paprika.
Put the fish into about ½ pint (1⅓C) of the fish stock. Simmer gently until just tender. Strain the fish from the liquid and put the stock into a saucepan. Blend the rest of the

fish stock with the cornflour, put into the saucepan, add the butter, a little more seasoning if required and the lemon rind. Bring to the boil, cook until slightly thickened, stirring well. Add the milk and cream and the flaked fish. Heat for a few minutes only, *without boiling*. Top with the garnish and serve. *Serves 4–6.*
To vary To make a thicker soup, either decrease the amount of fish stock (which gives a creamier result) or increase the amount of cornflour to 1½–2 oz. (up to ½C).
Creamed shell fish soup Use prepared or canned mussels, shelled prawns or flaked crabmeat instead of white fish.
Slimmers Soup Cook the fish as above. Add to *very well flavoured* fish stock and blend in a little yoghourt instead of milk and cream.

Spiced Fish Soup

2 tablespoons oil; 1–2 cloves garlic; 1 large onion; 3 large tomatoes; 1½ pints (4C) fish stock (see Blue Print); ½ teaspoon paprika; pinch allspice; good pinch saffron*; pinch turmeric; about 12 oz. white fish; seasoning. *To garnish:* croûtons or garlic croûtons (see page 53); parsley.
*If using a few saffron strands instead of saffron powder infuse this in the stock for about 30 minutes, then strain and use the stock.
Heat the oil in a pan, fry the crushed garlic, the chopped onion and skinned chopped tomatoes until a thick purée. Blend the fish stock with all the flavourings, add to the purée, together with the finely diced, skinned raw white fish. Simmer until the fish is tender. Season to taste and garnish with the croûtons and parsley just before serving. *Serves 4–6.*

Genoese Fish Soup

Follow the recipe for the Spiced Fish Soup and add a few shelled prawns and mussels just before serving.

Crab Bisque

1 medium-sized cooked crab; ¾ pint (2C) fish stock (see Blue Print) or water; 1 lemon; seasoning; *bouquet garni*; 1 onion; 2 oz. (½C) mushrooms; 2 oz. (¼C) butter; ½ pint (1⅓C) thin cream; 2 egg yolks; 2 tablespoons sherry. Remove all the meat from the crab, put on one side. Put the crab shell into a pan with the stock or water, the pared lemon rind, a little lemon juice, seasoning and *bouquet garni*. Cover the pan tightly and simmer for about 30 minutes. Chop the onion, slice the mushrooms and toss in the hot butter. Add the strained crab stock and crabmeat and heat gently. Blend the cream with the egg yolks, add to the crab mixture and heat, *without boiling*. Stir in the sherry, heat for 1–2 minutes and serve. (Illustrated on page 49.) *Serves 4–5.*

Lobster Bisque

1 medium-sized cooked lobster; ¾ pint (2C) water; 1 onion; 1 lemon; small piece celery;

seasoning; ½ pint (1⅓C) thin cream; 2 egg yolks; 2 tablespoons dry sherry or brandy. Remove all the flesh from the lobster and put on one side. Put the crushed shell into a pan with the water, chopped onion, pared lemon rind and a little juice and chopped celery. Season, cover the pan tightly and simmer for 30 minutes. Strain the lobster stock into a pan, add the flaked lobster and the cream, blended with the egg yolks, and heat *without boiling*. Add the sherry or brandy, heat for about 2 minutes and serve. Garnish with the tiny claws. *Serves 4–6.*
To vary Prawns, shrimps, scallops or oysters may be used instead of lobster. Scallops need cooking, so slice or dice and simmer in the strained fish stock for about 8 minutes before adding the cream.

Storing and Freezing *Fish is highly perishable so do not store any of these soups. Frozen fish may be used in making the soup, but I find the flavour of fish rather disappointing if frozen.*

Chicken chowder

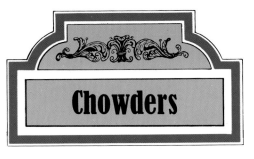

Chowders

The term Chowder is used to describe a really thick soup, which is very like a rather liquid stew, full of interesting ingredients. Chowders make excellent light meals. Serve with toast or fresh rolls.

Blue Print Recipe

Salmon Chowder

1 pint (2⅔C) milk · medium-sized can sweet corn · medium-sized can salmon · 1 oz. butter · seasoning · chopped parsley

To cook Put the milk and sweet corn into a pan. Bring almost to the boil. Add the

To make croûtons
1. Either dice toasted bread or dice bread and fry in hot oil or fat until crisp and golden brown.
2. Drain on absorbent paper.

To make garlic croûtons
3. Fry as above, then roll in garlic salt.

flaked salmon, butter, seasoning and parsley. Heat gently for a few minutes. *All recipes based on this serve 4.*
To vary Use tuna, crabmeat, chopped prawns or flaked white fish in place of salmon.
Omit the corn and add raw diced vegetables (potatoes, onions, peas, carrots) to the milk. Simmer steadily for about 15 minutes. Add a little extra milk or white stock, then the remaining ingredients.

Chicken Chowder

2 or 3 rashers bacon; 1 onion; ¾ pint (2C) chicken stock; about 12 oz. (1½C) diced raw root vegetables; ½ pint (1⅓C) milk; about 6 oz. (nearly 1C) diced cooked chicken; 3–4 tablespoons sweet corn; seasoning. *To garnish:* chopped parsley; paprika.
Chop the bacon and the peeled onion. Fry the bacon for a few minutes, add the onion then cook together until the bacon is crisp. Add the stock. Bring to the boil, put in the vegetables and cook until just tender. Add the milk, chicken, sweet corn and seasoning.

Salmon chowder

Simmer for a few minutes then serve, topped with parsley and paprika. *Serves 4–6.*

To vary
Lobster Chowder Use the recipe above, but add flaked lobster in place of chicken. You can make the chowder with chicken stock or simmer the lobster shells to give a fish stock.
Ham Chowder Use stock from boiling bacon or ham in place of chicken stock. Increase the amount of bacon slightly and reduce the amount of chicken.
Clam Chowder Use fish stock in place of chicken stock and use about 8 oz. bacon. Add a medium-sized can clams instead of chicken.

Storing and Freezing *Store in the refrigerator and reheat gently. These chowders freeze well but should be used within several weeks.*
To use any left over *Heat for a short time only, do not over-cook.*

There are three basic ways in which one can make a vegetable soup.

The first is to chop, shred or grate the vegetables and cook them in clear stock (or water, if the vegetables have sufficient flavour). Most vegetables are suitable for this type of soup, either by themselves or mixed with others, see Blue Print 1.

The second type of vegetable soup is a purée. Cook the vegetables in stock or water until tender, then emulsify in the liquidiser goblet, or sieve. The 'starchy' vegetables, such as potatoes, give a thick purée soup, other vegetables a thinner purée. Blue Print 2 describes this type of soup.

In Blue Print 3 you have a creamed vegetable soup. Here the vegetables are blended with a creamy white sauce and cream if wished.

Blue Print Recipes

1. Onion and Capsicum Soup

2 large onions · 1–2 cloves garlic (optional) · 2 tablespoons oil or 2 oz. ($\frac{1}{4}$C) butter or margarine · 1 large green and 1 large red pepper (capsicums) · 1$\frac{1}{2}$ pints (4C) brown or white stock or water · 2 large tomatoes · 2–4 oz. ($\frac{1}{2}$–1C) mushrooms · seasoning. To garnish: chopped herbs, grated cheese or croûtons (see page 53).

To make Peel the onions and cut into narrow strips. Peel and crush the garlic cloves.
To cook Heat the oil or butter and toss the onion and garlic in this until nearly transparent. Take care the onions do not brown. Discard the cores and seeds from the peppers and cut the pulp, or flesh, into small strips. Blend with the onion but do not fry if you like a firm texture. Add the liquid, bring steadily to the boil, add the skinned chopped tomatoes and sliced mushrooms. Continue cooking until the vegetables are soft. Season well.
To serve While very hot. Garnish with chopped fresh herbs, grated cheese or croûtons. *All recipes based on this serve 4–6.*
To vary Use all onions and brown stock. Use all mushrooms and brown stock.

2. Green Pea and Potato Soup

2 large old potatoes · 1 large onion · 2 oz. ($\frac{1}{4}$C) margarine or butter · 1$\frac{1}{2}$ pints (4C) white stock or water · 8 oz. (1$\frac{1}{4}$C) shelled peas or frozen peas · *bouquet garni* · sprig mint or pinch dried mint · seasoning · little cream (optional). To garnish: parsley, mint, watercress or chives.

To make Peel and dice the potatoes and onion.

Cream of mushroom soup

To cook Toss the vegetables in the hot margarine or butter for a few minutes, take care they do not brown. Add the stock, bring to the boil, simmer for about 15 minutes. Add the peas, herbs and seasoning. Continue cooking gently for 30 minutes. Remove the *bouquet garni* and either emulsify in a warmed liquidiser or sieve the soup. Reheat, stir in the cream, if liked.
To serve Top with chopped and/or sprigged herbs. *All recipes based on this serve 4–6.*
To vary Use 3–4 potatoes and 2 onions.

Lentil Soup

Method as Blue Print 2. Put 6 oz. ($\frac{3}{4}$C) lentils into a pan with 2 pints (5$\frac{1}{3}$C) stock, preferably from simmering a ham bone or boiling bacon. Add 1–2 chopped onions, a little chopped celery (optional), 1–2 chopped tomatoes, a *bouquet garni* and seasoning.

Simmer steadily for about 1$\frac{1}{2}$ hours or allow 15 minutes at 15 lb. in a pressure cooker. Remove *bouquet garni* and either emulsify in a warmed liquidiser or sieve. Return to the pan, add 1–2 oz. butter or margarine and/or a little cream. Taste and season well, if necessary. Reheat and garnish with chopped parsley.

Leek and Potato Soup

Follow Blue Print 2, but use 1 lb. leeks in place of the onion. Wash the leeks, cut into rings and cook with the potatoes as the Blue Print. Top with paprika and a few pieces of reserved leek before serving.

3. Cream of Mushroom Soup

4–6 oz. (1–1$\frac{1}{2}$C) mushrooms · 1 onion · $\frac{1}{2}$ pint (1$\frac{1}{3}$C) white stock · *bouquet garni* · 2 oz. ($\frac{1}{4}$C) butter or margarine ·

2 oz. ($\frac{1}{2}$C) flour · 1 pint (2$\frac{2}{3}$C) milk seasoning · 3–4 tablespoons thick cream (optional). To garnish: chopped parsley.

To make Wash and slice the mushrooms, do not peel if good quality. Peel, but do not chop, the onion.
To cook Put the vegetables into a saucepan with the stock and *bouquet garni*. Simmer for 15 minutes. Meanwhile heat the butter or margarine in another pan, stir in the flour, cook for 2–3 minutes, stirring well. Gradually add the milk, bring to the boil and cook until a thickened sauce.

For a delicate mushroom soup, strain just the liquid from cooking the mushrooms into the sauce, then add seasoning, some of the cooked mushrooms and the cream. For a soup with more flavour emulsify *all* the mushrooms, onion and stock in the warmed liquidiser goblet, or sieve and add to the sauce, together with seasoning and cream. The third version is to remove the onion, then add *all* the cooked mushrooms, and stock to the sauce with seasoning and cream.
To serve Top with chopped parsley. *All recipes based on this serve 4–6.*
To vary Use Jerusalem artichokes, celery, spinach, etc. If using 'starchy' vegetables, such as potatoes, in a creamed soup reduce the flour to 1–1$\frac{1}{2}$ oz.

Tomato Soups

Tomatoes are extremely versatile in soup. You can make a clear tomato soup as Blue Print 1; use about 1 lb. additional tomatoes in place of peppers and mushrooms. On the other hand a creamed tomato soup is delicious. Use Blue Print 3. Simmer 1 lb. tomatoes, 1–2 onions and $\frac{1}{2}$ pint (1$\frac{1}{3}$C) white stock with a *bouquet garni* of herbs. Sieve or emulsify, reheat then blend the very hot tomato purée into the very hot white sauce (as Blue Print 3), season well.

Tomato and Pasta Soup

1$\frac{1}{2}$ lb. tomatoes; 2 onions; 2 oz. ($\frac{1}{4}$C) margarine or butter; 1$\frac{1}{2}$ pints (4C) white stock; *bouquet garni*; seasoning; 1 tablespoon concentrated tomato purée; 1–2 diced carrots; 2–3 tablespoons uncooked pasta.

Chop the tomatoes and onions. Toss the onions in the hot margarine or butter for 2–3 minutes. Add the tomatoes, stock, *bouquet garni* and seasoning. Simmer for 20 minutes, sieve or emulsify, return to the pan with the rest of the ingredients. Cook for 15 minutes. Add extra liquid if the soup becomes too thick. *Serves 6.*

Storing and Freezing *Store soups for 2–3 days only in the refrigerator. The puree soups freeze best.*
To use any left over *Heat; this can be done quickly unless there is cream in the soup. A creamed soup with tomatoes must be heated gently to prevent the soup curdling.*

Take a pride in making interesting and varied salads. All too often a salad consists of the same mixture of vegetables; be adventurous and add fruits and nuts. We are told that 'salads are good for you', that is true, but they are also capable of being some of the most delicious dishes.

Blue Print

To Prepare Some Salad Ingredients

Beetroot Peel and dice or slice cooked beetroot. Put in seasoned vinegar. Grated raw beetroot makes a change.

Cabbage and similar greens Wash and shred finely.

Celery, Chicory and Seakale Wash, discard the very outer leaves or sticks. Chop neatly or as the particular recipe.

Cucumber Slice thinly, peel if wished, leave for a while in seasoned vinegar or lemon juice, or oil and vinegar or lemon juice.

Fruit Wash and slice if necessary. If adding the fruits that discolour easily (apples, peaches, avocado pears, etc.), then toss in lemon juice or well seasoned oil and vinegar or coat with mayonnaise.

Green Vegetables—Lettuce, Endive, Watercress and Cress Wash lettuce and similar vegetables, pull apart gently and then pat dry in a cloth or shake in a cloth or salad shaker. Use ice cold water for washing them. Shred or use the leaves whole. Watercress is sprigged and washed. Cress is cut with scissors, washed and the black seeds discarded.

Peppers (Capsicums) Cut the pulp or flesh into rings or dice. Discard cores and seeds. Some people like to 'blanch' peppers for a few minutes in boiling, salted water to soften slightly. Drain well.

Potatoes and Root Vegetables Cook in skins where possible, and do not over-cook. Skin when cooked, dice and toss in dressing while warm if possible, so the vegetables absorb the flavour. Add other ingredients to the salad while warm, but leave fresh herb garnishes and any 'crisp' additions, such as celery until cold.

Radishes Wash, discard the green stalk, slice or cut into shapes.

Rice Boil long grain rice, rinse well if sticky, but if boiled carefully this should not be necessary. I like to toss the *warm* rice in mayonnaise or oil and vinegar so it absorbs the flavourings.

Tomatoes Skin if wished, slice or quarter or cut into 'water-lilies'.

● **AVOID** *Adding dressings to most green vegetables too early, otherwise they lose their crispness. The more robust cabbage, used in coleslaw, is not spoiled by being coated with mayonnaise or oil and vinegar and left for some time before serving.*

Green Salad

Choose a selection of green ingredients only. These can be lettuce, endive, chicory, green pepper, celery, cucumber, cress and watercress. Prepare the vegetables, it makes the salad more interesting if you mix more than one type of lettuce, then toss in well seasoned oil and vinegar. This is an ideal salad to serve with steaks and other cooked meats or fish.

Mixed Salad

You can use as many and varying ingredients in this salad as wished.

Choose a lettuce or other similar green vegetable. Add sliced or diced cucumber, sliced tomatoes, radishes (whole or sliced), green or red pepper, cut into strips or dice, chopped celery or leaves of chicory, cress, spring onions and sliced hard boiled egg. To make the mixed salad more interesting, add chopped nuts, diced dessert apples and cooked sweet corn. Avoid too many solid vegetables, such as potatoes if the salad is being served with a fairly substantial dish. Obviously you can change the 'emphasis' of the mixed salad according to the type of food with which it is being served. If serving with fish I would be very generous with cucumber, and use chopped fresh tarragon in the dressing.

Quantities to Allow

Obviously the quantities allowed depend upon the quantity of other vegetables used, but this may be a guide to buying salads.

Beetroot 1 large one serves 4–6 (unless being served by itself, when it is enough for about 3 people).

Cabbage—a small cabbage cuts up to make coleslaw for about 6–8 people.

Celery—a head serves about 6. A **chicory** head serves 2–3.

Cucumber—a medium-sized one is enough for about 6.

Green or red pepper—serves 4–6.

Lettuce or other green vegetable—allow 1 small to medium-sized lettuce for 4–6.

Potatoes and other root vegetables—allow about 4 oz. for each person.

Radishes—2–3 per person.

Rice—allow about 1 oz. rice before cooking for each person.

Tomatoes—1 medium-sized per person.

Storing and Freezing *Unfortunately salads do not store particularly well when once prepared. The salad ingredients keep well in covered containers in the refrigerator, but as soon as they are mixed together, particularly with dressing, they lose their crispness. Salads do not freeze.*

Endive

Chicory

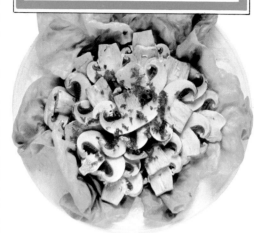

Mushroom salad

The recipes for two 'basic' salads are given on the left, but remember you can serve one vegetable alone for a salad, or mix two or three. These simple salads are excellent as an hors d'oeuvre as well as an accompaniment to hot or cold meats.

For Family Occasions

Chicory and Pepper Salad

There is often confusion about the word 'chicory'. In Britain this means the white vegetable which looks like a delicate head of celery and has a slightly similar flavour. In many countries this is called 'endive' and chicory means the vegetable that looks like a curly lettuce, see sketches.

Wash and separate the chicory leaves. Cut a raw red pepper into narrow strips. Wash and slice a few button mushrooms. Toss the pepper and mushrooms in a little oil and vinegar dressing, put into a bowl and arrange the chicory leaves round. Serve this salad with cold meats, or cheese.

Coleslaw

This salad is based on shredded cabbage. Choose white (often called Dutch) cabbage or use the heart of cabbage, not the tougher outer leaves. Wash and shred the cabbage very finely. Blend with mayonnaise.

This is a very basic coleslaw. It can be varied by adding grated raw carrots, chopped celery, chopped apple, raisins, green and/or red pepper and chopped nuts. It can be tossed in soured cream or oil and vinegar rather than mayonnaise. Serve this with cold meats, cheese or with grilled meats and fish.

Mushroom Salad

Raw mushrooms are delicious in a salad. Choose firm small button mushrooms, wash and trim the stalks, but do not peel. Slice

neatly and season or toss in an oil and vinegar dressing. Put on to crisp lettuce and top with chopped parsley or a mixture of fresh herbs. Serve this salad with hard boiled eggs or cheese, or as part of a mixed hors d'oeuvre.

For Special Occasions

American Salad

The salad illustrated on this page is typically an American one, for it has a colourful and delicious variety of ingredients, including sweet corn.

Mix cooked green beans, cooked or canned sweet corn, finely diced red pepper, sliced raw mushrooms, sliced firm tomatoes, and black olives. Toss in oil and vinegar. Put into a dish and top with rings of raw onion. Serve this salad with cold chicken or turkey.

Oil and Vinegar (French) Dressing

The proportions of oil and vinegar can be varied according to personal taste, but the most usual quantities are as follows:

Put a little salt, pepper, pinch dry mustard or little made or French mustard and a pinch sugar on to a plate. Gradually blend in 2 tablespoons olive or other first-class salad oil. Add 1 tablespoon white wine, white malt, red wine or brown malt vinegar. The choice of vinegar can be varied according to the type of salad. You can add chopped herbs or part of a crushed clove of garlic if wished.

It is sensible to make up large quantities of this dressing (mix in the liquidiser goblet), then store it in screw-topped jars. Shake just before use.

Storing and Freezing *See comments about storing on the left. I find peppers freeze well. Freeze without wrapping, wrap when very hard. Use in salads when only just defrosted.*

To use any left over *Cover, store in a refrigerator or cool place and use as soon as possible.*

American salad

Fruit blends with most other ingredients. You can use fresh, canned or defrosted frozen fruit. Choose citrus fruits to serve with rich foods, for example orange with duck, grapefruit with boiled bacon. Fruit blends well with all types of cheese salads, but particularly with cottage cheese. Dried prunes are an excellent accompaniment to cold beef or pork, so add these with raw apple to a green salad.

Emphasis on Fruit

For All Occasions

Orange Salad

Lettuce; large oranges; oil and vinegar dressing; chopped parsley.

Arrange the lettuce on a dish, cut away the peel from the oranges and cut into segments. Moisten with dressing and top with chopped parsley if wished. Serve with duck, pork or goose.

You can add a little chopped green pepper, chicory or celery, but do not make this salad too elaborate, as the oranges are very important to counteract the richness of the meat.

Carrot and Apple Salad

Top prepared lettuce and watercress or other green salad vegetable with coarsely grated carrot, as shown in the picture. Arrange segments of apple, dipped in oil and vinegar dressing, as a garnish. This salad can be made more interesting if finely chopped apple and chopped nuts are mixed with the carrot. Serve with cooked sausages, pork, goose or other fairly rich meats or with cheese.

Chicken peach salad (top)
Carrot and apple salad (below)

For Special Occasions

Avocado Pear Salad

2 avocado pears; oil and vinegar dressing; lettuce; 1–2 oranges; 2 tomatoes; cucumber. Halve the avocado pears, remove the stones, then peel away the skin from the pears. Slice and put into the dressing immediately, so the fruit does not discolour. Arrange a bed of lettuce on a dish. Cut the peel from the oranges, then cut into segments, and slice the tomatoes. Arrange the pears, oranges and tomatoes on the lettuce. Garnish with twists of cucumber. Serve this salad with cold poultry or meat or with hot roasts. (Illustrated on page 49) *Serves 4–6.*

Chicken Peach Salad

Cooked chicken has a very delicate flavour and a salad has to complement this. The salad shown on this page is an ideal blending of flavours. Arrange the prepared lettuce, watercress and chicory in a bowl. Top with neatly diced pieces of cooked chicken, sliced fresh pear, dipped in oil and vinegar dressing, sliced canned peaches and fresh or dried dates. Serve with mayonnaise or oil and vinegar dressing and garnish with lemon.

Storing and Freezing *Store as other salads. Frozen chicken can be used, but do not freeze the completed salad. Ripe avocado pears freeze well, but use immediately they are defrosted.*

To use any left over *Cover, store in a refrigerator and use as soon as possible.*

Practically every kind of cheese can be served in a salad. The cheese may be sliced, diced, grated or cut into neat wedges. Cottage cheese should be piled neatly on the bed of salad, or used as a filling for ham, as in the pictures on this page.

Eggs are generally hard boiled for salads, but scrambled egg, mixed with mayonnaise and finely chopped chives or other fresh herbs is delicious. The scrambled egg can be put on top of the salad ingredients or used as a filling for tomato cases or tiny boat shapes of well seasoned cucumber, see the sketches.

Hawaiian Salad

1 lettuce; 1–2 heads chicory; about 8 oz. (1C) cottage cheese; fresh or canned pineapple rings; 2–3 oranges; 1 apple; piece cucumber; oil and vinegar dressing.

Prepare the lettuce, put on a flat dish. Wash and separate the chicory leaves, arrange at either end of the dish. Spoon the cottage cheese into the centre of the lettuce, garnish with halved pineapple rings, orange segments, apple and cucumber slices (both dipped in oil and vinegar). *Serves 4.*

Note About 2 tablespoons mayonnaise can be blended into the cheese if wished.

Californian Cottage Cheese Salad

Arrange lettuce on individual plates. Top with cottage cheese, halved walnuts, cooked, well drained prunes and radish slices.

This salad can be served on buttered bread or crispbread as an open sandwich.

Stuffed Ham Rolls

1 lettuce; 6 large slices lean ham or mortadella; about 8 oz. cottage cheese; 1–2 tablespoons chopped nuts; 1–2 tablespoons chopped gherkins. *To garnish:* 4–6 slices of cucumber.

Prepare the lettuce and arrange on 4 or 6 small dishes. Halve the ham or mortadella slices. Blend the cottage cheese with the nuts and gherkins, spread over the ham and roll neatly. Put 2–3 rolls on each plate, garnish

Hawaiian salad (right)
Californian cottage cheese salad, Stuffed ham rolls and Cheese and mushroom salad (below)

with watercress and twists of cucumber. *Serves 4–6.*

This salad can be served on buttered bread or crispbread as an open sandwich.

Cheese and Mushroom Salad

Arrange slices of cucumber on a dish, top with cottage cheese, then arrange sliced raw mushrooms over the cheese. Garnish with parsley.

This salad can be served on buttered bread or crispbread as an open sandwich.

Egg and Carrot Salad

3 hard boiled eggs; 2 medium-sized carrots; 3–4 tablespoons salted peanuts; 2 teaspoons chopped parsley; mayonnaise; lettuce.

Chop the eggs coarsely, peel and grate the carrots. Mix with the peanuts, chopped parsley and mayonnaise to moisten. Use the larger lettuce leaves as cups and spoon some of the egg mixture into the centre of each cup. Serve the lettuce heart in the middle of the dish of filled lettuce leaves. *Serves 4.*

To vary
Egg and Prawn Salad Use shelled prawns instead of peanuts.
Egg and Potato Salad Use diced cooked new potatoes instead of grated carrots, add chopped chives and chopped parsley.
Egg and Corn Salad Omit the nuts and use cooked corn in the salad.

Storing and Freezing *See comments on other salads. Cottage cheese can be stored for several days in a refrigerator or for a limited time in a freezer—it tends to dry-out if kept for too long.*
To use any left over *Cover, store in a cool place and use as quickly as possible.*

1. Use scrambled egg in salads to fill tomato cases.

2. Scrambled egg also makes an interesting filling for cucumber 'boats'.

One of the most appetising ways to serve cold meat and fish is mixed with other ingredients in a salad, rather than just having sliced meat or a piece of fish on a plate.

By mixing the meat or fish with other foods you make it look more appetising, often it gives added moistness and it can make the meat or fish 'go further'. Our traditional meat pie (opposite) is a perfect accompaniment to salads.

Ways to Serve Meat in Salads

Cut the meat into neat pieces (as the chicken on page 57) and mix with the salad.
Cut the meat thinly, roll round a stuffing and serve on a bed of salad.

Beef Rolls

Mix horseradish cream with cream cheese or mayonnaise. Spread on slices of cooked beef and roll. Or blend chopped mustard pickle and a little mayonnaise, spread over the beef and roll.

Pork or Ham Rolls

Cottage cheese is an excellent filling for these meats, since it is not too rich. Flavour the cheese with a little chopped onion and freshly chopped sage. Spread over the meat and roll.
Cover the pork or ham with diced raw apple, mixed with diced cooked prunes, roll firmly. Blend cottage, cream or Demi-sel cheese with a little curry powder. Spread on the meat and roll firmly.

Tongue Rolls

Blend mayonnaise with chopped gherkins and capers. Spread over the tongue and roll. A sweet chutney also blends well with tongue. Spread thinly, top with chopped cucumber and roll.
Some meats, lamb and veal for example, have the wrong texture to roll neatly.

Meat and Fish Salads

Ham and Pâté Cones

8 good-shaped slices ham; 8 cooked or canned asparagus tips; about 4 tablespoons coleslaw (see page 56); approximately 2–3oz. ($\frac{1}{2}$C) canned or home-made pâté; stuffed olives. *To garnish:* lettuce; radishes.
Spread a slice of ham on a board and lay an asparagus tip diagonally on the meat. Add the coleslaw. Roll into a cone. Put the pâté into a piping bag with a $\frac{1}{4}$- or $\frac{1}{2}$-inch rose (potato) pipe. Press out rosettes at the top of each ham cone and top with a slice of stuffed olive. Serve on a bed of lettuce and garnish with radishes. *Serves 4.*
Note If the pâté is rather firm blend with a little mayonnaise or cream.

Mixed Meat Rolls

A good mixture of meats to serve would be pressed beef filled with asparagus, mortadella filled with coleslaw (see page 56) and the ham and pâté cones above.

Ways to Serve Fish in Salads

Flaked white fish or shell fish may be mixed with other ingredients in a salad. The fish and potato salad below is a good basic recipe that can be varied in many ways.

Fish and Potato Salad

About 1–1$\frac{1}{4}$ lb. white fish; about 1 lb. potatoes, preferably new; seasoning; piece cucumber; few radishes; few capers; 1 dessert apple (optional); mayonnaise. *To garnish:* lettuce; tomatoes; 1 lemon.
Cook the fish and the potatoes in well seasoned water. Dice the potatoes neatly when cooked and flake the fish. Blend with the diced cucumber, sliced radishes, capers and diced apple. Add just enough mayonnaise to bind, about 4–5 tablespoons. Put into a plain mould or basin and leave until ready to serve. Turn out on to a bed of lettuce and garnish with sliced tomatoes and lemon. *Serves 4–6.*
To vary Chopped hard boiled eggs can be added to the above ingredients and white and shell fish can be mixed together.

Prawn and Rice Salad

6 oz. ($\frac{3}{4}$C) long grain rice; nearly $\frac{3}{4}$ pint (nearly 2C) water; seasoning; 4–5 tablespoons oil and vinegar dressing; little chopped parsley; little chopped rosemary (optional); about 8 oz. (1$\frac{1}{2}$–2C) shelled prawns; about 8 oz. (1$\frac{1}{4}$–1$\frac{1}{2}$C) diced cooked chicken; few mushrooms; 1–2 dessert apples; lettuce. *To garnish:* few prawns.
Put the rice, water and seasoning into a saucepan. Bring the water to the boil, stir briskly, cover the pan, lower the heat and cook for 15 minutes. By this time the liquid should have evaporated and the rice cooked, without being sticky. Toss the rice in dressing while hot. Cool and add the herbs, prawns, chicken, chopped mushrooms and diced apples. Shred the lettuce finely, put at the bottom of a salad bowl. Add the rice salad, and garnish with prawns. *Serves 4–6.*

Storing and Freezing *Although meat and fish may be frozen or stored, the salad ingredients on this page, including rice, do not freeze well.*
To use any left over *Cover, store in the refrigerator and use as quickly as possible.*

Prawn and rice salad

The term 'raised pies' refers to the fact that the traditional way of making these was to mould (or raise) the pastry dough, rather like a sculptor moulds clay. The sketches indicate how this is done, but if preferred you can make and bake the pie in a cake tin. If possible choose a tin with a loose base or a side lock so the pie may be removed without fear of the pastry breaking. The Blue Print gives the correct pastry for this type of pie, but short crust could be substituted.

Blue Print Recipe

Hot Water Crust Pastry

4 oz. ($\frac{1}{2}$C) fat, preferably lard · $\frac{1}{4}$ pint ($\frac{2}{3}$C) water · 12 oz. (3C) flour, preferably plain · good pinch salt · 1 egg yolk (optional).

To make Put the fat and water into a saucepan, heat until the fat has melted. Sieve the flour and salt into a mixing bowl, add the melted lard and water, knead lightly, add the egg yolk. This is not essential, but gives a better colour to the pastry and helps it to crisp. If omitting the egg yolk you may need just a little more water, for the dough should be a soft rolling consistency. Keep warm and use as shown in the sketches.

● **AVOID** *Letting the pastry cool, it is called a 'hot water crust' because the fat and water are heated, but the dough should be used while warm, soft and pliable.*
● **TO RECTIFY** *If the dough does become cold, put it into a warm place for a short time.*

Pork Pie

Ingredients as Blue Print PLUS $1\frac{1}{2}$–$1\frac{3}{4}$ lb. pork (choose about $1\frac{1}{4}$–$1\frac{1}{2}$ lb. fillet and the rest belly of pork, to give a little fat), seasoning, 1–2 teaspoons grated lemon rind, good pinch chopped fresh or dried sage, about 6 tablespoons stock and 1 teaspoon powdered gelatine. *To glaze:* 1 egg.
Dice or mince the meat, add the flavourings and 2–3 tablespoons stock. Make the pastry case, as the Blue Print. Mould or cut out. Put the filling into the pastry case, place the lid in position; *do not press down too firmly* as you must leave room for the jelly. Make a slit on top, decorate with leaves and fork the edge as in the picture. Beat the egg and brush the top, or top and sides in the moulded version of the pie. Bake in the centre of a moderate oven, 350–375°F, Gas Mark 4–5, for 1 hour. Lower the heat to very moderate, 325–350°F, Gas Mark 3–4, for a further 1–1$\frac{1}{4}$ hours. Take the pie out of the oven, allow to cool. Meanwhile soften the gelatine in the cold stock, stand over hot water and allow to dissolve. Let the jelly mixture cool and begin to stiffen *very slightly*. Put a plastic funnel or

cone of foil or greaseproof paper into the slit on top of the pie and pour the jelly through this. Leave in a cold place until set. *Serves 6.*
Note In the traditional Melton Mowbray pork pie, 6–7 chopped anchovy fillets are added to the pork.

A home-made veal and ham, or chicken and ham pie is an excellent choice for summer. Follow the directions in the Blue Print for the pastry and the proportions and flavourings for the filling as the pork pie but use.

Veal and Ham Pie

$1\frac{1}{4}$ lb. diced fillet veal and 4–8 oz. diced or minced ham or gammon in place of the pork and 2–3 hard boiled eggs.

Chicken and Ham Pie

12 oz. diced breast chicken, 8 oz. diced or minced dark meat and 4–8 oz. diced or minced ham or gammon in place of the pork and 2–3 hard boiled eggs.
Put half the filling in the pastry case, add the shelled eggs, then the rest of the filling and bake as the pork pie.

Storing and Freezing *This type of pie cannot be reheated and must be used when fresh. If freezing use as soon as the pie is defrosted.*

To Mould a Pie
1. Use about $\frac{3}{4}$ of the dough, flatten this slightly with your hand. Keep remaining dough in a warm place.
2. Now place a round or oval mould or tin on this and gradually pull and mould the dough round this to give the right shape, and an even thickness. Remove the mould or tin.
3. Put the filling into the pastry case, see recipes, then damp the top edges of pastry.
4. Mould a lid of pastry, place on to the top of the pie, make a slit, decorate and bake as pork pie.

To Make a Pie in a Tin
5. Roll out the pastry and cut 2 rounds the size of the cake tin. Put one into the base of the greased tin; damp the edges. Keep the second round warm.
6. Roll the remaining pastry into a band, the circumference and depth of the tin. Insert into the tin.
7. Put in the filling, pull the side band of pastry gently up as you do so to give a neat appearance.
8. Damp the edges of the pastry, place the 'lid' into position, make a slit, decorate and bake as pork pie.

HORS D'OEUVRE, SAVOURIES & SAUCES

In this particular part of the book you will find the first course of a meal, the hors d'oeuvre, or 'meal starters', as they are often called today. This course is a very important one, for it can turn an every day meal into something special. It is a leisurely course, where everyone should relax, ready to enjoy their meal.

Although an hors d'oeuvre generally consists of a light cold or hot dish, and could be fruit juice only, the choice is important. If the hors d'oeuvre is too solid and highly flavoured then it spoils one's appetite for the main course to follow. The hors d'oeuvre, like the dessert, should complement the main course. It should have a refreshing flavour, so that if your family and guests are not particularly hungry, the piquant flavour of this 'beginning to the meal' whets their appetites. In order to enjoy the first course, time the cooking carefully for your main dish, so you can linger over the start of a pleasant meal. Almost any kind of food could be served as an hors

d'oeuvre and pages 61–67 give a very varied selection, together with ideas of *just when* that particular kind of meal starter would be ideal.

A savoury after, or instead of, the dessert is an attractive idea. If you want a very special meal then add this course. If your family are not particularly fond of puddings and desserts then serve

something savoury at the end of the meal. The recipes on pages 68–69 give you many suggestions. These savouries are ideal also to serve for light luncheon or supper dishes, particularly when you plan a 'meal on a tray'. They are easy to eat, quick to prepare and most important of all, are highly nutritious.

Can you make perfect sauces? All too often when I pose this question I am told that it is 'so difficult to make a smooth sauce'. That is not true. It takes both time and patience to achieve perfection in sauce making but it is *not* difficult. It is important to appreciate *why* sauces curdle or *why* they become lumpy and these points are dealt with in the last section of this part. It is also important to know *how* to put right an error when making a sauce, whether it is to correct seasoning, texture or consistency.

Interesting and well flavoured sauces can turn a simple dish into a superb one and mastering the art of sauce making is an important part of good cooking.

Fruit Plus

When you plan a really substantial main course and a rather creamy dessert, choose a 'fruity' hors d'oeuvre. The refreshing flavour will give everyone an appetite to appreciate the meat or fish course that follows.

Certain fruits and fruit juices are served so frequently that they could be dull. Melon, grapefruit, orange juice, all of these are very pleasant, but there are many occasions when they would be improved with a 'new look'.

Blue Print

Serving Fruit for an Hors d'Oeuvre

Never over-sweeten the fruit or fruit juice. If you do it makes it rather like a dessert.

Present it in an interesting way, i.e. melon should be cut as the sketches opposite, fruit juices should be served in frosted glasses and topped with mint leaves, which both smell and look attractive.

Try to have an unusual mixture of flavours when serving fruit, as the recipes on these pages.

● **AVOID** *Making your fruit hors d'oeuvre too sweet.*
● **TO RECTIFY** *Sprinkle a little lemon juice or dry sherry over the fruit if you have added too much sugar.*
● **SHORT CUT** *Use canned grapefruit segments and mix the liquid from the can with a little sherry or lemon juice.*
● **TO SLIMMERS** *An ideal hors d'oeuvre on most diets.*

Melon balls with lemon sauce

Melon

Throughout most of the year one is likely to be able to purchase some kind of melon. The most usual are Honeydew, Charentais, Cantaloupe and Ogen (the small melons that are generally served halved). The pink fleshed water melon is less suitable for a first course, except in a melon cocktail.

To buy melon, feel it and it should appear heavy for its size. Press gently but firmly and the melon should 'give' at either end, so indicating it is ripe.

Prepare by slicing or halving and removing the seeds. The usual accompaniments are sugar and ground ginger.

Although melons may not be kept in the refrigerator they are improved by being chilled before serving or serving on a bed of crushed ice.

Melon Balls with Lemon Sauce

1 melon (see below); 2 lemons; little water; 1–2 tablespoons sugar. *To garnish:* sprigs of mint; lemon twists.

Buy a ripe Honeydew, Charentais or Cantaloupe melon, or a rather large Ogen melon. Halve the melon, remove the seeds. Take a vegetable scoop and make balls of the flesh, see Sketch 4. Chill these. The rather untidy pieces of melon at the bottom of the fruit can be used for the sauce. Grate enough rind from the lemons to give about 2 teaspoons. Squeeze the juice, measure and add enough water to give $\frac{1}{4}$ pint ($\frac{2}{3}$C). Simmer the rind with the liquid and sugar for about 5 minutes. Pour over the odd pieces of melon, then sieve or emulsify in the liquidiser. Taste and add more sugar if wished. This is not really necessary, for the sauce should be both thick and fairly sharp. Spoon into the bottom of 4–6 glasses and top with the melon balls. Garnish with mint and lemon. *Serves 4–6.*

Melon and Crème de Menthe

Sprinkle balls of melon or a slice of melon with a little crème de menthe.

Melon and Pineapple

Freeze canned pineapple juice until lightly frozen; do not allow it to become too hard. Put at the bottom of glasses and top with diced melon or melon balls.

Melon and Parma Ham

Put slices of melon, this time with the skin removed, on plates with curls of Parma ham. Garnish with a slice of lemon and serve with paprika or cayenne pepper.

Grapefruit

This is one of the most refreshing hors d'oeuvre and particularly good if you are slimming. Grapefruit, like melon, should feel heavy for its size. Do not buy very light coloured fruit unless you can store them for a while, for they are inclined to be under-ripe and lacking in sweetness and flavour. Halve the grapefruit and separate the segments, discard the pith and seeds. Serve with sugar and decorated with cherries.

Jamaican Grapefruit

Halve the fruit, remove the segments, put into a basin. Blend with a little brown sugar and rum. Pile back into the grapefruit case, chill and serve very cold, or put back into the case, top with a little brown sugar and butter and heat under the grill.

Grapefruit and Avocado Pear

2 grapefruit; 2 avocado pears; 2 tablespoons oil; good pinch dry mustard; pinch salt; shake pepper; pinch sugar; 1 tablespoon white vinegar; lettuce.
Cut the peel away from the grapefruit, then cut into segments. Make the dressing before halving the avocado pears. Blend the oil with the seasonings and sugar, then the vinegar (this can be wine or malt). Halve the avocado pears, remove the stones and skin. Cut into slices. Put in the dressing, so they do not discolour. Arrange small lettuce leaves on 4 or 6 individual plates. Top with the sliced grapefruit and avocado pears. *Serves 4–6.*

Avocado Vinaigrette

2 ripe avocado pears (see method); lemon juice; dressing as above, but you need to make a little more. *To garnish:* lettuce.
To choose avocado pears, feel gently, not just at the tip but all over the fruit; it should yield to the gentlest pressure.

Halve the pears, remove the stones, sprinkle lightly with lemon juice if there is even a slight delay in serving, as the fruit discolours badly. Fill the 'holes' where the stones were with the dressing. Garnish with lettuce leaves. *Serves 4.*

A New Look at Fruit

The recipes pictured and described on this page use fruits in unusual ways. The dishes are equally as suitable for an informal party as for an hors d'oeuvre. If serving as an hors d'oeuvre, pass each dish round the table with crisp biscuits, as shown in the picture, to counteract the rather rich flavour of the fillings.

Avocado Cream Dip

2 avocado pears; 2 tablespoons lemon juice; 3 tablespoons mayonnaise; 1 very small onion or 2–3 spring onions; 2 tablespoons soured cream; 2 tablespoons thick cream; seasoning. *To garnish:* shelled prawns or salted peanuts.
Halve the pears, remove the stones. Spoon the pulp into a basin; be careful not to break the skins, as these will be used for holding the filling. Add the lemon juice at once, so the pulp does not have an opportunity to discolour. Mash thoroughly, then blend in all the other ingredients; the onion or onions should be chopped very finely. Return the mixture to the 4 halved shells and top with prawns or nuts. *Serves 4, or 8–12 if part of a mixed hors d'oeuvre.*
To vary Add 2–3 oz. chopped prawns to the mixture.
Use cream cheese instead of thick cream and add finely chopped nuts to the mixture.

Kipper and Grapefruit Dip

2 rashers lean bacon; 1 small onion; 2 fairly large grapefruit; 12 oz. (1½C) cottage cheese; 6 tablespoons thick cream; 2 tablespoons chopped parsley; 1 can kipper fillets; seasoning.
Fry or grill the bacon until crisp, leave two larger pieces for garnish, then chop finely.

Chop or grate the onion. Remove the tops from the grapefruit and scoop out all the pulp. Press this through a sieve to extract the juice. Mix the juice with the cottage cheese, the chopped bacon and onion and the cream. Blend thoroughly, then add the parsley and the well drained flaked kipper fillets. Keep two pieces of kipper for garnish. Season the mixture very well, then pile back into the grapefruit cases. Garnish with the pieces of bacon and kipper. *Serves 4, or 8–12 if part of a mixed hors d'oeuvre.*

Melon and Pineapple Dip

1 Charentais or large Ogen melon; 1 lb. (2C tightly packed) cream cheese; 5 oz. (⅔C) natural yoghourt; 1 tablespoon concentrated tomato purée; 1 can pineapple pieces; 2 tablespoons chopped parsley; seasoning.
Cut the top off the melon, scoop the flesh from this slice. Remove the seeds then scoop out all the pulp; use a dessertspoon or a vegetable scoop, as shown in Sketch 4 opposite. If using a scoop, save a few melon balls for garnish. Blend the cream cheese, yoghourt and tomato purée until smooth. Stir in the melon pulp, well drained pineapple pieces and parsley. Mix thoroughly, add a little pineapple syrup from the can if the mixture is too stiff. Season well. Spoon back into the melon case and top with melon balls. *Serves 8, or 12–16 if part of a mixed hors d'oeuvre.*

Storing and Freezing *Grapefruit and melon store well for some time, although melons ripen quickly in hot weather. Put into a refrigerator for a short time before serving. Whole melons and whole grapefruit do not freeze well, but segments of grapefruit or melon balls, packed in sugar and water syrup, freeze very well for a limited time. Avocado pears also ripen quickly, so use soon after purchase. They can be kept for a few days in a refrigerator and can be frozen whole. Use as soon as they have defrosted. The avocado pear must be ripe when frozen.*
To use any left over *Left over fruit can be added to salads.*

1. Cut a large melon into slices, remove the seeds, but not the skin.
2. Cut the slice into sections.
3. Pull the sections alternately to left and right so breaking the straight line of the slice. Garnish with a slice of lemon, or a grape or cherry on a cocktail stick.
4. To make melon balls. Insert the vegetable scoop into the melon, turn to give a ball.

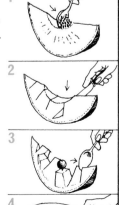

Avocado dip, Kipper and grapefruit dip and Melon and pineapple dip

Fish Hors D'Oeuvre

Hors d'oeuvre, based upon fish, are an excellent choice. Fish is basically a light food and, as such, is ideal to start a meal.

Blue Print

Choosing Fish Hors d'Oeuvre

The fish dish may be cold or hot, but it should consist of a small portion only. Many fish dishes normally served for a main course could be offered as hors d'oeuvre, but allow half-sized portions. Some of the best fish dishes to choose are:
Fish cocktail, see below, and shell fish dishes.
Herrings, either rollmop or Bismarck with salad, or some of the canned savoury herring dishes.
Anchovy fillets, served with hard boiled egg.
Sole or other white fish, served in sauces or grilled or fried.
Light fish moulds, see below.

● **AVOID** *The rather substantial fish, such as turbot, unless used in a very small quantity as the Prawn and Turbot Salad.*
● **SHORT CUTS** *Use canned salmon, tuna or sardines in salads.*
● **TO SLIMMERS** *Choose fish salads with a low calorie dressing (see page 74).*

Haddock mousse

Prawn and turbot salad

For Family Occasions

Herring Salad

2 rollmop herrings; 1 dessert apple; 1 small onion; 2 medium-sized cooked potatoes; 2 hard boiled eggs; either $\frac{1}{4}$ pint ($\frac{2}{3}$C) soured cream or use thick cream plus 1 tablespoon lemon juice; seasoning. *To garnish:* lettuce; diced beetroot; chopped dill or parsley.
Cut the herrings into neat pieces. Mix with the diced apple (this need not be peeled), the grated or finely chopped onion, diced potatoes and eggs. Blend with the soured cream or thick cream and lemon juice. Season very well. Put into a plain basin or mould and leave in a cool place for several hours. Turn out on to a bed of lettuce, garnish with diced beetroot and dill or parsley. *Serves 4–6, or 8–12 if part of a mixed hors d'oeuvre.*

Potted Tuna Fish

Blend a medium-sized can well drained tuna fish with enough mayonnaise to make a smooth texture. Add 1–2 teaspoons chopped gherkins, 1–2 teaspoons chopped capers and 1 tablespoon chopped parsley. Season well. Form into a neat shape on a bed of lettuce and garnish with wedges of lemon and tomato. Serve with hot toast and butter. *Serves 4.*

For Special Occasions

Fish Cocktail

Although most fish can be used in a cocktail, it is usual to select shell fish. A mixture of different shell fish (cooked mussels, crab, prawns) makes a more interesting cocktail than if one variety only is used. Pay attention to the flavouring of the sauce, for this is very important; shred the lettuce finely, since the cocktail is eaten with a small spoon and fork and large pieces of lettuce can be difficult to manage.
For the sauce: 5–6 tablespoons mayonnaise; 1 tablespoon thick cream; $\frac{1}{2}$ tablespoon lemon juice; 1 tablespoon fresh or canned tomato purée or use tomato ketchup if you like a slightly sweet flavour; few drops Worcestershire and/or Tabasco sauce and/or soy sauce; 1 tablespoon dry sherry (optional). Approximately 6 oz. ($\frac{3}{4}$C) shelled prawns or other shell fish or a mixture of fish; $\frac{1}{2}$ small lettuce. *To garnish:* 1 lemon; parsley; paprika.
Blend all the ingredients together for the sauce; this should pour easily, so if too thick add a little more cream. Blend most of the sauce with the fish, but save a little for the topping. Shred the lettuce finely, put into 4–5 glasses, top with the fish and sauce. Spoon the remaining sauce on top. Top with wedges of lemon, sprigs of parsley and paprika. Serve as cold as possible. It is ideal if the cocktail can be served on crushed ice. *Serves 4–5.*

Prawn and Turbot Salad

1 piece turbot, weighing about 6 oz.; seasoning; 3–4 oz. (generous $\frac{1}{2}$C) shelled prawns; sauce as given in the Fish Cocktail or use mayonnaise with a little lemon juice; 1 small green pepper; 1 small red pepper; lettuce or watercress. *To garnish:* black olives.
Poach the fish in well seasoned water until just tender. Do not over-cook for the fish

continues to soften as it cools. Cut into small cubes, blend with the prawns. Prepare the sauce or mix mayonnaise with lemon juice. Add the diced flesh from the green and red peppers (discard the cores and seeds) and the fish. Put lettuce or watercress on to 4–6 individual dishes or use scallop shells, as shown in the picture. Spoon the fish mixture on top and garnish with olives. *Serves 4–6, or 8–12 if part of a mixed hors d'oeuvre.*

Haddock Mousse

1 lb. fresh haddock (weight without bones); ½ pint (1⅓C) water; seasoning; aspic jelly to set 1 pint (2⅔C); 2 eggs; 1 lemon; 1 tablespoon dry sherry; ½–1 teaspoon anchovy essence; ¼ pint (⅔C) thick cream. *To garnish:* sliced tomatoes; watercress or lettuce; sliced cucumber.

Poach the fish in the water with seasoning. Do not over-cook as the fish continues to become soft as it cools. Measure the liquid and make up to ½ pint (1⅓C) again. Soften then dissolve the aspic jelly in this. Separate the eggs. Beat the yolks in a basin with the grated rind and juice of the lemon, sherry and anchovy essence. Pour the warm aspic liquid over, whisking hard as you do so. Add the flaked fish and allow the mixture to cool and stiffen slightly. Whip the cream until it just holds its shape, do not over-whip, otherwise it is difficult to fold this into the jellied mixture. Fold the cream, then the stiffly whisked egg whites into the mixture. Put into a 7-inch deep plain mould or tin, brushed with a little oil. Leave to set, then turn out on to a serving dish and garnish with tomatoes, watercress or lettuce and twists of cucumber. *Serves 4–6, or 8–12 if part of a mixed hors d'oeuvre.*

To vary Omit the anchovy essence and add 1 tablespoon tomato purée to the aspic jelly.

Increase the amount of anchovy essence or add finely chopped anchovy fillets to the flaked white fish; be sparing with the salt if you do this.

Use flaked shell fish, simmer the shells in water to give a good flavour to the liquid. If using shell fish omit anchovy essence.

Smoked Fish Hors d'Oeuvre

Smoked fish makes a pleasing meal starter. There is no cooking or special preparation. Arrange on a plate with the garnishes suggested. Serve with thin brown bread and butter.

Smoked trout, mackerel, sprats and eel are served with horseradish cream, lemon wedges and cayenne pepper. Garnish with lettuce. Smoked salmon is served with lemon, cayenne pepper and garnished with lettuce. All these smoked fish can be served with lightly scrambled egg, which makes a pleasing contrast in colour and texture.

Allow 1 trout or *small* mackerel (or 2 fillets from a larger mackerel) per person or about 3–4 oz. smoked eel (a little less if boned fillet) or sprats or 2 oz. smoked salmon.

Hot Fish Hors D'Oeuvre

The dishes on this page are served hot; they would be a good choice when the main dish is a cold one.

For Family Occasions

Eskimo Risotto

4 oz. (½C) long grain rice; seasoning; about 8 oz. smoked haddock (weight without bones); pint (1⅓C) milk; 2 eggs. *For the parsley sauce:* 1 oz. butter or margarine; 1 oz. flour; little extra milk if necessary and 1–2 tablespoons chopped parsley (or use a packet of parsley sauce mix); 2 large tomatoes; cayenne pepper.

Cook the rice in well seasoned water until tender, drain, unless all the water has been absorbed. Meanwhile poach the fish in the milk and hard boil the eggs. Lift the fish from the milk, save this for the sauce. To make the sauce, heat the butter or margarine in a pan, stir in the flour and cook over a low heat for 2–3 minutes. Gradually add the milk in which the haddock was cooked, bring to the boil and cook until thickened. Add a little extra milk, if necessary and the parsley (if using the parsley sauce mix follow the directions on the packet). Add the rice, flaked fish and most of the sliced egg to the sauce together with the diced tomatoes and a little seasoning, including cayenne pepper. Heat without boiling, then put into a hot dish and top with the remaining sliced egg. *Serves 4–6.*

For Special Occasions

Mussels in Mustard Brandy Sauce

5–6 pints mussels; 2 onions; 1–2 cloves garlic; 2 oz. (¼C) butter; ¼ pint (⅔C) water; seasoning; *bouquet garni*; scant 1 oz. flour; ¼ pint (⅔C) white wine; 2 teaspoons made mustard; 5 tablespoons brandy; ¼ pint (⅔C) thin or thick cream.

Eskimo risotto

Scrub the mussels well, remove any weeds on the side of the shells. Discard any mussels whose shells do not close when tapped sharply. Chop the onions and crush the garlic. Heat 1 oz. butter in a large pan, toss the onions and garlic in this, then add the mussels, water, seasoning and herbs. Heat gently until the mussels open, this takes only a short time, so watch the pan carefully. Strain, but keep all the liquid and onions. Remove the mussels from the shells. Heat the remaining butter in a pan, stir in the flour and cook gently for 2–3 minutes. Add the onions and liquid and the white wine. Bring slowly to the boil, stirring all the time. Stir in the mustard. Add the mussels, brandy and cream and heat *very gently without boiling.* Taste and add any extra seasoning required. Serve as soon as the mussels are hot. *This can serve up to 8 people, particularly if accompanied by crusty French bread.*

Salmon Mould

1 lb. uncooked salmon; 2 eggs; 1 oz. butter; 1 oz. flour; ½ pint (1⅓C) milk; 1 lemon; 2 tablespoons dry sherry; seasoning. *To garnish:* lemon; cucumber.

Put the fish through a fine mincer and pound until very soft and smooth. Add the eggs and beat well. Make a coating white sauce with the butter, flour and milk (see page 70). Add the finely grated lemon rind and juice and sherry to the sauce, when thickened, together with seasoning. Blend with the fish and eggs. Put into a well oiled mould, cover with oiled paper. Put into a steamer over hot, but not boiling, water and cook for 1 hour. Allow to stand for a few minutes then turn out on to a hot serving dish and garnish with lemon and rings of cucumber. Serve with tartare sauce (page 74). *Serves 4–6.*

To vary For a more economical dish use white fish plus a few drops anchovy essence.

Storing and Freezing *Cooked or uncooked fish must be stored in a refrigerator for the shortest time possible. Frozen fish can be chosen for most of the recipes. The Haddock Mousse and Salmon Mould freeze well. The salads and cocktails do not freeze, although defrosted shell fish is very satisfactory as the main ingredient.*

Fry the liver in the hot fat or butter until just tender. Hard boil the eggs. Mince or chop the liver with the onion. Add to the chopped hard boiled eggs and season well. Allow to cool, pile on to a dish and garnish with lemon and parsley. Serve with hot toast and butter. *Serves 4–5.*

Fried Garlic Sausage

Many garlic sausages can be served hot, particularly the Spanish Chorizo, and sliced black pudding makes an excellent hors d'oeuvre. It is important that the sausage is not dry so fry quickly.

Dip the slices of sausage into a very little flour and fry in hot fat for a few minutes. Serve garnished with tomatoes and lettuce.

For Special Occasions

Five Minute Pâté

8–10 oz. calves' liver; 2 oz. ($\frac{1}{4}$C) butter; seasoning; 2 tablespoons cream; 2 tablespoons sherry or brandy.

Cut the liver into small pieces. Heat the butter in a pan and fry the liver in this for several minutes only. Either mince or chop very finely while warm and blend with the other ingredients, or emulsify in the liquidiser with the seasoning, cream and sherry or brandy. Allow to cool and serve with hot toast and butter. *Serves 4–5.*

Note If the mixture seems too stiff for the liquidiser blades then add a very little extra hot liquid (cream, stock or brandy). If you add the liver gradually to the cream, etc. though it should emulsify easily.

To vary Add 1 crushed clove garlic to the liver when frying in the pan.

Add 1–2 gherkins to the mixture in the liquidiser.

Use chickens' livers instead. Pig's or lambs' liver could be used, but this needs slightly longer cooking.

Cover with a layer of melted butter to prevent it from drying.

Ham Mousse

Aspic jelly to set 1 pint (2$\frac{2}{3}$C); $\frac{1}{2}$ pint (1$\frac{1}{3}$C) chicken or ham stock; 2 eggs; 12 oz. lean ham; $\frac{1}{4}$ pint ($\frac{2}{3}$C) mayonnaise. *To garnish:* lemon; tomatoes; lettuce.

Soften and then dissolve the aspic jelly in the stock. Separate the eggs and beat the egg yolks for a few minutes. Add the warm aspic liquid, whisking hard as you do so. Cool, then add the minced or finely chopped ham and mayonnaise. Leave until the mixture stiffens slightly then fold in the whisked egg whites. Spoon into an oiled mould and allow to set. Turn out and garnish with wedges of lemon, tomato and lettuce. *Serves 4–6.*

To vary Add lightly whipped cream flavoured with sherry or lemon juice in place of mayonnaise.

Use tomato juice instead of stock in which to dissolve the aspic jelly.

Meat Hors D'Oeuvre

You will find that meat hors d'oeuvre are extremely popular, even when the main course consists of meat or poultry.

Blue Print

Choosing Meat Hors d'Oeuvre

With the very wide selection of garlic sausages, salami, etc. available, this can be a very simple course to prepare. Arrange the various kinds of salami (or choose all one kind) on a dish and garnish with lettuce and tomato. Serve with mustard or, to add a touch of originality, serve with Cumberland sauce (see page 73).

Parma or other smoked ham makes a luxurious meal starter. It can be served by itself or it blends well with melon, fresh figs, or dessert pears.

Undoubtedly pâté is popular with most people. Various recipes are to be found in this book, but the recipe on this page is particularly quick and easy.

Small portions of some of the meat or chicken salads given on page 59 would also be very suitable. Modern food is often very informal and the slightly unusual version of sausage rolls would be a practical and inexpensive beginning to a meal.

Sausage twists and Sausage cheese savouries (above)

For Family Occasions

Sausage Twists

1 lb. small chipolata sausages. *Puff pastry made with:* 4 oz. (1C) plain flour; pinch salt; 4 oz. ($\frac{1}{2}$C) butter and water to mix (or buy 8 oz. frozen puff pastry). *To glaze:* little beaten egg.

Grill, fry or bake the sausages for about 6 minutes, until partially cooked. Allow to cool. Make the pastry and roll out until wafer thin. Cut into strips and roll round the sausages, as shown in the picture. Put on a baking tray. Brush with beaten egg. Bake for 15 minutes towards the top of a very hot oven, 450–475°F, Gas Mark 7–8. Reduce the heat after 7–8 minutes if necessary. Serve with mustard or one of the sauces below. *Serves 8 as an hors d'oeuvre.*

These sauces are all cold, but could be heated in the top of a double saucepan or basin over hot water.

Onion mustard sauce Blend $\frac{1}{4}$ pint ($\frac{2}{3}$C) mayonnaise with 2–3 tablespoons chopped spring onions (use the white part only) and 3–4 teaspoons French mustard or use half this quantity of made English mustard. Top with the chopped green stems of the onions.

Devilled tomato sauce Blend $\frac{1}{4}$ pint ($\frac{2}{3}$C) mayonnaise with 2 tablespoons tomato purée or ketchup and 2 tablespoons top of the milk or thin cream. Flavour with a few drops chilli and/or Worcestershire sauce. Top with parsley.

Pineapple sweet sour sauce Blend $\frac{1}{4}$ pint ($\frac{2}{3}$C) mayonnaise with 2–3 tablespoons syrup from a small can pineapple. Add 2–3 teaspoons vinegar, 1 teaspoon made mustard and the diced pineapple.

Chopped Liver

8–10 oz. calves' or chickens' liver; 2 oz. ($\frac{1}{4}$C) chicken fat or butter; 2 eggs; 1 small onion; seasoning. *To garnish:* lemon; parsley.

Many vegetables are served as an hors d'oeuvre, the most usual and appropriate being globe artichokes and asparagus. These vegetables can be served hot with melted butter or cold with a vinaigrette dressing. Many other vegetables are served as part of salads and these may be chosen to suit individual tastes.

Cheese is not often part of an hors d'oeuvre, but it is included in both the recipes pictured on this page. The cheese is used delicately so it does not make too substantial or too strongly flavoured a dish.

For Family Occasions

Vegetable Cheese Pie

2 oz. ($\frac{1}{4}$C) butter or margarine; 4 large tomatoes; 2 onions; 2 oz. ($\frac{1}{2}$C) mushrooms; small can asparagus tips; seasoning; 12 oz. ($1\frac{1}{2}$C) mashed potatoes. *For the cheese sauce:* 1 oz. butter or margarine; 1 oz. flour; $\frac{1}{2}$ pint ($1\frac{1}{3}$C) milk; 4 oz. (1C) grated Cheddar cheese. *To garnish:* 1–2 tomatoes.

Heat 1 oz. butter or margarine and fry the skinned chopped tomatoes, onions and mushrooms until softened. Mix with the drained asparagus tips and seasoning. Put into 4 individual dishes. Add the rest of the butter or margarine to the potatoes and season. Put into a piping bag with a $\frac{1}{4}$-inch rose pipe and pipe a border round the edge of the dishes. Make the cheese sauce as page 71. Spoon over the vegetables. Brown under the grill or in the oven and serve at once, garnished with sliced tomato. *Serves 4.*
To vary Use flaked cooked fish instead of the selection of vegetables.
Use one vegetable only instead of the selection in the recipe.
Use a béchamel sauce (see page 71) for the base rather than the white sauce given above.

Vegetable cheese pie

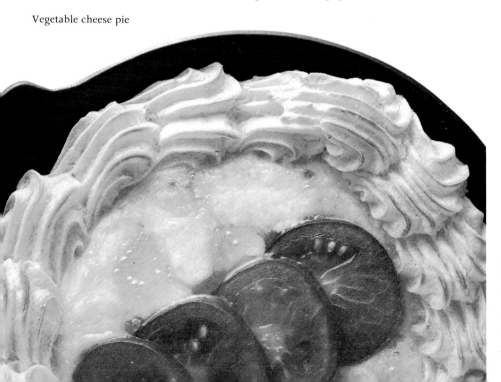

For Special Occasions

Cucumber Cheese Mould

1 lemon; $\frac{1}{2}$ oz. powdered gelatine (enough to set 1 pint ($2\frac{2}{3}$C)); $\frac{1}{2}$ pint ($1\frac{1}{3}$C) water; 1 large cucumber; $\frac{1}{4}$ pint ($\frac{2}{3}$C) mayonnaise; 8 oz. cream cheese; seasoning. *To garnish:* cucumber; watercress; lettuce; tomatoes.
Grate the rind from the lemon, use only the top 'zest'. Soften the gelatine in the lemon juice. Add the lemon rind to the water, heat and pour over the gelatine. Stir until the gelatine has dissolved. Strain, if wished, to remove the pieces of lemon rind. Allow to cool, but not set. Dice the cucumber finely, remove the peel if this is tough. Blend the cucumber with the mayonnaise and cream cheese. Gradually beat in the cool liquid gelatine mixture. Season well. Spoon into an oiled mould and allow to set. Turn out and garnish with cucumber, watercress, lettuce and sliced tomatoes. Serve with mayonnaise or tartare sauce (page 74). *Serves 6–8, or 12–16 if part of a mixed hors d'oeuvre.*
To vary Use a lemon flavoured jelly instead of powdered gelatine. This gives a slightly sweet flavour which is very pleasant. Add 2–3 tablespoons very finely chopped or grated onion to the gelatine liquid.

Mushroom Cocktail

4–6 oz. (1–1$\frac{1}{2}$C) button mushrooms; $\frac{1}{4}$ pint ($\frac{2}{3}$C) natural yoghourt; $\frac{1}{2}$ tablespoon olive oil; 1 tablespoon lemon juice or white wine vinegar; 1 tablespoon chopped chives; 1 tablespoon chopped parsley; seasoning (optional); lettuce. *To garnish:* paprika.
Wash, dry and slice the mushrooms very thinly. Blend the yoghourt, oil, lemon juice or vinegar and herbs. Add seasoning if wished. Shred the lettuce very finely. Put into 4–6 glasses. Blend the mushrooms with the sauce. Spoon on top of the lettuce, garnish with paprika. *Serves 4–6.*

Cucumber cheese mould

Mainly Vegetable Hors D'Oeuvre

To vary Thin cream or mayonnaise may be used in place of yoghourt. The latter is rather thick, so blend with a little top of the milk.
Mix mushrooms and prawns in the recipe above.

Danish Cucumber Boats

1 medium-sized, but fairly thick, cucumber; 2 tablespoons oil; seasoning; 2 tablespoons lemon juice; 4 oz. smoked salmon; little horseradish cream; 3 eggs; 2 tablespoons thick cream; 1 oz. butter. *To garnish:* $\frac{1}{2}$ red pepper; lettuce.
Remove the peel from the cucumber and slice lengthways. Cut into about 12 segments and remove the seeds, so giving small boat shapes. Chop the seeds and pieces removed very finely. Blend the oil, seasoning and lemon juice. Sprinkle the cucumber with this dressing and leave for about 20 minutes. Drain the cucumber. Fill each 'boat' with chopped smoked salmon, spread with a little horseradish cream. Season the beaten eggs, add the chopped cucumber and cream. Heat the butter in a saucepan. Scramble the eggs and spoon over the smoked salmon. Garnish with thin strips of red pepper and serve on a bed of lettuce. While the scrambled egg may be served cold, this is a very pleasant hors d'oeuvre with *cold* cucumber and salmon and *hot* egg topping. *Serves 4–6.*

Storing and Freezing *All these recipes should be served freshly cooked or freshly prepared.*

There are many kinds of savouries that can be served at the end of a meal and on this, and the following pages, are some of the most interesting.

Blue Print

Choosing After Dinner Savouries

Cheese and other soufflés are ideal to end the meal – they *look* and *taste* exciting.

Egg, cheese, fish and other savoury mixtures may be served on toast or fried bread.

Small pastry shapes or cases made of choux pastry can be filled with a variety of fish, meat, vegetable or cheese mixtures.

Allow small portions only when you serve these savouries at the end of the meal; large slices of toast should be cut.

Toasted savouries

Toast the bread, remove the crusts and divide large slices of toast into two fingers, rounds or squares. Spread with butter or margarine then top with the other ingredients.

If keeping hot do not cover, otherwise the toast becomes soft. Put on a hot dish and keep in the oven with the heat turned very low.

Blue Print Recipe

Scotch Woodcock

4 large slices bread · 2 oz. ($\frac{1}{4}$C) butter · 6–8 eggs · seasoning · 2–3 tablespoons thick cream · 8 anchovy fillets · about 16–20 capers ·

To cook Toast the bread, halve each slice if serving for an after dinner savoury and spread with half the butter. Heat the rest of the butter in a pan. Beat the eggs and seasoning with the cream. Scramble lightly, then spoon on top of the toast. Divide the anchovy fillets into thin strips. Arrange on top of the egg with the capers.

To serve At once. *All recipes based on this serve 4 as a snack or 8 as a savoury.*

Canapés Brillat Savarin

Ingredients as Blue Print PLUS 2–3 oz. ($\frac{2}{3}$–1C) grated Gruyère cheese.
Mix the cheese with the eggs, and scramble as the Blue Print.

Asparagus Toasts

Ingredients as Blue Print PLUS cooked or canned asparagus and MINUS the anchovies and capers.
Chop the tender stalks of the asparagus, save the tips for garnish. Heat the stalks in the hot butter, add the beaten eggs and scramble as the Blue Print. Top with asparagus tips.

Devils on Horseback

2 large slices bread; $\frac{1}{2}$ oz. butter; 8 large cooked, but fairly firm prunes; 4 long or 8 short rashers streaky bacon.
Toast the bread, quarter each slice and spread with butter. Stone the prunes. Cut the rinds from the rashers of bacon, halve the long slices. Stretch the bacon as the sketch. Wrap round the prunes and secure with wooden cocktail sticks. Cook under a hot grill until the bacon is crisp and golden brown. Turn once or twice to ensure even cooking. Remove the cocktail sticks. Put on the toast and serve. *Serves 8.*
To vary Fill the prunes with flaked almonds.

Fill the prunes with liver pâté.

Angels on Horseback Use oysters instead of prunes. Season the oysters and sprinkle with lemon juice then wrap in the bacon and cook as above.

Sausage Cheese Savouries

Grill small sausages until just brown. Spread one side with French mustard and press a finger of Cheddar or Gruyère cheese against this. Wrap in halved or short rashers of bacon. Secure with wooden cocktail sticks. Grill as the Devils on Horseback above. Remove the cocktail sticks. Serve very hot. The savouries may be put on toast or fingers of fried bread if wished. (Illustrated on page 66).

To stretch bacon, hold one end of the halved rasher with your left hand, and 'stroke' the bacon with a knife to make it less rigid and longer.

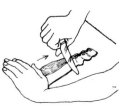

Crab and Tomato Toasts

4 small rounds bread; 2 oz. ($\frac{1}{4}$C) butter; $\frac{1}{2}$ lemon; small crab or can crabmeat; 2 tablespoons fresh or 1 tablespoon concentrated tomato purée; seasoning. *To garnish:* $\frac{1}{2}$–1 lemon; watercress or lettuce.

Toast the bread, spread with half the butter. Squeeze the juice from the $\frac{1}{2}$ lemon, blend with the flaked crabmeat, the tomato purée and the rest of the butter. Season well and spread on to the hot toast. Heat for a few minutes, then serve hot garnished with lemon and watercress or lettuce. *Serves 4.*

The best known of all cheese savouries is a Welsh Rarebit. The 'old fashioned' rarebit was of a sauce-like consistency, rather than the firmer texture we know today. I have given the softer mixture under Blue Print 2, for I find this particularly good when it is covering other ingredients, such as in the York Rarebit.

Blue Print Recipes

1. Welsh Rarebit

4 slices bread · 2 oz. ($\frac{1}{4}$C) butter or margarine · $\frac{1}{2}$ level tablespoon flour · $\frac{1}{4}$ teaspoon dry mustard · 3 tablespoons milk · 2 tablespoons ale (or use all milk) · 1 teaspoon Worcestershire sauce · seasoning · 6–8 oz. (1$\frac{1}{2}$–2C) grated cheese*. To garnish: parsley and/or sliced tomatoes. * For a strongly flavoured mixture use mature Cheddar or Gruyère or add just a little Parmesan cheese. For a delicately flavoured mixture use mild Gouda or Edam cheese. Although it is not considered a cooking cheese, Double Gloucester makes a splendid rarebit, so does a golden Cheshire which cooks well.

To cook Toast the bread, halve each slice if required, spread with half the butter or margarine and keep hot, or toast while preparing the rarebit. Heat the rest of the butter or margarine in a pan, stir in the flour and mustard and cook for 2–3 minutes. Blend in the milk and ale, stir well as the mixture heats, as it is very thick. Add the sauce, seasoning and nearly all the cheese. Spread on the hot toast, sprinkle with the remainder of the cheese and brown under the grill.

To serve As hot as possible with mustard. Garnish with parsley and/or sliced tomatoes. *All recipes based on this give 8 small portions or 4 larger slices.*

Note If wished increase the amount of Worcestershire sauce by up to 1 tablespoon, particularly if using all milk. The true rarebit should have a definite 'spicy' flavour.

2. Creamy Welsh Rarebit

To make Cream together 1 oz. butter, 1 egg or 2 egg yolks, seasoning, 1 teaspoon made mustard and 6–8 oz. (1$\frac{1}{2}$–2C) grated Cheddar or other cheese. Gradually blend in 6 tablespoons milk or thin cream (or use partially ale and partially milk). Add a little Worcestershire sauce.

To cook Put this mixture into a pan, heat *gently* for 2–3 minutes only. Spread on toast as Blue Print 1, but keep well away from the edges, so it does not run off the toast when grilled. Grill until golden as Blue Print 1.

To serve Garnish and serve as Blue Print 1. If wished you can heat the mixture until a sauce-like consistency, put on to the toast and serve at once without placing under the grill.

York Rarebit

Ingredients as Blue Print 1 or 2 PLUS a little made mustard and 4 slices lean ham.

Toast the bread, spread with butter or margarine and a very little made mustard. Top with the ham, heat for 1 minute under the grill, then add the cheese mixture and brown.

Buck Rarebit

This is far too substantial for an after dinner savoury, although excellent for a light snack. It consists of a Welsh Rarebit topped with a poached egg, but if you wish to combine Welsh Rarebit and egg for a savoury use the following recipe.

Rarebit Scramble

Ingredients as Blue Print 2 PLUS 2–3 eggs, seasoning, 1 teaspoon chopped fresh herbs and an extra 1 oz. butter.

Prepare the toast and prepare, but do not cook, the rarebit mixture. Beat the eggs with the seasoning and herbs. Scramble lightly in the extra 1 oz. butter then spoon on to the hot toast. While the eggs are cooking heat the cheese mixture. Spoon over the scrambled eggs the moment they are set and grill quickly or serve without grilling.

Toasted Cheese

This has an entirely different texture from a Welsh Rarebit, but is very good. Slice Cheddar, Gruyère or other good cooking cheese. Put on to the hot buttered toast and heat until the cheese melts.

Grated cheese may be mixed with a good knob of well seasoned butter or margarine and spread on to the toast or blended with a little, very well seasoned, perfectly smooth creamed potato. It is then sprinkled with cheese and grilled until golden brown. This is both economical and interesting in texture.

Mushrooms on Toast

Choose small button mushrooms. Fry or grill with butter and put on to fingers of toast. Top with paprika and parsley.

Soft Roes on Toast

1 lb. soft herring roes; 2–3 oz. ($\frac{1}{4}$–$\frac{3}{8}$C) butter; seasoning; 3 tablespoons milk or thin cream (see Method 2); 3–4 large slices bread. *To garnish:* parsley; cayenne pepper or paprika.

Wash, dry and separate the roes.

Method 1 Heat 2 oz. ($\frac{1}{4}$C) of the butter and fry the roes in this until just tender, season well.

Method 2 (You need only 2 oz. ($\frac{1}{4}$C) butter in all for this method.) Put 1 oz. of the butter into a pan with the milk or cream. Add the roes and seasoning and simmer gently until nearly tender, then lift the lid so the liquid evaporates.

Toast the bread, spread with the remaining butter. Top with the roes and garnish with parsley and cayenne or paprika. *Serves 3–4 as a snack or 6–8 as an after dinner savoury.*

Storing and Freezing *These savouries must be eaten when fresh. Welsh Rarebit mixture stores well for 1–2 weeks in a covered container in the refrigerator. It could be frozen but dries out if kept for too long.*

Toasted cheese

Making Sauces

Throughout the various chapters of this cookbook are recipes for sauces that are needed for a particular dish. In this, and the next pages, basic savoury sauces are described, with easy and interesting variations that can be served with various foods. An indication of the dishes with which they blend is given with each sauce.

Making Sauces

The following points are the most important when making any sauce.
1. Use the correct proportions for the consistency required, but if you have misjudged the amount of flour or liquid, this can be adjusted:
a) If too thick add more liquid.
b) If too thin let the sauce evaporate and thicken by cooking in an open pan.
2. Cook the flour adequately. If a sauce is cooked for too short a time there is a 'floury' taste which spoils the flavour. The times given in the Blue Print Recipe are minimum and a little longer cooking will be an advantage.
3. Stir the sauce as you add the liquid.
4. Stir as the sauce thickens to keep it smooth and prevent it sticking to the pan.
5. Taste to make sure the sauce is adequately seasoned.
6. Never let a sauce boil if adding egg or egg yolk, the sauce would curdle (become lumpy). Cook very gently. Other ingredients can cause curdling to a white or similar sauce, i.e. lemon juice, vinegar, wine.
7. Do not let a skin form on a sauce. There are two ways of preventing this:
a) Cover with very damp greaseproof paper. Remove the paper when ready to heat the sauce.
b) Use less liquid in making the sauce than stated in the recipe. Make the sauce, allow to thicken, then pour the cold liquid on top. This acts as a barrier between the sauce and the air. You will need a good layer of liquid so hold back about 25%. Stir the liquid slowly into the sauce before heating.

● **AVOID** *A lumpy sauce: An under-cooked sauce: A greasy sauce.*
● **TO RECTIFY** *Whisk a lumpy sauce hard and the lumps should come out. If not, sieve the sauce or emulsify in a liquidiser and reheat: Taste a sauce and if it has the roughness of uncooked flour or cornflour return to the heat for a little longer: A greasy sauce indicates too much butter (or other fat) to the amount of flour, so blend a little extra flour with cold liquid, stir into the sauce and continue stirring until thickened.*
● **SHORT CUTS** *Use the quick method of sauce making or sauce mixes.*
● **TO SLIMMERS** *Sauces should be avoided.*
Storing and Freezing *A sauce can be kept for 1–2 days then reheated. Cover with damp paper to keep it as moist as possible. Heat gently to serve. You will probably need to add a little extra liquid to give the desired consistency. It is a good idea to emulsify the sauce in the liquidiser after or before heating. Sauces can be frozen but they may separate as they are reheated. The possibilities of this happening are less if you make the sauce with cornflour (allow $\frac{1}{2}$ oz. cornflour in place of each 1 oz. flour) or potato flour (allow the same weight as when using flour). Whisk or emulsify the defrosted sauce if it does separate or add a little extra flour or cornflour blended with cold liquid and cook slowly, stirring all the time, until the sauce thickens again.*

Caper sauce

Terms Used in Sauce Making

Roux This means the butter and flour mixture, which can be called a liaison. Stages 1–3 in the Blue Print Recipe for white sauce show how this is used.
Consistency The thickness of a sauce.
Coating consistency The sauce coats the back of a wooden spoon (shown in the picture).
Thin consistency The sauce pours easily. This is often used when adding a sauce to vegetables to make a soup. Follow the Blue Print Recipe but use 1 pint ($2\frac{2}{3}$C) milk instead of $\frac{1}{2}$ pint ($1\frac{1}{3}$C) to the 1 oz. butter or margarine and 1 oz. flour.
Panada or binding consistency The sauce is very thick. This is used to bind ingredients together, e.g. in rissoles, and fish cakes (instead of an egg). Follow the Blue Print Recipe but use $\frac{1}{4}$ pint ($\frac{2}{3}$C) milk instead of $\frac{1}{2}$ pint ($1\frac{1}{3}$C) to the 1 oz. butter or margarine and 1 oz. flour.

Blue Print Recipe

White Sauce

For a coating consistency
1 oz. butter or margarine · 1 oz. flour · $\frac{1}{2}$ pint ($1\frac{1}{3}$C*) milk · seasoning ·
* This is fractionally less than $\frac{1}{2}$ pint so be fairly generous with filling the cup.

1. Heat the butter or margarine in a fairly small saucepan. Do not over-heat, otherwise the butter or margarine darkens in colour.
2. Remove from the heat, stir in the flour.
3. Return to a low heat and stir for several minutes, until the 'roux' forms a dry looking ball.
4. Once again take the pan off the heat and gradually blend in the liquid.
5. Stir briskly with a wooden spoon as you do so.
6. Return once again to the heat and bring steadily to the boil, stirring or whisking all the time as the sauce thickens.
7. Add *a little* seasoning and continue stirring for 4–5 minutes. Taste and add more seasoning if required.
To serve A white sauce blends with most foods – eggs, fish, poultry, vegetables. *All recipes based on this serve 3–4.*

Adaptations

Blending method Use the same proportions as in the Blue Print Recipe for white sauce. Blend the flour carefully with the liquid. Put into a saucepan. Add the butter or margarine. Bring gradually to the boil, stirring all the time. Cook as Stage 7 of the Blue Print Recipe. This is found to be an easier method of making the sauce for some people.

Making white sauce

Quick method Use the same proportions as in the Blue Print Recipe for white sauce. Proceed as Stages 1–3. Take the pan off the heat, add *all* the liquid. Return to the heat. Allow the liquid to come to the boil and whisk sharply. Continue as Stage 7.

Using cornflour If you wish to use cornflour instead of flour, remember cornflour thickens more than flour, so use ½ oz. cornflour in place of 1 oz. flour. Although a sauce made with cornflour thickens more quickly than one made with flour, it is important to cook it for some minutes.

When all milk should not be used in a white sauce

I prefer using half milk and half vegetable stock, or at least some vegetable stock, when making a sauce to coat vegetables. In this way you retain more of the flavour of the particular vegetables.

Use *some* fish, meat or poultry stock in the sauce when making a white sauce to serve with these foods, see velouté sauce below.

Recipes Based on White Sauce

In each case the proportions for the basic sauce are as the Blue Print Recipe. The flavourings are added at Stage 7, unless stated to the contrary.

Admiral sauce—for fish dishes.
Add 2 teaspoons capers, 2 teaspoons chopped parsley, few drops anchovy essence, ½ teaspoon grated lemon rind and 2 teaspoons lemon juice.

Anchovy sauce—for fish dishes.
Add enough anchovy essence to give a definite flavour and colour to the sauce. Be sparing with the salt.

Aurore sauce—for fish dishes.
Make white or béchamel sauce. Flavour with a little paprika and ½ teaspoon chopped tarragon. For luxury occasions, add 2 table-spoons pounded red lobster coral (roe).

Béchamel sauce A more sophisticated version of white sauce and used as a basis for other sauces in place of white sauce. Warm the milk with a piece of celery, carrot, onion and bay leaf for 2–3 minutes. Leave in the pan for about 30 minutes, strain, then add enough milk to give ½ pint (1⅓C) again. Proceed as white sauce. If desired you can flavour with a little grated nutmeg at Stage 7 of the Blue Print Recipe.

Bohemian sauce—for meat dishes (particularly beef).
Use half milk and half white stock. Add 1–2 teaspoons grated horseradish or horseradish cream. This sauce can be made by omitting the flour, heating the butter or margarine and milk and thickening with 1½ oz. (½C) soft white breadcrumbs, then adding seasoning, grated horseradish and a little cream.

Caper sauce—generally served with boiled lamb, but can be used with fish, ham or chicken.
Add 2–3 teaspoons capers (chopped or left whole) and a little vinegar from the bottle.

Cardinal sauce—for fish dishes.
Blend pounded lobster coral into a very creamy béchamel sauce.

Celery sauce—excellent with chicken or turkey.
Make white sauce with half milk and half celery stock (from boiling finely chopped celery). Add 4–5 tablespoons chopped cooked celery and a little thick cream.

Cheese sauce—to serve with fish, vegetables, meat, eggs.
Add a little made mustard to the thickened sauce or good pinch dry mustard to the flour. Stir in 3 oz. (¾C) grated cheese (Cheddar, Dutch Gouda or Gruyère—or use rather less Parmesan). Heat, do not boil.

Duchesse sauce—for boiled ham.

Blend 2–3 tablespoons chopped tongue and 2 oz. (½C) sliced mushrooms fried in 1 oz. butter into the sauce.

German sauce—for chicken or veal.
Make the sauce with half milk and half white stock. When thickened blend 2 egg yolks with 2–3 tablespoons thick cream. Stir into the sauce. Cook gently, *without* boiling, for several minutes.

Mornay sauce—as cheese sauce above or for a richer sauce use a béchamel sauce foundation.
Add 1–2 tablespoons cream blended with 1 egg yolk with the cheese.

Mustard sauce—to serve with herrings, very good with fried or grilled chicken.
Blend from 1 teaspoon to 1 tablespoon made mustard with the sauce or add from ½–2 teaspoons dry mustard to the flour.

Onion (soubise) sauce—excellent with many meat dishes, particularly roast mutton.
Boil 2 finely chopped onions until tender. Strain the liquid. Use ¼ pint (⅔C) of this and ¼ pint (⅔C) milk to make the sauce. Add the chopped onions to the thickened sauce. Add a little cream, cayenne pepper and/or grated nutmeg if desired.

Shrimp sauce—for fish or egg dishes.
Add 3–4 tablespoons whole or chopped shrimps (chopped prawns may be used instead) to the sauce.

Velouté sauce—for steamed or boiled chicken or other meat dishes.
Make béchamel sauce with half chicken stock and half milk or all chicken stock if preferred. When thickened blend in 3–4 tablespoons thick cream mixed with 1–2 tablespoons dry sherry. Heat gently *without* boiling.

White wine sauce—for fish, chicken or veal dishes.
Flavour a white or béchamel sauce with a little white wine.

A brown sauce is generally served with meat dishes and while most of the essential points in making the sauce are the same as for a white sauce the ingredients differ and are very important.

In order to give a very good flavour to a brown sauce, add 1–2 tablespoons of the meat jelly that forms under the dripping.

Blue Print Recipe

Brown Sauce

1 oz. (generous weight) fat (well clarified dripping, lard, cooking fat, margarine or butter) · 1 oz. flour · ½ pint (1⅓C) brown stock (see page 114) or water and 1 beef stock cube · seasoning.

To cook Put the selected fat into a pan. Stir in the flour and blend thoroughly. Allow the 'roux' to cook over a low heat, stirring occasionally, until it turns a golden brown. Do not over-cook at this stage, otherwise the sauce will be spoiled. If you are in a hurry, omit the browning of the flour and add a few drops of gravy browning instead. Add the brown stock or water and stock cube as described in the Blue Print Recipe for white

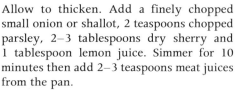

Brown, Vegetable and Fruit Sauces

sauce on page 70 and cook until a smooth thickened sauce. Taste and season as required.

To serve Hot with grilled or fried meats or as a basis for casseroles (see below). *All recipes based on this serve 3–4.*

Consistency This may be varied in the same way as a white sauce (see page 70). The thin brown sauce is used as the liquid in some casseroles.

Flavouring Add a chopped onion, a little chopped celery and/or carrot and a *bouquet garni* to the sauce *with* the liquid or heat 2 oz. (¼C) fat and toss the vegetables in this, *then* add the flour. Either strain the sauce before serving or remove the *bouquet garni* and sieve or emulsify the vegetables and sauce then reheat. You may need a little extra stock or use sherry or red wine for additional flavour.

Recipes Based on Brown Sauce

Beefsteak sauce—serve with grilled or fried steak.
Make the brown sauce as the Blue Print.

Bressoise sauce

Allow to thicken. Add a finely chopped small onion or shallot, 2 teaspoons chopped parsley, 2–3 tablespoons dry sherry and 1 tablespoon lemon juice. Simmer for 10 minutes then add 2–3 teaspoons meat juices from the pan.

Bordelaise sauce—serve with grilled or fried lamb or beef.
Make the brown sauce as the Blue Print. Allow to thicken. Add 2 teaspoons finely chopped onion or shallot, 1–2 teaspoons chopped parsley, ½–1 teaspoon chopped tarragon and 4 tablespoons red wine. Simmer for approximately 10 minutes.

Cavalier sauce—a pleasant alternative to tomato sauce to serve with pasta, meat, fish or poultry dishes.
Make the brown sauce as the Blue Print. Allow to thicken. Add 2 tablespoons sieved tomato purée, or use 1 tablespoon concentrated tomato purée, 2 teaspoons tarragon vinegar and 1 teaspoon French mustard. Heat, then add 1 tablespoon chutney, 2 teaspoons chopped gherkins and 2 teaspoons chopped capers.

Garibaldi sauce—to serve with fish or meat.
Make the brown sauce as the Blue Print, but toss 1–2 crushed cloves garlic in the fat. When the sauce has thickened add 1–2 teaspoons capers (do not chop), ½ teaspoon curry paste, few drops anchovy essence and 1 teaspoon made mustard.

Espagnole (Spanish) Sauce

This is a more elaborate type of brown sauce, more difficult to make, but much more delicious than the Blue Print. The vegetables give a subtle flavour and pleasant colour to the sauce. This sauce can be served with meat, poultry and pasta dishes.

1–2 oz. (⅛–¼C) fat (see Blue Print); 1 rasher bacon; small piece chopped onion; 1 oz. (¼C) chopped mushrooms; 2 large chopped tomatoes; 1 oz. flour; ½ pint (1⅓C) brown stock; *bouquet garni*; seasoning; 1–2 tablespoons sherry.

Melt the fat (use the larger quantity if the bacon is lean). Add the chopped bacon and heat for a few minutes, then add the vegetables. Toss in the fat with the bacon. Stir in the flour and cook for 3–4 minutes. Add the stock, as the Blue Print Recipe for white sauce on page 70, together with the herbs. Bring to the boil, stirring all the time, and cook until thickened. Season to taste. Simmer for 10 minutes. Remove the herbs. This sauce is generally sieved (or it can be emulsified in the liquidiser). If preferred serve without sieving, in which case the tomatoes should be skinned. Heat with the sherry. *Serves 3–4.*

Recipes Based on Espagnole Sauce

Bressoise sauce—excellent with roast poultry, particularly duck, or with pork chops or cutlets.
Make the espagnole sauce (using an *extra*

medium-sized onion for a stronger flavour). Sieve or emulsify, put into the pan and add 2–3 tablespoons orange juice and the finely chopped cooked duck or chicken liver (naturally this cannot be added with pork).

Burgundy sauce—serve with meat particularly tongue).

Make the espagnole sauce but use half brown stock and half red Burgundy wine. Sieve or emulsify. A quicker version is to make the brown sauce as the Blue Print with half brown stock and half red Burgundy wine.

Chateaubriand sauce—to serve with grilled steaks, but excellent with veal or venison.

Make the espagnole sauce. Sieve or emulsify, then reheat with 3 tablespoons white wine, 1–2 tablespoons meat jelly (from under the dripping), 1–2 teaspoons chopped parsley and 1 tablespoon red currant jelly.

Madeira sauce—serve with most meat (particularly tongue).

Make either the espagnole, or the brown sauce but use half brown stock and half Madeira wine. Sieve or emulsify the espagnole sauce. Heat the sauce with $\frac{1}{2}$ teaspoon made mustard; 1 tablespoon red currant jelly may be added as well.

Poivrade sauce—serve with meat, excellent with steaks.

Make the espagnole sauce, but simmer with about 12 peppercorns. Sieve or emulsify *with* the peppercorns—beware it is very hot. Reheat with a little brandy.

Blue Print Recipe

Tomato Sauce

Tomato sauce is one of the most versatile sauces, for it can be served with many foods.

1 small onion · $\frac{1}{2}$ small dessert apple · 1 rasher bacon or several bacon rinds · 1 clove garlic · $1\frac{1}{2}$ lb. *ripe* tomatoes · 1 oz. butter · $\frac{1}{4}$ pint ($\frac{2}{3}$C) white stock or water · seasoning.

To make Peel the onion and apple and grate or chop finely. The rasher of bacon may be left whole if you wish to remove this. Crush the peeled garlic clove. Skin and chop the tomatoes.

To cook Heat the butter and bacon rasher or rinds then toss the onion, apple and garlic in the butter and bacon fat. Take care these do not discolour. Add the tomatoes and stock or water and heat until the tomatoes are tender. Remove the bacon rasher or rinds. Season well.

To serve This sauce can be served hot or cold. *All recipes based on this serve 5–6.*

To give a smooth textured sauce Sieve or emulsify. Blend 1 oz. flour or $\frac{1}{2}$ oz. cornflour with $\frac{1}{4}$ pint ($\frac{2}{3}$C) extra white stock or water. Add to the tomato mixture, return to the pan and heat steadily, stirring all the time, until smooth and thick. Taste and add any extra seasoning. Serve hot.

Cumberland sauce

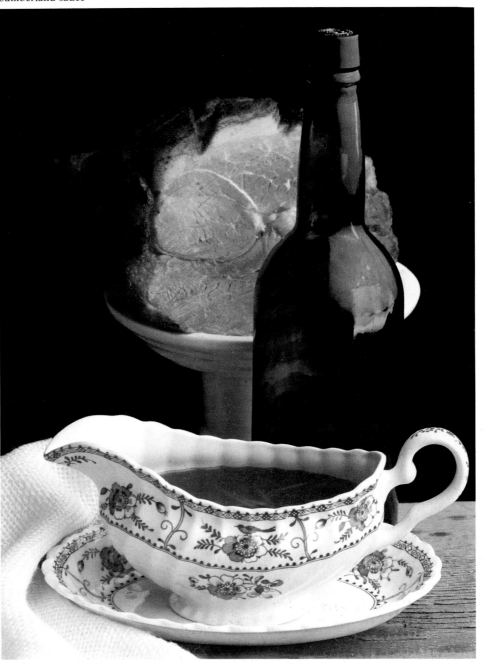

To add extra flavour The Blue Print gives a very mild flavoured sauce, so to add extra flavour:

Blend 1–2 tablespoons concentrated tomato purée (from a can or tube) with the fresh tomato mixture.

Add a generous amount of cayenne pepper to the sauce.

Flavour with a *bouquet garni* of herbs and a little chopped celery. Omit the apple.

Add 1–2 teaspoons brown sugar.

Cumberland Sauce

This sauce is an ideal accompaniment to hot or cold ham or boiled bacon. There are many ways of making it but the sauce should contain orange and lemon juice, red currant jelly, mustard and port wine. Here is a recipe I find particularly good.

2 small oranges; 1 lemon; $\frac{1}{4}$ pint ($\frac{2}{3}$C) water; 2 teaspoons arrowroot or cornflour; $\frac{1}{4}$ pint ($\frac{2}{3}$C) ham or white stock; 2 teaspoons made mustard; 2 tablespoons port wine; 4–5 tablespoons red currant jelly; seasoning.

Cut the peel from the oranges. Remove the white pith then cut into thin matchsticks. A very little lemon rind may be treated in the same way if wished. Squeeze the juice from the fruits. Put the rind into a pan with the cold water. Soak for 1 hour then simmer very gently in a covered pan until nearly tender (about 15–20 minutes). Remove the lid towards the end of the cooking time so the liquid is reduced to 3 tablespoons. Blend the arrowroot or cornflour with the ham or white stock. Put into the pan with the fruit juice, mustard, wine and jelly. Stir over a low heat until thickened and clear. Season well. Serve hot or cold. *Serves 4–5.*

Storing and Freezing *See the comments on page 70. Espagnole and tomato sauce freeze well, particularly if not sieved.*

To use any left over *Store carefully in the refrigerator or cool place reheat gently.*

73

Cold Sauces

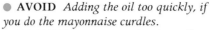

The most famous of all cold sauces is mayonnaise, and while excellent commercial mayonnaise is available the home-made variety has a flavour that it is difficult to surpass.

Blue Print Recipe

Mayonnaise

2 egg yolks · ½–1 teaspoon made English mustard or French mustard · ¼–½ teaspoon salt · good shake pepper · pinch sugar (optional) · ¼ pint (⅔C) olive oil · 1–2 tablespoons vinegar (white or brown malt or wine vinegar) or lemon juice · 1 tablespoon boiling water (optional).

To make Put the egg yolks, seasonings and sugar into a mixing bowl or basin. Beat well with a wooden spoon or with a whisk. Add the oil drop by drop, beating all the time. When the oil has been incorporated whisk in the vinegar or lemon juice. Taste once or twice to make sure you are not adding too much for *your* taste. Add the boiling water gradually at the end to give a very light creamy taste.
To serve Cold with salads.
To make a piping mayonnaise Add up to ½ pint (1⅓C) oil; the more oil added the thicker the mayonnaise.

Mayonnaise

● **AVOID** *Adding the oil too quickly, if you do the mayonnaise curdles.*
● **TO RECTIFY** *Put another egg yolk into a basin and whisk the curdled mayonnaise very gradually into this. Be sure the egg yolks and oil are at room temperature. If the eggs come from the refrigerator the mayonnaise is more likely to curdle.*
● **SHORT CUTS** *Use an electric whisk or a liquidiser (blender) is even quicker.*
● **TO SLIMMERS** *Avoid the oily mayonnaise and use the yoghourt dressing on this page.*

Mayonnaise in a Liquidiser

Ingredients as the Blue Print but the order of adding these is different. Put the egg yolks, seasonings and sugar into the liquidiser goblet, switch on for a few seconds. Add the vinegar or lemon juice. I would use the smaller amount the first time you make this. Switch on until blended. Switch to a low speed and pour the oil in *very steadily*. Taste and add any more vinegar or lemon juice required on low speed, then add the water.

Sauces Based on Mayonnaise

Andalouse sauce—especially good with shell fish.
Add 1–2 tablespoons fresh or concentrated tomato purée and 1 finely chopped red pepper (discard the core and seeds) to the thickened mayonnaise.
Aioli (garlic) mayonnaise—for all salads. Add 1–2 cloves finely chopped or crushed garlic to the thickened mayonnaise. Taste and add a little extra lemon juice if desired.

Green mayonnaise—especially good with fish salads.
Add freshly chopped herbs plus a little green colouring, or put a spinach leaf and the herbs into the liquidiser when the mayonnaise has thickened. Switch on until the herbs are chopped and the spinach blended.
Lemon mayonnaise—to serve in place of mayonnaise.
Add extra lemon juice and a little finely grated lemon rind to the thickened mayonnaise.
Tartare sauce—for all fish dishes.
Add up to 1 tablespoon chopped parsley, ½–1 tablespoon chopped gherkins and 1–2 teaspoons whole or chopped capers to the thickened mayonnaise. If making the mayonnaise in the liquidiser add the sprigs of parsley and whole gherkins to the thickened mayonnaise. Switch on until 'chopped' then add the capers.
Tomato mayonnaise—especially good with cheese or meat salads.
If making in a liquidiser, add 1–2 skinned tomatoes to the mayonnaise when thickened. Switch on until the tomatoes are blended. If mixing by hand sieve the tomatoes or use concentrated tomato purée.

Yoghourt Dressing

Blend seasoning, a little made mustard and 1 crushed sugar substitute tablet into ¼ pint (⅔C) natural yoghourt. Add ½–1 teaspoon finely grated lemon rind and 1 tablespoon lemon juice. 1 tablespoon olive oil may also be blended into the yoghourt to give a richer flavour. *Serves 4.*

French Dressing

Gradually blend 2 tablespoons olive or other good salad oil (corn oil if wished) into a little dry or made mustard (½–1 teaspoon). Add a good pinch of salt, shake of pepper, a pinch of sugar and 1 tablespoon vinegar or lemon juice.

Vinaigrette Dressing

This is often given as another name for French dressing, but this is not quite correct—it is French dressing plus 1–2 teaspoons freshly chopped herbs. A teaspoon finely chopped shallot or onion and 2 teaspoons chopped gherkin may also be added.

Storing and Freezing *Mayonnaise keeps well in the refrigerator for several weeks. Keep well covered so the mixture does not dry. French dressing keeps almost indefinitely which is why you can make a large quantity and store it in a screw topped bottle. Shake before using. I prefer to make vinaigrette dressing freshly. Mayonnaise will not freeze, it separates badly.*

EGG COOKERY, PIES AND FLANS

This part covers a wide variety of cookery skills and dishes. Pages 76–85 and page 94 deal with eggs in cooking. An egg is probably the most versatile ingredient in cooking. It forms the basis of main dishes that can be served at all meals of the day, it gives light cakes, puddings, soufflés, omelettes and it is the 'thickening agent' in many classic sauces. If you consider the price of an egg, it is still very inexpensive compared to other foods. Remember eggs are not only invaluable in cooking, they also have a very high food value.

One often hears the expression, (describing a not very talented cook), she (or he) 'cannot boil an egg'. You know boiling eggs cannot be said to be difficult, but they do need care in timing. You will therefore find the Blue Print on the next page deals with the right way to boil an egg so the white is light and not tough. The page also gives some new ways of serving boiled eggs.

The rest of the egg cookery section covers pancakes, soufflés and some very interesting egg dishes (such as the French classic, Piperade). If you have never made Hollandaise sauce, fearing it is too difficult, may I suggest you follow the Blue Print on page 94. It is a surprisingly simple sauce—and quite delicious. Here you will also find the Italian classic dessert Zabaione.

Page 86 commences the section on savoury pies and flans. These can be served hot or cold for main meals, quick family or party snacks. The fillings for flans can be 'cheesey', 'fishy', 'meaty' or full of colourful vegetables.

Some of the best known tarts and flans for tea have been popular for several centuries. The recipe on page 92 is for the *real* Maid of Honour, which has been known since Tudor times. There is a more modern recipe that I find very popular on the same page.

During the past years the Italian Pizza, which is a savoury yeast flan or tart, has grown in popularity. This can be a very inexpensive or quite luxurious dish, according to the topping selected. If you do not wish to make the yeast dough (which is very simple), then try the other variations on page 89.

Can you make perfect puff pastry? The Blue Print on page 92 gives the 'do's and don'ts' for success. Of course if you do not have the time to spare you can make all the recipes with the frozen puff pastry that is readily available.

75

Boiling an Egg

The flavour of an egg, when boiled, is very pronounced and therefore one should be ultra-fussy that the eggs are very fresh.

Blue Print Recipe

To Boil an Egg

Regular boiling of eggs can darken a pan slightly, so you may like to keep a small pan specially for this purpose. There are two ways in which you can boil an egg. Method 1 gives a lighter texture to the egg white and is therefore ideal for small children and invalids.

Method 1 Put the eggs carefully in enough *cold* water to cover. Bring the water to the boil *as quickly as possible*, and time the cooking from the moment the water is boiling. Since the egg cooks slightly *as the water heats*, the cooking time is shorter than that for Method 2.

Method 2 Lower the eggs into boiling water and time the cooking.

Timing	Method 1	Method 2
Lightly set egg	2½–3 min.	3½–4 min.
Firmly set egg	4 min.	5 min.
Hard boiled egg	8–9 min.	10 min.

● **AVOID** *Boiling any eggs that have even the finest cracks, for these could develop into larger cracks and some of the egg could be wasted: Over-cooking eggs when you wish them to be hard boiled; if over-cooked they develop a dark ring round the yolk and an unpleasantly strong flavour.*

● **TO RECTIFY** *Put a teaspoon vinegar in the water if you have to boil a slightly cracked egg, this helps the egg white to stop spreading out into the pan: Put hard boiled eggs into cold water as soon as they are set, then crack the shells. This cools the eggs quickly, so stops continued cooking and should prevent the dark line round the yolk (unless the egg has been cooked for too long a period).*

● **TO SLIMMERS** *A boiled egg is very low in calories, as there is no added fat or sauces, so is ideal for a 'slimmer's meal'.*

Storing and Freezing *Boiled eggs do not store well and they are one of the few things that do not freeze, they become like 'rubber'.*

For Family Occasions

Eggs Mornay

4 eggs; 1 oz. butter or margarine; 1 oz. flour; ½ pint (1⅓C) milk; seasoning; 4 oz. (1C) grated Cheddar cheese.

Boil the eggs, these can be firmly set or hard boiled, according to personal taste. Plunge into cold water to cool, crack the shells, then remove these. Heat the butter or margarine in a pan, stir in the flour and cook for several minutes. Gradually blend in the milk and bring to the boil, then cook until the sauce has thickened. Season well, stir in the grated cheese. Do not continue cooking after the cheese has melted. Arrange the whole or halved eggs in a dish, top with the cheese sauce and serve at once. *Serves 4 as an hors d'oeuvre or 2 as a main dish.*

Eggs Florentine

Ingredients as above (or use poached eggs if preferred). Put on a bed of cooked spinach, coat with the sauce as above.

Eggs au Gratin

These are the same as Eggs Mornay, but topped with a layer of fine breadcrumbs and grated cheese, so you have a crisp topping. If the sauce is hot the dish may just be browned under the grill. If the sauce and eggs have become cold, then heat and brown in a moderately hot oven for about 15–20 minutes.

Scotch Eggs

4 eggs; little flour; seasoning; 12 oz.–1 lb. sausagemeat. *To coat:* 1 egg; 2–3 tablespoons crisp breadcrumbs. *To fry:* fat or oil.

Hard boil the eggs and cool, as the Blue Print. Coat each egg in a little seasoned flour, this makes the sausagemeat 'stick' round the egg better. Divide the sausagemeat into four portions, press out into neat squares on a floured board. Wrap round the eggs, then seal the ends and roll until neat shapes. Coat in beaten egg and crumbs.

These may be fried in deep fat or oil, in which case turn once to brown and fry for about 5–6 minutes. If using shallow fat or oil then turn several times and cook for about 10–12 minutes. Remember it is essential to ensure that the sausagemeat is thoroughly cooked. If preferred, bake for about 25 minutes in the centre of a moderate to moderately hot oven, 375–400°F, Gas Mark 5–6. Serve hot or cold. *Serves 4.*

For Special Occasions

STUFFED EGGS

These can be used for a main dish with salad or as an hors d'oeuvre.

Cold stuffed eggs

The quantities of filling are enough for 4 hard boiled eggs.

Hard boil, cool and shell the eggs as the Blue Print, remove the egg yolks, mash or sieve and continue as the suggestions below. In each case the yolks are put back into the white cases.

For Hot Stuffed Eggs
Creamed eggs Mix the yolks with 3 tablespoons thick cream and seasoning. Top with fine crumbs and melted butter, brown under the grill.

Cheese eggs Mix the yolks with 3 oz. ($\frac{3}{4}$C) grated Cheddar or Parmesan cheese and 1–2 tablespoons thick cream. Top with fine crumbs and brown under the grill.

Curried eggs (good cold as well as hot) Blend the yolks with 2 tablespoons mayonnaise, 2–3 teaspoons chutney and 1–2 teaspoons curry powder. Top with fine crumbs and brown under the grill.

For Cold Stuffed Eggs
Anchovy eggs Blend the yolks with a little mayonnaise and a few drops anchovy essence if wished. Top with rolled anchovy fillets. or with anchovy stuffed olives.

Corn eggs Blend the yolks with well drained canned corn, seasoning and a little mayonnaise (grated cheese can be added if wished). Top with strips of fresh or canned red pepper (capsicum).

Crabmeat eggs Blend the yolks with flaked crabmeat, use some of the dark as well as the light flesh. Moisten with a little cream or mayonnaise and lemon juice, season well. Top with paprika and piped rosettes of really thick mayonnaise if desired.

Seafood eggs Flavour the yolks with anchovy essence and a few drops soy sauce if wished. Add chopped prawns or other fish if wished, then top with shelled prawns.

Other fillings can be caviare, mashed sardines, diced ham and tongue or flaked salmon. Always use a moist filling or moisten with mayonnaise or a little thick cream. Season well.

Cover with foil or greaseproof paper so the eggs do not dry.

Scotch eggs

A perfect omelette should be moist in texture, very light and served 'piping hot'. In order to achieve this, cook the mixture quickly so the eggs set in a short time; too slow cooking toughens them. Never keep omelettes waiting; they should be cooked *as* required then served immediately, this means all fillings and garnishes should be prepared before you start to cook the omelette. Omelettes are suitable for serving either as an hors d'oeuvre or as a main dish for any meal.

● **AVOID** *Putting too many eggs into the pan, this 'slows up' the cooking. A 5–6-inch omelette pan should be used for a 2–3 egg omelette: Using too large a pan for the number of eggs, for this means you have a wafer thin layer which becomes dry and slightly hard in cooking: Washing the pan after use, it is the main reason why omelettes stick.*

● **TO RECTIFY** *Make several small omelettes if you have only a small pan. This does mean the first omelettes are kept waiting, unless you can persuade your family to eat them as they are cooked, rather than serving them altogether. If you make a lot of omelettes it is worth while investing in two omelette pans, so you can cook two omelettes simultaneously: If the only pan you have is really too big for the number of eggs then*

To Make an Omelette

work on half the pan, *Sketches 4, 5 and 6 illustrate this: Treat an omelette pan with great respect, season it when new, see Sketch 1 and wipe out with soft paper or a soft cloth after use.*

Blue Print Recipe

To Make a Plain Omelette

2 or 3 eggs · seasoning · 1 tablespoon water · 1 oz. butter · filling or flavouring (see individual recipes) · garnish as recipes.

To make Beat the eggs, seasoning and water lightly. I use a fork only for a plain omelette like this, for I find over-beating gives a less moist result.

To cook Heat the butter in the omelette pan, make quite sure it is hot, but do not let it darken in colour, otherwise it spoils the look of the omelette. Pour the eggs into the hot butter then *wait* $\frac{1}{2}$–1 minute until the eggs have set in a thin film at the bottom. Hold the handle of the omelette pan quite firmly in one hand, then loosen the egg mixture from the sides of the pan with a knife and tilt the pan slightly (it should be kept over the heat all this time). This is known as 'working' the omelette and it allows the liquid egg from the top of the mixture to flow to the sides of the pan and cook quickly. Continue tilting the pan, loosening the sides and moving the mixture until it is as set *as you like*. People vary considerably in the way they like their omelettes cooked, some prefer them just set, others fairly liquid in the centre. Add any filling mentioned in the recipe.

To serve Fold or roll the omelette away from the handle of the pan, see Sketch 2. Hold the pan firmly by the handle, then tip the cooked omelette on to the very hot serving dish or plate, see Sketch 3. Garnish as the recipe and serve at once. *All recipes based on this serve 1 person as a main course or 2 people as an hors d'oeuvre unless stated otherwise.*

Storing and Freezing *Omelettes cannot be stored or frozen.*

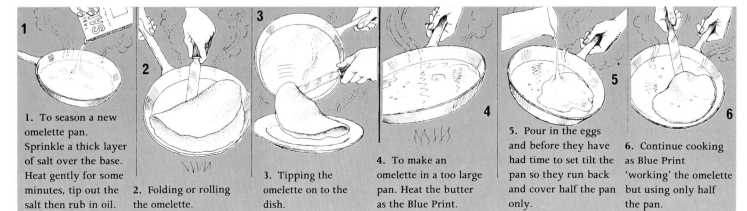

1. To season a new omelette pan. Sprinkle a thick layer of salt over the base. Heat gently for some minutes, tip out the salt then rub in oil.

2. Folding or rolling the omelette.

3. Tipping the omelette on to the dish.

4. To make an omelette in a too large pan. Heat the butter as the Blue Print.

5. Pour in the eggs and before they have had time to set tilt the pan so they run back and cover half the pan only.

6. Continue cooking as Blue Print 'working' the omelette but using only half the pan.

SOME FLAVOURINGS AND FILLINGS FOR OMELETTES

Omelette aux Fines Herbes

Ingredients as Blue Print PLUS 1–2 teaspoons freshly chopped herbs or $\frac{1}{4}$–$\frac{1}{2}$ teaspoon dried herbs. Mix the herbs with the beaten eggs. Cook and serve as the Blue Print. Garnish with freshly chopped herbs.

Bacon Filled Omelette

Ingredients as Blue Print PLUS 2 rashers of bacon and 1 tomato. Chop and fry the bacon, keep hot. Cook the omelette as the Blue Print, add the bacon then fold or roll. Serve as the Blue Print, garnished with cooked or raw tomato slices.

Cheese Omelette

Ingredients as Blue Print PLUS 1–2 oz. ($\frac{1}{4}$–$\frac{1}{2}$C) grated cheese. Cook the omelette as the Blue Print but add the cheese just before it is completely set. Fold or roll and serve as the Blue Print. Garnish with a little more grated cheese and parsley.

Ham Omelette

Ingredients as Blue Print PLUS 2 oz. ($\frac{1}{4}$C) diced cooked ham. Mix the ham with the beaten eggs. Cook as the Blue Print.

Mushroom Omelette

Ingredients as Blue Print PLUS 1–2 oz. ($\frac{1}{4}$–$\frac{1}{2}$C) chopped fresh mushrooms and a little extra butter. Cook the mushrooms in some of the butter. Mix with the beaten eggs. Cook as the Blue Print. Garnish with more mushrooms or parsley.

Prawn Omelette

Ingredients as Blue Print PLUS 2 oz. ($\frac{1}{4}$C) chopped shelled prawns. Mix the prawns with the beaten eggs. Cook as the Blue Print. Garnish with a thick slice of lemon.

Pastel de Tortillas (Omelette Cake)

8 eggs; seasoning; 3 tablespoons water; about 2 oz. butter. *For the sauce:* $1\frac{1}{2}$–2 lb. tomatoes; 2 oz. ($\frac{1}{4}$C) minced raw beef; 1 clove garlic; 1 onion; seasoning; good pinch dried or fresh basil. *Layer one:* about 4 oz. (1C) mixed cooked vegetables; little butter. *Layer two:* 4 oz. (1C) mushrooms; 1–2 oz. butter. *Layer three:* 4 oz. (about 1C) cooked shrimps or other shell fish; little butter.

This is an unusual variation of the Spanish omelette or Tortilla.

The omelettes are made just as the Blue Print, but do not cook these until all the fillings and sauce are ready. To make the sauce, chop the tomatoes, put into a pan and simmer until the juice flows, then add the beef, crushed garlic, chopped onion, seasoning and herbs. Simmer for about 30 minutes, sieve if wished, then reheat. The sauce must be fairly stiff, so allow any surplus liquid to evaporate in an uncovered pan.

Heat the vegetables in the minimum of butter (they must not be greasy). Slice or chop the mushrooms, simmer in the butter. Toss the shrimps or shell fish in butter.

Make four omelettes as the Blue Print. Put the first omelette on a hot dish, cover with the vegetable layer, then add the second omelette and the mushroom layer, the third omelette and the shell fish and the final omelette to cover. Top with some of the sauce and serve the rest separately. *Serves 4–5 as a main course, 8–10 as an hors d'oeuvre.*

Store Cupboard Omelette

Ingredients as Blue Print (using 3 eggs) PLUS can asparagus spears, can diced potatoes, little extra butter or use 1–2 tablespoons oil, 1–2 oz. ($\frac{1}{4}$C) diced Cheddar cheese and parsley.

Open the cans, cut the tips from the asparagus spears. Chop the stalks. Heat the tips and put on one side for garnish. Fry the drained diced potatoes in hot butter or oil until golden, drain. Mix the chopped asparagus stalks, fried potatoes and cheese. Make the omelette as the Blue Print but add the potato mixture while it is still fairly soft. Fold. Slide out of the pan (as you have a very generous filling) on to a hot dish. Garnish with hot asparagus tips and parsley. *Serves 2 as a main dish.*

Bacon filled omelette (opposite)
Pastel de Tortillas (Omelette Cake), below left
Store cupboard omelette (below)

Poached and Scrambled Eggs

All too often a poached or scrambled egg is spoiled by over-cooking. This produces a tough hard poached egg or a dry scrambled egg, or one that 'curdles' and becomes 'watery' due to too much heat.

Blue Print Recipes

1. Poached Eggs

METHOD 1. To Make Half fill a shallow pan or frying pan with water. Add a good pinch salt and bring to boiling point. Pour in 1–2 teaspoons vinegar if wished, this helps to prevent the white spreading in the water, but does give a faint vinegar taste to the eggs. Break the first egg into a cup or saucer, slide into the water. Continue like this, adding the number of eggs required.

To cook Lower the heat once the eggs have been added, so it bubbles very gently. Move the water round the eggs in a 'whirling' movement, this, like the vinegar, assists in keeping the eggs a good shape. Cook for 2–3 minutes only until set.

To serve Lift each egg out with a fish slice or perforated spoon, allow to drain over the water. Serve on hot buttered toast or as the suggestions below.

METHOD 2. To Make Put water into the base of an egg poacher. Add a small knob of butter or margarine to each small metal cup and allow to melt as the water boils. Break an egg into each cup, season lightly if wished.

To cook Until just set, be careful they do not become too firm.
To serve As above.

● **AVOID** *Boiling the water too rapidly, this produces a very badly shaped egg and one where the white breaks away.*
● **TO RECTIFY** *If this has started to happen, reduce the heat at once and gather the white together with a metal spoon or spatula.*
● **TO SLIMMERS** *Choose Method 1 for poaching the eggs.*

2. Scrambled Eggs

3 or 4 eggs · seasoning · 1–2 tablespoons milk or thin cream (see method) · 1 oz. margarine or butter.

To make Beat the eggs with seasoning and the milk or cream. It is not essential to add milk or cream, although this gives a lighter scrambled egg.
To cook Melt the margarine or butter in a saucepan. Add the eggs, make sure the heat is low then leave the eggs for about 1 minute. Stir gently with a wooden spoon until lightly set.
To serve Spoon on to hot buttered toast or fried bread or serve as the suggestions below. Scrambled eggs make a light meal served with piped creamed potatoes. *All recipes based on this serve 2–3.*

● **AVOID** *Leaving the eggs too long without stirring, for they then set too firmly.*
● **TO RECTIFY** *If the eggs have become rather firm, add either another raw, seasoned egg, or a little milk or cream and blend gently with the firm egg.*
● **TO SLIMMERS** *Omit the cream.*

For Special Occasions

Eggs Hollandaise

Make Hollandaise sauce as page 94. Poach 6 eggs as Blue Print 1, put on rounds of fried bread or buttered toast. Coat with the Hollandaise sauce. Top with paprika or sliced cooked mushrooms. *Serves 3 as a main dish or 6 as an hors d'oeuvre.*

Oeufs en Matelote

Poach the eggs as Blue Print 1, but use meat stock instead of salted water. Top with a thick, well seasoned onion purée and serve on rounds of toast. Garnish with anchovy fillets. The mixture of meat and fish in this particular recipe is most interesting and a very pleasant combination.

Piperade

1–2 oz. butter or use half butter and half olive oil; 1 green pepper; 1 red pepper (optional—or use half a green and half a red pepper); 1–2 onions: 1–2 tomatoes; 1 clove garlic; 6 eggs; seasoning.
Heat the butter, or butter and oil in a pan. Add the prepared peppers, either diced or cut into thin rings, (discard the seeds and core), the peeled sliced or chopped onions and tomatoes and the crushed clove of garlic. Cook gently until tender, then add the beaten seasoned eggs and scramble as Blue Print 2; *do not add milk or cream.* Serve with crusty French bread or with crisp toast. *Serves 2–3 as a main dish or 6 as a light hors d'oeuvre.*

Eggs with Asparagus

Heat the tips of canned or cooked asparagus in butter or margarine, then add the eggs, beaten with cream or milk, and scramble as Blue Print 2.
To vary Add diced ham or cooked chicken or prawns in place of asparagus.

Storing and Freezing *You can store the cooked, scrambled eggs for sandwich fillings and they can be frozen although they do become slightly tough. Poached eggs are quite unsuitable for freezing, they can however be stored then chopped to add to sauces etc. in place of hard boiled eggs. Naturally they must be poached until firm for this purpose.*

Piperade

Scrambled eggs

Fried bacon and eggs

egg and makes it difficult to 'dish-up'. Too cool fat also produces a greasy egg.

● **TO RECTIFY** *Check cooking progress carefully and 'dish-up' as soon as the eggs are set. Remember they continue cooking if kept warm for any length of time.*

● **TO SLIMMERS** *Choose a 'non-stick' pan so you need the minimum of fat.*

2. Baked Eggs

½–1 oz. butter or margarine · 2 eggs seasoning.

To make Put half the butter or margarine into one or two containers (use one container for a main dish, two for hors d'oeuvre).

To cook Heat the butter or margarine for a few minutes in a moderate to moderately hot oven, 375–400°F, Gas Mark 5–6. Break the eggs over the hot butter or margarine, add a little seasoning, then the rest of the fat in one or two small knobs. Bake for just over 10 minutes towards the top of the oven.

To serve With a teaspoon, while still very hot. *All recipes based on this serve 2 as an hors d'oeuvre or 1 as a main meal.*

To vary This is a very basic way of baking the eggs, you can:

Put grated, cottage or cream cheese into the dish or dishes, with the butter or margarine. Heat this for a few minutes, then add the egg or eggs, seasoning, more grated (not cream or cottage) cheese and butter or margarine. Cook as Blue Print 2.

Put a layer of thin or thick cream over the hot butter or margarine, then add the egg or eggs, seasoning, another layer of cream and the remaining butter or margarine. Cook as Blue Print 2.

Add chopped ham, chicken, prawns or asparagus tips to the butter or margarine, heat, then add the egg or eggs, seasoning and the rest of the butter or margarine. Cook as Blue Print 2.

All these variations make excellent light dishes.

● **AVOID** *Cooking the eggs too slowly, they become 'leathery'.*

● **TO RECTIFY** *Check on the cooking after about 6–7 minutes, the egg whites should be setting, if they are still very transparent raise the oven temperature.*

● **TO SLIMMERS** *Use as little butter as possible and choose low calorie flavourings.*

Fried Eggs Hussarde

4 small slices bread; 2 oz. (¼C) fat; 2 slices cooked ham; 1–2 tomatoes; seasoning; 4 eggs. Cut the bread into neat rounds. Heat most of the fat, fry the bread until crisp and golden brown on both sides. Lift out of the pan on to a hot oven-proof dish. Top with chopped ham, thickly sliced tomatoes and seasoning. Put into the oven to soften the tomatoes while frying the eggs. Heat the remainder of the fat in the pan. Fry the eggs as Blue Print 1, put on top of the tomato slices and serve at once. *Serves 2 as a main dish, 4 as a snack.*

Savoury Snow Eggs

4 thick slices Gruyere or Cheddar cheese; little made mustard; 4 slices cooked ham; 4 eggs; seasoning. *To garnish:* paprika; chopped parsley.
Put the cheese into a shallow oven-proof dish. Spread with the mustard and top with the ham. Put into a moderate to moderately hot oven, 375–400°F, Gas Mark 5–6 for about 10 minutes. Meanwhile, separate the egg yolks and whites. Beat the yolks with seasoning, pour over the ham and cheese. Bake for 5 minutes. Whisk the egg whites until very stiff, add seasoning and pile over the egg yolk mixture. Return to the oven, lower the heat to very moderate and leave for about 10–15 minutes. Garnish with paprika and chopped parsley. *Serves 4.*

Fried Eggs Turque

4–6 chickens' livers; 2 oz. (¼C) butter; ½ tablespoon chopped parsley; 4 large tomatoes; seasoning; 4 eggs; French bread.
Slice the chickens' livers and fry in half the hot butter until tender. Add the chopped parsley and arrange in the centre of a hot dish. While the livers are cooking, heat the skinned chopped tomatoes with seasoning until a thick purée. Spoon over the livers. Fry the eggs in the remaining hot butter as Blue Print 1 and arrange round the tomato and liver mixture. Serve with hot French bread. *Serves 4.*

Storing and Freezing
None of these dishes store or freeze.

Perfectly fried eggs with grilled or fried bacon are one of the best and quickest dishes to serve at breakfast time, or any other meal of the day. The soft yolk of the egg gives moistness to grilled meat or fish. I enjoy hot fried eggs on thick slices of cold boiled bacon or ham or as a topping on Welsh Rarebit (instead of poached eggs).

Baked eggs are equally good for a light main dish, or an hors d'oeuvre. They can be varied in many ways. As the baked eggs are generally served in the cooking container it is worth while investing in interesting oven-proof dishes if you serve them frequently.

Blue Print Recipes

1. Fried Eggs

To cook If you have fried bacon or sausages there may be enough fat left in the pan; if insufficient then heat a small knob of fat, check it is not too hot. Break the first egg into a cup or saucer or directly into the hot fat. Tilt the pan for a few seconds to encourage the white to set in a neat shape. Add the second egg, tilt the pan, then continue like this. If very fussy about the shape, you can put an old round metal pastry cutter into the pan and heat this as you heat the fat, then break the egg into it. When set, lift away the cutter and use for each egg.

Lift the eggs from the pan with a fish slice so they are drained of any surplus fat.

Some people like the yolk covered with a layer of white, in which case spoon the fat over the yolk as its sets.

To serve As soon as possible after cooking.

● **AVOID** *Over-cooking, fried eggs cook very quickly: Too hot fat, if you dislike a crisp skin at the bottom of the eggs: Too cool fat, as this allows the white to spread over the pan which gives a bad shape to the*

Do not imagine that pancakes 'belong' just to Shrove Tuesday. It is an old and cherished tradition to make pancakes, served with sugar and lemon, for this special day, but they are excellent as a savoury or pudding throughout the year.

Blue Print Recipe

To Make Pancakes

To Make Pancakes

For the batter: 4 oz. (1C) flour, preferably plain · pinch salt · 1 egg · $\frac{1}{2}$ pint (1$\frac{1}{3}$C) milk or milk and water. **For frying:** oil or fat (see method).

To make Sieve the flour and salt, add the egg and a little milk or milk and water. Beat or whisk thoroughly to give a smooth thick batter. Gradually whisk in the rest of the liquid.

To cook For each pancake you cook, put about 2 teaspoons oil or a knob of fat the size of an unshelled almond into the pan. If using a 'non-stick' pan then brush with oil or melted fat before cooking each pancake. This is essential if you want really crisp pancakes. Heat the oil or fat until a *faint* blue haze is seen coming from the pan. Pour or spoon in a little batter, then move the pan so the batter flows over the bottom, it should give a paper thin layer, see Sketches 1 and 2. Cook fairly quickly until set on the bottom. This takes about 1$\frac{1}{2}$–2 minutes. To test if ready to toss or turn, shake the pan and the pancake should move easily if cooked on the under surface. Toss or turn carefully as directions given with the sketches. Cook for about the same time on the second side.

To serve Lift or slide the pancake out of the pan. Keep hot (see below), while cooking the rest of the pancakes. *This batter should give enough pancakes for 4 people, but you may*

1. Spoon or pour a little thin batter from a jug.

2. Immediately turn and tilt the pan to allow the batter to coat the bottom of the pan in a paper-thin layer.

3. To turn the pancake, slip a palette knife under the pancake and turn carefully.

4. To toss a pancake, hold the pan in a relaxed fashion pointing slightly downwards.

5. Flick the wrist very briskly upwards so the pancake lifts from the pan, turns and drops back again.

be able to serve a greater number if using a substantial filling, as in the Savoury Pancake Boat and Orange Pancake Gâteau opposite.

To keep pancakes hot Either put a large plate over a pan of boiling water and place each cooked pancake on this or keep hot on an uncovered dish in a cool oven.

● **AVOID** *Making the batter too thick: Insufficient heating of the oil or fat before cooking each pancake: Pouring too much mixture into the pan: Trying to turn or toss before the pancake is properly set (this is the main reason why pancakes break): Washing the pan after use.*

● **TO RECTIFY** *Follow the proportions in the Blue Print. This gives a very thin batter. Always whisk the batter just before cooking, as it tends to separate slightly as it stands; so that the batter at the bottom of the basin is slightly thicker than at the top: Check the heat of the oil or fat very carefully: Learn the 'knack' of pouring a little batter into the pan, see the sketches: Shake the pancake well before trying to toss or turn; if it does not move easily it is* not *ready: Wipe the used pan with soft paper immediately after use. If using a 'non-stick' pan follow the maker's directions.*

● **SHORT CUTS** *There are commercial pancake mixes, or blend the ingredients in the liquidiser. Emulsify the liquid and egg first, then add the flour and salt. In this way you prevent the flour sticking round the sides of the goblet.*

Storing and Freezing *The uncooked batter may be stored for several days in a refrigerator and can be frozen for a few weeks. Wrap cooked unfilled pancakes in aluminium foil (separate each pancake with squares of greaseproof or waxed paper). Store for several days in a refrigerator or 10–12 weeks in a freezer. Most filled pancakes can be frozen.*

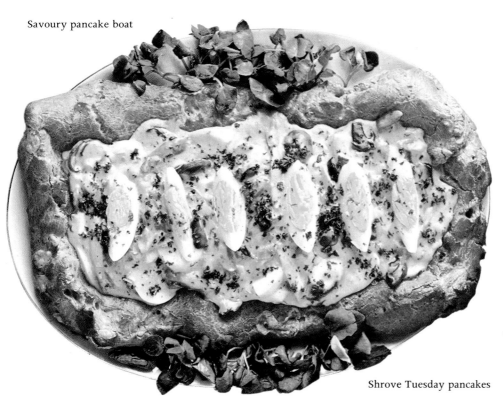
Savoury pancake boat

Red Currant Pancakes

Ingredients as Blue Print opposite PLUS red currant jelly and caster sugar.

Make the pancakes as the Blue Print. Fill with hot red currant jelly and top with sugar. *Serves 4–6.*

To vary Use hot jam or fruit purée instead of jelly.

Crisp Coated Pancakes

Ingredients as Blue Print opposite PLUS jam, jelly or fruit purée, oil or fat for deep frying and sugar.

Put a little of the pancake batter on one side, make and cook the pancakes with the remainder of the batter as Blue Print. Keep warm. Spread with a little jam, jelly or fruit purée, then fold in the sides of the pancakes and roll firmly. Dip each rolled pancake in the reserved batter and fry in hot deep oil or fat until very crisp and golden brown. Put on to a hot dish, top with sugar and hot jam, jelly or fruit. *Serves 4–6.*

To vary Dip in batter, then in fine soft breadcrumbs or chopped nuts before frying.

Shrove Tuesday pancakes

The pancake batter, covered by the Blue Print opposite, enables you to make a variety of savoury and sweet dishes.

Savoury Pancake Boat

Ingredients as Blue Print opposite MINUS fat for frying and PLUS 1 oz. fat; 3–4 hard boiled eggs; 3 oz. ($\frac{3}{8}$C) butter or margarine; 2 oz. ($\frac{1}{2}$C) flour; $\frac{1}{2}$ pint (1$\frac{1}{3}$C) chicken stock; $\frac{1}{4}$ pint ($\frac{2}{3}$C) milk; seasoning; about 4–6 oz. (1C) diced cooked chicken; 2–3 tablespoons thin cream; 2–4 oz. ($\frac{1}{2}$–1C) button mushrooms; chopped parsley. To garnish: sprigs of watercress.

Make the batter as the Blue Print opposite. Heat the fat in a shallow tin, pour in the batter and bake for approximately 25–30 minutes towards the top of a hot to very hot oven, 450–475°F, Gas Mark 7–8. Reduce the heat after about 15 minutes to moderate. Meanwhile slice the eggs, make a sauce with 2 oz. ($\frac{1}{4}$C) of the butter or margarine, the flour, chicken stock and milk. When thickened and smooth, add the seasoning, chicken and cream; do not allow to boil. Heat the remainder of the butter or margarine, fry the whole or sliced mushrooms. Add most of the sliced eggs and mushrooms to the chicken mixture. Lift the batter from the tin on to a hot serving dish, spoon the sauce mixture over this. Top with the remainder of the eggs, mushrooms and chopped parsley. Garnish with watercress. *Serves about 6.*

Orange Pancake Gâteau

Ingredients as Blue Print opposite PLUS 2 cans mandarin oranges, fresh orange juice (optional—see method), 2 tablespoons honey, 2 tablespoons sieved apricot jam, 3 teaspoons

arrowroot or cornflour and 1 glacé, fresh or canned cherry.

Cook the pancakes as the Blue Print opposite and keep hot. Strain the syrup from the cans of oranges, measure and allow $\frac{3}{4}$ pint (2C). If insufficient add a little fresh orange juice. Put most of the fruit syrup into a saucepan with the honey and jam, heat gently until the jam has melted. Blend the arrowroot or cornflour with the remainder of the syrup, add to the mixture in the pan, stir until thickened and clear. Put the first pancake on to a hot dish, top with some mandarin oranges and sauce. Continue like this, ending with a pancake. Arrange a few orange segments and the cherry on top and coat with a little sauce. Serve cut into slices, like a cake. *Serves 6–8.*

Shrove Tuesday Pancakes

Make the pancakes as the Blue Print opposite, serve in the traditional way with sugar and lemon slices. *Serves 4–6.*

A New Look to Pancakes

1 Flavour the batter with $\frac{1}{2}$ teaspoon ginger, cinnamon, allspice or grated lemon rind.
2 Fill the cooked pancakes, fold the ends in and roll. This prevents the filling coming out. Dip in a stiffly beaten egg white blended with 1 teaspoon cornflour and fry in deep fat or oil. If the filling is savoury, roll in grated cheese after frying. If the filling is sweet, roll in chopped nuts or desiccated coconut.
3 Use pancakes instead of omelettes in the recipe for Pastel de Tortillas (page 79).

A savoury soufflé is ideal for a light meal or can be served at the end of a formal dinner. For serving as a savoury at the end of a meal, the best flavours to choose are cheese, ham or smoked haddock.

The Blue Print gives a fairly firm textured soufflé. If you are having this with vegetables, as a main course, I would increase the amount of liquid by up to an extra $\frac{1}{4}$ pint ($\frac{2}{3}$C). This means that you have a very soft texture in the centre which serves as a sauce with any vegetables.

Blue Print Recipe

Cheese Soufflé

1 oz. butter or margarine · 1 oz. flour · $\frac{1}{4}$ pint ($\frac{2}{3}$C) milk (see introduction above) · seasoning · 4 eggs · approximately 3 oz. ($\frac{3}{4}$C) grated cheese*.

*You can vary the cheese—Dutch Gouda gives a pleasant mild, creamy texture, a Cheddar or Gruyère a fairly definite taste and Parmesan a very strong taste and a drier texture.

To make   Heat the butter or margarine in a large saucepan, stir in the flour then gradually blend in the milk. Cook until a thick sauce (if using the higher percentage of

Savoury Soufflés

liquid it will be a coating consistency). Season well. Remove from the heat and add the egg yolks, then the cheese and finally fold in the stiffly beaten egg whites. Put into a greased soufflé dish.

To cook   Bake in the centre of a moderate to moderately hot oven, 375–400°F, Gas Mark 5–6, for approximately 30 minutes. If using the larger quantity of liquid use the lower temperature so the mixture does not over-brown before it is cooked.

To serve   As quickly as possible. *All recipes based on this serve 4 for a main dish or 6 as a savoury.*

● **AVOID** *Handling the mixture too much when putting in the egg whites, for this destroys the fluffy texture.*
● **TO RECTIFY** *You can tell if you are overhandling the mixture because you lose the very light appearance. If by chance you have been too rough, the best remedy is to incorporate an extra whisked egg white.*
● **SHORT CUT** *Instead of making the sauce, use $\frac{1}{4}$–$\frac{1}{2}$ pint ($\frac{2}{3}$–$1\frac{1}{3}$C) condensed soup,*

either mushroom, chicken or asparagus, to blend with the other flavouring.
● **TO SLIMMERS** *This is a relatively low calorie, high protein dish.*
Storing and Freezing   *You cannot freeze or store a hot soufflé.*

Spinach Soufflé

Ingredients as Blue Print but substitute spinach purée for the milk. Cheese may be added if wished. Make and bake as the Blue Print.

Fish Soufflé

Ingredients as Blue Print but use flaked cooked fish (white fish, salmon or shell fish) in place of cheese and flavour the sauce with a few drops of anchovy essence. Make and bake as the Blue Print.

Smoked Haddock and Cheese Soufflé

This is a very pleasant combination.
Follow the Blue Print recipe but use only 2 oz. ($\frac{1}{2}$C) grated Parmesan cheese and 2–3 oz. cooked flaked smoked haddock. Substitute fish stock (or liquid from cooking the fish) for milk if possible.

Cream Soufflé

Follow the Blue Print recipe using the smaller quantity of milk and add 3–4 tablespoons thick cream to the sauce with the egg yolks.

Soufflé omelette

A soufflé omelette is made by separating the egg yolks and the whites, then whisking the whites until very stiff and folding them into the egg yolks. In this way you produce a thick, ultra-light type of omelette.

A soufflé omelette makes an excellent basis for a hot dessert. Although you can add sweet fillings to the plain omelette on page 78, they blend better with the lighter texture of the soufflé type.

The savoury fillings given on pages 78 and 79 may be incorporated into this type of omelette, although I prefer more moist fillings as indicated by the suggestions on this page.

The points under AVOID and TO RECTIFY on page 78 also apply to this type of omelette.

Blue Print Recipe

To Make a Soufflé Omelette

2 or 3 eggs · seasoning or 1 teaspoon sugar for a sweet omelette · 1 tablespoon water · 1 oz. butter · filling or flavouring (see individual recipes).

To make Separate the yolks from the whites. Beat the yolks with seasoning or sugar, and water. Whisk the egg whites until very stiff, fold into the yolks.

Making a Soufflé Omelette

To cook Heat the butter in the pan (see page 78). Switch on or light the grill. Pour the fluffy egg mixture into the hot butter. Allow to set and 'work' as the Blue Print on page 78. You will find this more difficult as the mixture is less liquid. When the omelette is about half-cooked, put the pan under the grill (with the heat to medium) and complete the cooking.

To serve Add any filling required. This thicker omelette is more difficult to fold (you cannot roll it) so make a shallow 'cut' across the centre, then fold, see Sketches 2 and 3 (page 78). Slide or tip on to the hot serving dish or plate. *All recipes based on this serve 1 as a main dish or 2 as a light hors d'oeuvre or dessert.*

SWEET FILLINGS
Nut Omelette

Follow the Blue Print and blend 1–2 table-spoons chopped blanched almonds, hazel, pecan or walnuts with the egg yolks. Fill with hot sweetened apricot purée or jam.

Fruit Omelette

Use thin cream instead of the water in the Blue Print. Fill with hot fruit purée or sliced uncooked sweetened fresh fruit. The fruit can be flavoured with brandy or liqueur.

Jam Omelette

Make the omelette as the Blue Print and fill with hot jam (or jelly). A delicious omelette is made by adding finely grated orange or lemon rind to the egg yolks then filling with hot marmalade.

SAVOURY FILLINGS WITH SAUCES

Thick cheese, curry, mushroom, or tomato sauces all make excellent fillings.

Vegetable Filling

Blend diced cooked vegetables with any of the sauces above or with a thick fresh tomato purée (made more piquant with the addition of a little canned concentrated tomato purée).

Fish and Meat Filling

Blend cooked ham, tongue, chicken, white fish or shellfish with the selected sauce and flavour with chopped fresh herbs.

Storing and Freezing *You cannot store or freeze a soufflé omelette, but it is a good idea to freeze different fillings in small containers.* **To use any left over** *I quite like a cold soufflé omelette cut in strips and served in place of hard boiled egg.*

85

Making Short Crust Pastry

Short crust is undoubtedly the most useful of all types of pastry. It is quick to make, relatively simple, keeps well and is equally good with sweet as with savoury ingredients.

Blue Print Recipe

Short Crust Pastry

8 oz. (2C) flour, preferably plain · pinch salt · 4 oz. (½C) fat* · cold water to mix.
*This can be cooking fat, margarine, butter, shortening or a mixture.

To make   Sieve the flour and salt. Cut the fat into convenient-sized pieces, drop into the bowl. Rub in with the tips of your fingers until the mixture looks like fine breadcrumbs. *Do not overhandle.* Lift the flour and fat as you rub them together so you incorporate as much air as possible and keep the mixture cool. *Gradually* add water to give enough moisture to bind the ingredients together. Use a palette knife to blend. Flour varies a great deal in the amount of liquid it absorbs, but you should require about 2 tablespoons water. When blended, form into a neat ball of dough with your fingers. Put on to a lightly floured pastry board, and roll out to a neat oblong or round about ¼-inch in thickness unless the recipe states to the contrary. Always roll in one direction and do not turn the rolling pin, instead lift and turn the pastry. This makes sure it is not stretched badly.
To cook   As the individual recipes, generally short crust pastry needs a hot oven to set the pastry, but you may need to reduce the heat after a time.

● **AVOID** *Making the pastry too wet, this produces a tough instead of a crisp, short result: Overhandling the dough: Baking too slowly.*

● **TO RECTIFY** *If you have made the pastry over-moist either chill thoroughly, this does allow it to 'dry out' slightly, or use a generous amount of flour on the pastry board; unfortunately the latter remedy spoils the basic proportions of the pastry.*

● **SHORT CUT** *Use ready-prepared frozen short crust pastry for the various dishes in this section.*

For Special Occasions

Old English Chicken Pie

Short crust pastry made with 8 oz. (2C) flour etc. as Blue Print. *For the filling:* small quantity of sage and onion stuffing or ½ packet stuffing; 12 oz. (nearly 2C) diced raw chicken meat; 2 oz. (½C) flour; seasoning; 3 sausages (skinless if possible); 2 oz. (¼C) butter or fat; ¾ pint (2C) chicken stock or water and 1 chicken stock cube; 2 hard boiled eggs. *To glaze:* 1 egg.

Make the pastry as the Blue Print and put on one side while preparing the filling. Form the stuffing into 6 small balls. Toss the chicken meat in half the flour, blended with a little seasoning. Halve the sausages. Toss the stuffing balls, coated chicken and sausages in the hot butter or fat until golden brown. Remove from the fat and put into a 2-pint (5–6C) pie dish. Stir the remaining flour into any fat remaining in the pan, then gradually add the stock or water and stock cube. Bring to the boil, cook until thickened. Add the coarsely chopped eggs. Pour the sauce over the chicken, stuffing balls and sausages. Cool slightly, then cover with the pastry as the sketches below. Make a slit in the centre of the pie to allow the steam to escape. (This encourages the pastry to crisp.) Decorate with pastry leaves made from the trimmings. Brush with the beaten egg and bake in the centre of a hot oven, 425–450°F, Gas Mark 6–7, for about 20–25 minutes until the pastry is golden brown. Reduce the heat to moderate and cook for a further 20–25 minutes. Serve hot. *Serves 6.*

To make tartlets
1. Cut the pastry into rounds (about 2-inches in diameter, but depending upon the size of the patty tins). Use a plain cutter for savoury tarts and a fluted cutter for sweet tarts.
2. Put the rounds into the patty tins, press down and continue as the individual recipes.

Old English chicken pie

To make a pie
3. Put the filling into the pie dish. Cut a band of pastry to fit round the moistened edge of the pie dish. Brush the rim of pastry with a very little water.
4. Support the rest of the pastry over the rolling pin. Arrange on top of the pie (slip the rolling pin away).

5.   Press the edges together, then cut away the surplus pastry.
6. Decorate the edges by fluting.

Savoury Tarts and Pies

Corned Beef Plate Tart

Short crust pastry made with 8 oz. (2C) flour, etc. as Blue Print opposite. *For the filling:* 2 × 12 oz. cans corned beef; 2 medium-sized onions; 1 tablespoon oil; seasoning; 1 teaspoon Tabasco (pepper) sauce; 1 egg; 2–3 diced cooked or canned carrots; 4 oz. (about ½C) cooked or canned peas. *To glaze:* 1 egg. *To garnish:* parsley.

Make the pastry as the Blue Print opposite and put on one side. Flake the corned beef and put into a basin. Peel and chop the onions, toss in the hot oil until tender, blend with the corned beef, seasoning, Tabasco sauce, egg and vegetables. Roll out the pastry, use half to cover a 7–8-inch pie plate or tin. Cover with the filling and the rest of the pastry as sketches below and opposite. Decorate with leaves of pastry, made from the trimmings, and glaze with the beaten egg. Bake for 25–30 minutes in the centre of a moderately hot to hot oven, 400–425°F, Gas Mark 5–6, then lower the heat to moderate for a further 20–25 minutes. Serve hot or cold, garnished with parsley. *Serves 6.*
Note As you see, by comparing the cooking temperatures of this tart with the Old English Chicken Pie opposite, it is advisable to use a slightly lower oven temperature, and longer cooking time, when you have pastry above and below a substantial filling. This ensures that the bottom pastry sets and browns as well as the top pastry. If the filling is fairly dry in texture, as above, it is not essential to make a slit in the pastry 'lid'.

Chasseur Chicken Pie

Ingredients as Old English Pie opposite, but substitute 4–6 oz. mushrooms for the sage and onion balls and about 4 firm, halved skinned tomatoes for the hard boiled eggs.
Make as the Corned Beef Plate Tart with pastry above and below the filling. *Serves 6.*

Steak and Vegetable Pie

The pie shown on page 75 is made with steak and vetables. Cook the steak as in the Steak and Kidney pie on page 91 for about 1 hour, then add about 12 oz. diced uncooked vegetables and continue cooking until the steak is almost tender, i.e. approximately 2–2¼ hours. Put into the pie dish and cover with flaky or short crust pastry. Cook as the instructions for that pastry. *Serves 6.*

Golden Crust Pie

Short crust pastry made with 6 oz. (1½C) flour etc. as Blue Print opposite. *For the filling:* 2 oz. (¼C) butter; 1 large onion; 2 large tomatoes; 8 oz. (1C) minced cooked meat or chicken; seasoning; 1 tablespoon

chopped parsley; ½–1 teaspoon chopped thyme or pinch dried thyme; 2 eggs; 2 oz. (½C) grated Cheddar cheese.
Make the pastry as the Blue Print opposite. Roll out and line an 8-inch flan ring or tin. Bake 'blind' in the centre of a hot oven, 425–450°F, Gas Mark 6–7 until crisp and just golden in colour, this takes approximately 15–18 minutes. While the pastry is cooking, prepare the filling. Heat the butter in a frying pan and cook the peeled chopped onion and tomatoes until soft. Add the meat or chicken, seasoning and herbs and heat thoroughly. Add the beaten egg yolks then spoon the hot filling into the hot pastry case. Whisk the egg whites until very stiff, fold in the cheese and seasoning, pile this over the meat mixture. Lower the oven temperature to very moderate and cook for 10 minutes. Serve at once. *Serves 4–5.*
To vary Omit the meat or chicken and add the same quantity of cooked or canned haricot beans. Children love this variation.

Salmon Pie Florentine

Short crust pastry made with 6 oz. (1½C) flour etc. as Blue Print opposite. *For the filling:* 1 lb. fresh spinach or large packet frozen spinach; 2 oz. (¼C) butter; 2 tablespoons thick cream; seasoning; medium-sized can salmon; ¼ pint (⅔C) milk; 1 oz. flour. *To garnish:* 1 lemon.

Make the pastry as the Blue Print opposite. Roll out and line an 8-inch flan ring or tin. Bake 'blind' as the recipe above but allow a little longer until golden brown. Meanwhile cook the spinach, drain well, sieve or chop and blend with half the butter, the cream and seasoning. Open the can of salmon, strain this and blend the juice from the can with the milk. Make a thick sauce with the rest of the butter, flour and milk (plus salmon liquid). Add the flaked fish and seasoning. Put the creamy spinach at the bottom of the pastry, top with the salmon mixture. Garnish with lemon slices, serve at once. *Serves 4–5.*

To make a plate tart
7. Cover the baking tin or pie plate with pastry, neaten edges, add filling. Cover with pastry as described under the pie, Sketches 4–6.

To make a flan
8. Lower the pastry into the flan ring on an upturned baking sheet or tray, or put into a sandwich tin. Neaten edges by cutting or rolling. This is described in detail on page 99.

Corned beef plate tart

Savoury Cheese Flans

The best known of all the savoury flans is a Quiche Lorraine, i.e. an egg custard filling flavoured with cheese and crisp bacon. This is only one of the many interesting flans of the same type. A Quiche is an excellent hors d'oeuvre and ideal for buffet parties.

Blue Print Recipe

Making a Quiche

To make   Prepare the pastry, roll out and line the flan ring (put this on an upturned baking tray, for easy removal) or use a sandwich tin or oven-proof serving dish. Prepare ingredients for the filling.

To cook   Bake the pastry 'blind' (see page 99) in a moderately hot to hot oven, according to the type of pastry used, until just set and pale golden; do *not* over-cook. Remove the pastry from the oven and pour the *warm* filling into the *warm* pastry. Lower the heat to very moderate to moderate, as directed in the recipe and continue cooking until the filling is set. The *greater* the depth of filling, the *longer* the cooking time and the *lower* the oven setting.

To serve   Hot or cold.

● **AVOID**   *Having pastry that is not crisp: Allowing the custard filling to curdle.*

● **TO RECTIFY**   *Although not all recipes bake the pastry case 'blind', I find this the perfect solution. You have crisp pastry, by baking in a hot oven, and a custard filling that is perfectly set but does not curdle, by cooking the filled flan at a lower temperature, see the Blue Print.*

● **SHORT CUTS**   *Use frozen or ready-prepared pastry: Use the quick method of filling as in the Onion and Cheese Flan.*

For Family Occasions

Prawn and Cheese Quiche

For the pastry: 6 oz. (1½C) flour, preferably plain; pinch salt; 3 oz. (⅜C) margarine, butter or cooking fat; water to mix. *For the filling:* 2 eggs; seasoning; ¼ pint (⅔C) milk; 4 oz. (1C) crumbled Lancashire cheese; 4 oz. (½C) shelled chopped prawns. *To garnish:* few whole prawns; parsley.

Sieve the flour and salt, rub in the fat then add sufficient water to make a firm rolling consistency. Roll out and line a *shallow* 8-inch flan ring, sandwich tin or oven-proof baking dish. Bake 'blind' for about 15 minutes in the centre of a hot oven, 425–450°F, Gas Mark 6–7, until just set. Meanwhile beat the eggs with seasoning, add the *warmed* milk, cheese and chopped prawns. Pour into the partially baked pastry case, return to the oven and continue baking in a moderate oven, 350–375°F, Gas Mark 4–5, for about 25–30 minutes until the filling is firm. Serve hot or cold garnished with whole prawns and parsley. *Serves 4–5.*

Note   This filling is rather shallow, as shown in the picture. This means it will set fairly quickly and is a firm filling, so ideal to cut and serve for a buffet. For a less firm filling you can use *nearly* ½ pint (1⅓C) milk to the 2 eggs for an 8-inch, reasonably shallow, dish. Allow about 40–45 minutes to set the filling in a very moderate oven.

Quiche Lorraine

A simple Quiche Lorraine can be made in a very similar way to the Prawn and Cheese Quiche above. Use crisply fried bacon in place of the prawns. If preferred you can use grated Cheddar or Gruyère cheese in place of the crumbled Lancashire cheese.

For Special Occasions

Rich Quiche Lorraine

For the pastry: 8 oz. (2C) flour, preferably plain; good pinch salt; 4 oz. (½C) butter; 1–2 egg yolks and water to bind. *For the filling:* 4 large eggs; good pinch salt; shake pepper; pinch dry mustard; ¼ pint (⅔C) milk and ½ pint (1⅓C) thin cream or use all milk or all thin cream or partly milk and partly thick cream, but make the total amount ¾ pint (2C); 8 oz. (2C) grated Gruyère cheese; about 6 rashers lean bacon (chopped, fried until crisp and well drained). *To garnish:* parsley.

Make the pastry as the Prawn and Cheese Quiche, but binding with the egg yolks and water, then line a deep dish. I use a 2-pint (5–6C) pie dish or similar sized dish. Make sure you make the pastry sides fairly high. If you wish a more shallow Quiche then line a 9–10-inch tin instead. Bake 'blind' in a hot oven for about 15 minutes. Prepare the filling as the Prawn and Cheese Quiche, heating both the milk and the cream. Pour into the pastry case. Lower the heat and bake

in a slow to very moderate oven, 300–325°F, Gas Mark 2–3, if you have a deep Quiche. Allow about 1¼ hours. For a shallow filling, bake for about 40–45 minutes in a very moderate oven. Garnish with parsley. *Serves 6–8.*

To vary   Use shell fish in this filling in place of bacon.

Use cooked chopped ham, or cooked chicken in place of the bacon.

Use a mixture of cooked vegetables, sliced onions, mushrooms, potatoes, peas. Do not use tomatoes, for they might cause the filling to curdle.

Onion and Cheese Flan

For the pastry: 6 oz. (1½C) flour, preferably plain; good pinch salt; shake pepper; pinch dry mustard; pinch cayenne pepper; 3 oz. (⅜C) margarine or butter; 1 oz. (¼C) grated Parmesan cheese; 1 egg yolk and water to bind. *For the filling:* 2 large onions; little water; seasoning; 1 level tablespoon cornflour; ¼ pint (⅔C) milk; 2 eggs; 2 tablespoons cream; 4 oz. (1C) grated Cheddar or Gruyère cheese.

Sieve the flour and seasonings together. Rub in the fat, add the cheese, then bind with the egg yolk and water. Roll out and line an 8-inch tin or flan ring or dish. Bake 'blind' in a

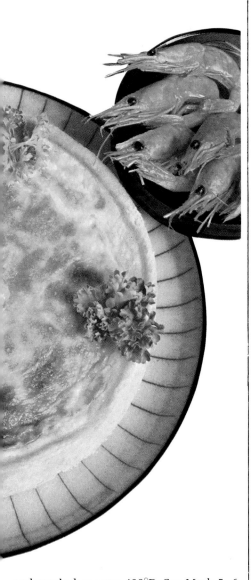

Making a Pizza Pie

The famous Italian Pizza Pie has a yeast base but can be made with a baking powder dough. It is also possible to fill a short crust pastry flan with the savoury mixture.

Blue Print Recipe

Pizza Pie

For the base: 12 oz. (3C) plain flour · pinch salt · 1 tablespoon olive oil · scant ½ oz. fresh or ¼ oz. (1 teaspoon) dried yeast · scant ¼ pint (barely ⅔C) water · **For the topping:** 2 large onions · 1–2 cloves garlic · 1 tablespoon olive oil · 1½ lb. tomatoes · 1–2 tablespoons concentrated tomato purée · seasoning · ¼ teaspoon dried or 1 teaspoon fresh chopped oregano or marjoram · 4–6 oz. Cheddar, Mozzarella or Gruyère cheese · few anchovy fillets · few black olives · sprinkling grated Parmesan cheese.

To make Sieve the flour and salt into a mixing bowl. Make a well in the centre and add the oil. Cream the fresh yeast and add the tepid water, or sprinkle the dried yeast over the water. Pour the yeast liquid over the oil. Sprinkle flour over the yeast liquid. Cover the bowl with a cloth and leave in a warm place for about 15–20 minutes until the yeast liquid bubbles. Blend all the ingredients together and knead until smooth. Return to the bowl and cover. Leave in a warm place for about 1½ hours until the dough has doubled its bulk. Knead again. Roll out to a 9–10-inch round then put on to a warmed greased baking tray. While the yeast dough is rising (proving) for the first time, prepare the topping.

Peel and chop the onions and garlic. Toss in the hot oil, then add the skinned chopped tomatoes, the purée and seasoning. Simmer until the mixture is thick in an uncovered pan. Stir in the oregano (wild marjoram) or marjoram. Spread the tomato mixture over the yeast round. Top with the sliced or grated Cheddar, Mozzarella or Gruyère cheese, the anchovy fillets, olives and a sprinkling of Parmesan. Allow to 'prove' for about 20 minutes (although this stage is not essential).

To cook Bake in the centre of a hot oven 425–450°F, Gas Mark 6–7 for about 15–20 minutes. If the yeast mixture is not quite cooked, then put a piece of foil over the topping to protect it, lower the heat to very moderate and leave a little longer.

To serve Hot or cold. *All recipes based on this serve 5–6 or up to 8 as an hors d'oeuvre.*

Speedy Pizza

Ingredients as Blue Print, but OMIT the yeast. Use self-raising flour or plain flour and 3 teaspoons baking powder. Blend the oil and water (or you can use milk) with the sieved flour and salt. Knead lightly, roll into a round, add the topping and proceed as the Blue Print recipe.

Seafood Pizza

Ingredients as Blue Print PLUS about 4 oz. (1C) shelled prawns and use a whole can of anchovy fillets. Prepare as the Blue Print but add the prawns and most of the anchovy fillets to the *cooked* tomato mixture. Proceed as Blue Print.

Ingredients for base as Blue Print, but OMIT the tomatoes and tomato purée from the topping and use double the amount of onions and garlic, and a whole can of anchovy fillets. Cook the onion and garlic as the Blue Print, add the seasoning and herbs and spread over the dough. Continue as Blue Print.

Pizza Flan

Another way of serving the delicious pizza topping is as follows.

Make a really deep 8–9-inch flan with short crust pastry using 8 oz. (2C) flour etc. Bake 'blind' until crisp and just golden, *do not over-cook.* Prepare the filling as the Blue Print. Spoon the hot tomato filling into the hot flan, top with the cheese, anchovies and olives as Blue Print. Return to the oven for a few minutes to melt the cheese.

Crisp Topped Pizza Flan

Make and fill the flan as above. Bring out of the oven when the cheese has almost melted and top with a layer of soft breadcrumbs and grated Gruyère or Cheddar cheese. Either return to the oven to crisp the crumbs, or protect the pastry with foil and crisp under a moderate grill.

Storing and Freezing *The dough and filling should be stored separately in the refrigerator before baking. The 'unproven' dough keeps for 12 hours and rises very slowly in the refrigerator. Allow to stand at room temperature for about an hour before topping and baking. You can freeze the uncooked or cooked pizza. Allow to thaw out before cooking, but reheat from the frozen state if wished.*

To use any left over *Heat gently so you do not dry the topping.*

---

moderately hot oven 400°F, Gas Mark 5–6, until quite cooked. Meanwhile cook the neatly sliced onions in just enough water to cover. Season, cover the pan tightly, so the liquid does not evaporate. When the onions are cooked, blend the cornflour with the milk, add to the onions and liquid and cook steadily until thickened. Remove the pan from the heat. Blend the beaten eggs with the cream, stir into the onion mixture and cook *without boiling* for about 3 minutes. Add the cheese and heat until melted. *If serving the flan hot:* put the hot filling into the hot pastry and serve as soon as possible. *If serving the flan cold:* allow the filling and pastry to cool then put the filling into the flan case. *Serves 4–5.*

Storing and Freezing *The uncooked pastry may either be stored overnight or for 1–2 days in a refrigerator or for some weeks in a freezer. The cooked Quiche keeps 2–3 days in a refrigerator or for some time in a freezer. The higher the proportion of cream used in the filling, the better the flan will freeze. Allow to defrost at room temperature.*

Quiche Lorraine (left)
Prawn and cheese quiche (above)
Pizza (right)

Making Flaky Pastry

Flaky pastry has a light texture, should rise well, and is easier and quicker to make than puff pastry.

Blue Print Recipe

Flaky Pastry

8 oz. (2C) flour, preferably plain · pinch salt · 6 oz. ($\frac{3}{4}$C) butter or other fat* · water to mix (as cold as possible).
*A favourite combination is half margarine and half lard.

To make   Sieve the flour and salt into a mixing bowl. Rub in one third of the fat. Add enough water to make an elastic dough. Roll out to an oblong on a lightly floured board. Divide the remaining fat in half, if hard soften by pressing with a knife, Sketch 1. Put over the top two thirds of the pastry in small pieces, Sketch 2. Bring up the bottom third of the pastry dough and fold like an envelope, Sketch 3. Bring down the top third, Sketch 4.

   Turn the pastry at right angles, seal the ends of the pastry then depress this at regular intervals with a lightly floured rolling pin—this is called 'ribbing' the pastry, Sketch 5. Roll the dough out into an oblong shape again. *If you find it feels sticky and is difficult to roll* then put away in a cool place for about 30 minutes. Repeat the process covered above and by Sketches 1–5. Put away in a cool place for another 30 minutes, or longer if wished. Roll out to the required shape.

To cook   As the individual recipe, but flaky pastry needs a hot to very hot oven to encourage the pastry to rise and to prevent it being greasy.

To serve   Hot or cold.

● **AVOID** *Overhandling the pastry both when rubbing the small amount of fat into the flour and when folding: Pressing too firmly when you roll out the dough: Allowing the pastry to become warm and sticky.*

● **TO RECTIFY** *Rub the fat into the flour carefully as for short crust pastry, (see page 86): Lift the dough as gently as you can when folding: Use short sharp movements when rolling out the pastry: Put the pastry away in a cool place from time to time.*

● **SHORT CUT** *Although given a different name, i.e. rough puff pastry this has the same proportions of fat to flour as flaky pastry and so can be considered a good alternative. The number of rollings and foldings for rough puff pastry is greater than when making flaky pastry, but the method of incorporating the fat is much quicker.*

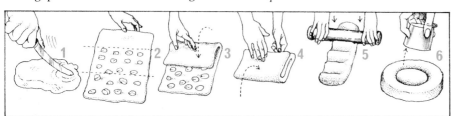

Rough Puff Pastry

Ingredients as the Blue Print.
Sieve the flour and salt into a basin. Drop in the fat, cut this into tiny pieces with 2 knives. Mix with water to an elastic dough. Roll out to an oblong as flaky pastry above, fold, as Sketches 3 and 4. Turn, seal the ends and 'rib' as Sketch 5. Continue as flaky pastry but allow a total of 5 rollings and 5 foldings. Use as flaky pastry.

For Special Occasions

Vol-au-Vent Cases

Choose flaky pastry as the Blue Print, rough puff pastry, as above, or puff pastry (see page 92).
Roll out the pastry until about $\frac{1}{2}$-inch in thickness for fairly shallow cases or up to 1-inch for deep ones. Cut into required shape, or shapes, i.e. either 1 large round or square or a number of smaller shapes. Take a smaller cutter and press into the pastry as Sketch 6; let this cutter mark the pastry about half-way through. Bake a large vol-au-vent case in the centre of a hot to very hot oven 450–475°F, Gas Mark 7–8 for about 25–30 minutes, reduce the heat to very moderate after about 15 minutes. Small cases take from about 10 minutes (for cocktail size) to 15–20 minutes for the size shown on this page. There should be no necessity to lower the heat. Remove the pastry case or cases from the oven. Lift out the pastry 'lid' very carefully. If you find there is a little uncooked mixture in the centre, return the cases to a very moderate oven until this is cooked.

   If serving the vol-au-vent cases cold, then put the *cold* filling into the cold pastry. Place the lids in position, if wished. If serving hot, make quite sure both pastry and filling are very hot. Put together and serve at once.

   Flaky or rough puff pastry made with 8 oz. (2C) flour etc. as the Blue Print will give 1 large vol-au-vent to serve about 6 people, 6–8 medium-sized cases or about 12–14 tiny ones. Puff pastry made with 8 oz. (2C) flour etc. produces rather more vol-au-vent cases.

Using Flaky Pastry

Although an excellent steak and kidney pie can be made with short crust pastry I always feel the lighter texture of flaky pastry blends rather better with the meat filling.

For Family Occasions

Steak and Kidney Pie

For the filling: $1\frac{1}{4}$–$1\frac{1}{2}$ lb. stewing steak; about 8 oz. ox-kidney; nearly 1 oz. flour; seasoning; 1–2 oz. fat; $\frac{3}{4}$ pint (2C) stock or water and 1 beef stock cube. *For the flaky pastry:* 6 oz. ($1\frac{1}{2}$C) flour; pinch salt; $4\frac{1}{2}$ oz. (just over $\frac{1}{2}$C) butter or other fat (see Blue Print opposite); water to mix. *To glaze:* 1 egg plus 1 tablespoon water or a little milk. Cut the steak and kidney into neat pieces. Blend the flour and seasoning. Roll the meat in the seasoned flour then fry gently in the hot fat. Use the higher amount of fat if the meat is exceptionally lean. Blend the stock into the mixture gradually. Bring to the boil and cook until thickened. Cover the pan *very* tightly and allow the meat to cook over a low heat until almost tender, 2–$2\frac{1}{4}$ hours. Make sure the liquid does not evaporate too much, add a little more stock if the gravy becomes too thick. Make the flaky pastry as the Blue Print opposite while the meat is cooking. Spoon the meat into a 2-pint pie dish, allow to cool, then cover with the pastry. Flake the edges with a knife to encourage the pastry to rise. Make a slit in the pastry so the steam escapes during baking and arrange pastry leaves, made from the trimmings, on top. Beat the egg (or use just the yolk) with the water. Brush over the pastry to give a shine when baked. Milk can be used in place of egg, but is not so effective. Stand the pie dish on a baking tray or baking sheet, this is a precaution in case any liquid boils out.* Bake in the centre of a hot to very hot oven 450–475°F, Gas Mark 7–8 for 15–20 minutes. Re-set the heat to moderate, 350–375°F, Gas Mark 4–5 and continue cooking for a further 30–35 minutes until the pastry is brown and firm and the meat very hot. *Serves 6.*
*If you like a generous amount of gravy then put a little into the pie with the meat and heat the rest to serve separately.
To vary Add sliced onions or other vegetables to the steak and kidney.
Use a little red wine in the gravy in place of all stock.

Chicken Pie

Use joints of raw chicken and diced vegetables in place of steak and kidney or a mixture of raw chicken and diced bacon.

Fillings for Vol-au-Vent

Savoury Blend diced cooked chicken, ham, cooked vegetables, flaked cooked fish or shell fish with a moderately thick sauce or with thick mayonnaise. The picture opposite shows chicken vol-au-vent.
Sweet Fill with jam, lemon curd or well drained fruit.

Using Trimmings of Pastry—

Often there are trimmings of pastry left, which can be used for unusual savoury or sweet 'tit-bits' which can be served either as cocktail snacks or with tea or coffee.
The baking temperature will be as the particular pastry, which is covered in the Blue Print on the various pages.

Sardine Cigars Mash sardines, season and flavour with lemon juice. Roll out narrow strips of pastry, put the fish mixture in the centre, fold as sausage rolls (page 92) and bake for about 12 minutes in a hot to very hot oven.
Jam fingers Roll out the pastry to a square or rectangle, spread half with jam. Fold the plain pastry over the top, brush with a very little water and sprinkle lightly with caster sugar. Bake for about 15 minutes in the

Steak and kidney pie

centre of a hot to very hot oven. Cut into fingers while warm. Mincemeat, honey and chopped nuts, chocolate spread and banana mashed with lemon juice and a little sugar, all make interesting sweet fillings. Use grated cheese and chopped dates or raisins, yeast extract and chopped peanuts for savoury fillings.
Nut crisps Roll out the pastry very thinly. Top with chopped nuts (fresh or salted peanuts, blanched almonds, walnuts, hazelnuts, brazils or pecans) and bake until crisp.

Storing and Freezing *Uncooked flaky pastry keeps well for several days in a refrigerator. Wrap in foil or polythene to prevent the outside hardening. It freezes very well. Cooked flaky pastry keeps for several days but needs to be crisped for a short time in the oven. It freezes well, but naturally the success depends upon the filling. A steak and kidney pie is excellent.*
It is better to freeze the uncooked or cooked vol-au-vent cases without the filling and freeze the fillings separately. You cannot freeze fillings containing mayonnaise, and sauces are better if made with cornflour rather than flour.

Puff is the richest of all pastries, yet, in spite of the high percentage of fat, it should not be greasy. The two important factors when making and cooking puff pastry are:

1 The way you roll the dough. Do not 'cut-down' on the number of rollings, for this blends the fat into the flour and incorporates air at the same time. You should see the bubbles of air forming in the dough as you roll. Read the comments about using the rolling pin in the same direction on page 86 and on handling flaky pastry on page 90. These are even more important when making puff pastry.

2 The baking temperature. Do not be afraid of using a very hot oven to encourage the pastry to rise and to 'seal-in' the fat. Reduce the heat as directed in the recipes to prevent over-browning.

Blue Print Recipe

Puff Pastry

8 oz. (2C) plain flour · pinch salt · water to mix (as cold as possible) · 8 oz. (1C) butter.* *preferably unsalted. Other fats could be substituted. Soften slightly with a knife if very hard.

To make Sieve the flour and salt into a mixing bowl. Gradually add enough water to make an elastic dough. Roll out to an oblong shape on a lightly floured board. Place the butter in the centre of the pastry dough, Sketch 1. Fold the bottom part of the dough over the butter, Sketch 2; bring down the top part, Sketch 3. Turn, seal the ends and 'rib' the pastry as described under flaky pastry (page 90). Continue rolling and folding as flaky pastry but allow a total of 7 rollings and 7 foldings. Puff pastry must be kept cool, so put away between rollings.

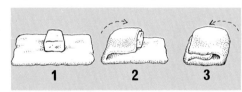

To cook As individual recipes, but puff pastry needs a very hot oven at the beginning of the cooking period. This enables it to rise well and prevents it being greasy. It is suggested sometimes that puff pastry is cooked on damp baking sheets but I have never found this necessary.

To serve Hot or cold. With sweet or savoury ingredients.

● **AVOID** *Overhandling the pastry—see the comments on page 90.*
● **TO RECTIFY** *See page 90.*
● **SHORT CUT** *Frozen puff pastry is one of the most successful convenience foods. Remember though that when a recipe says puff pastry made with 8 oz. (2C) flour etc., or 8 oz. puff pastry you need to buy 1 lb. frozen pastry.*

Puff Pastry

The following recipes all use puff pastry, several are equally successful with flaky or rough puff. An indication is given where the less rich pastries could be substituted.

Vanilla Slices (Mille Feuilles)

Puff pastry made with 8 oz. (2C) flour etc. as Blue Print. *For the filling*: $\frac{1}{2}$ pint ($1\frac{1}{3}$C) thick cream; sugar to taste; few drops vanilla essence; jam or jelly; little sieved icing sugar (optional).
Roll the pastry out until wafer thin. Cut into about 15 or 18 fingers. Put on to baking trays or sheets, leave in a cool place for about 30 minutes; this makes sure they keep a good

shape. Bake just above the centre of a very hot oven, 475°F, Gas Mark 8–9. Bake for approximately 10 minutes at this high temperature until well risen and golden, then lower the heat to very moderate or switch the oven off for about 5 minutes. Allow to cool, then trim the edges with a very sharp knife. Whip the cream, add a little sugar and vanilla essence. Spread one third of the slices with the cream, top with another slice, then the jam or jelly and a final pastry slice. Dust with sieved icing sugar. (Illustrated opposite.) *Makes 5 or 6.*
Note Flaky or rough puff are not as good in this recipe as puff pastry.
To vary The three layers of pastry gives a tall and very impressive slice, but two layers of pastry are often used, in which case spread the bottom layer of pastry with jam and then with cream and top with the second layer of pastry.
Coat the top of the slices with glacé icing.
Fill the slices with Vanilla cream (page 124) instead of whipped cream.

Maids of Honour

Puff, flaky or rough puff pastry made with 6 oz. ($1\frac{1}{2}$C) flour etc. (see above and page 90).
For the filling: little jam; 6 oz. ($\frac{3}{4}$C) cottage

cheese; 2 oz. (nearly $\frac{1}{3}$C) sultanas; $\frac{1}{2}$ teaspoon almond essence; 2 tablespoons ground or finely chopped almonds; 2 eggs. *For the topping*: 4 oz. (nearly 1C) icing sugar; little water; few drops almond essence.
Roll out the pastry until wafer thin. Cut into 12–15 rounds, to fit into fairly deep patty tins about 3-inches in diameter. When gathering-up the 'pieces' lay these carefully one over the other, and re-roll to use for some of the rounds. Do not squeeze into a ball, as this spoils the pastry. Put a teaspoon of jam into each pastry case. Sieve the cheese, add the other ingredients for the filling and beat well until a smooth mixture. Spoon into the pastry cases and bake for 10 minutes in the centre of a hot to very hot oven, 450–475°F, Gas Mark 7–8. Lower the heat to moderate and cook for a further 15 minutes, or until both pastry and filling are set. Allow to cool. Blend the icing sugar with enough water to make a flowing consistency. Add a few drops of almond essence. Spoon a little into the centre of each tartlet and leave to set. *Makes 12–15.*

Traditional Maids of Honour

Blend 4 oz. (1C) ground or finely chopped blanched almonds with 2 oz. ($\frac{1}{4}$C) caster sugar, the yolks of 2 small eggs and the white of 1 egg. Add 1 oz. plain flour or fine cake crumbs, then a teaspoon orange flower water or orange or lemon juice and a very little finely grated lemon rind. Use this filling in place of that given above. Do not ice.

Sausage Rolls

Puff, flaky or rough puff pastry made with 8 oz. (2C) flour etc.* (see above and page 80); 8–12 oz. sausagemeat. *To glaze*: 1 egg plus 1 tablespoon water.
*this gives a very thin layer of pastry only.
Roll out the pastry and cut into strips, these should be sufficiently wide to cover the sausagemeat. The pastry must be very thin if using the larger quantity of sausagemeat. Form the sausagemeat into long rolls. Lay on the pastry strips. Moisten the edges of the pastry and fold over the sausagemeat. Press the edges together and 'flake' these with the knife. Cut into the required lengths and make several slits on top if wished. Brush with the egg mixed with the water. Put on to baking sheets or trays and bake in the centre of a hot to very hot oven, 450–475°F, Gas Mark 7–8 for 10–15 minutes, then lower the heat to moderate and cook for another 5–10 minutes, depending upon the size of the sausage rolls. Serve hot or cold. *Makes 8 large, 12 medium-sized or about 18 tiny rolls.*

Storing and Freezing *See the comments on page 91 about uncooked pastry.*
Vanilla Slices freeze extremely well, but they should be served as soon as they have been defrosted at room temperature, otherwise the pastry becomes very soft.
Maids of Honour, Sausage Rolls etc., all freeze extremely well.

Maids of honour (above left) Vanilla slice (right)

Eggs in Sauces

An egg is an invaluable ingredient in many sauces. It adds flavour, food value and is either the sole thickening agent or helps the flour or cornflour to thicken the mixture. Although Zabaione (often known as Zabaglione) is really a complete dessert rather than just a sauce, I have given it on this page, for the principles of making this frothy egg mixture are the same as the Blue Print recipe.

● **AVOID** *Having the water under the mixture too hot; this is essential, otherwise the eggs could set or curdle, instead of being light and fluffy: Leaving the eggs without whisking, they could become hard around the sides of the cooking utensil.*

● **TO RECTIFY** *If the water begins to boil, remove from the heat and add a little cold water.*

● **SHORT CUT** *Soften the butter for the sauce, this means it is incorporated more readily.*

● **TO SLIMMERS** *Although no sauces can be 'slimming' the simple egg-thickened sauces are less fattening than those with a high percentage of flour.*

Hollandaise sauce with asparagus

Blue Print Recipe

Hollandaise Sauce

3 egg yolks · salt · pepper · cayenne pepper · 2 tablespoons lemon juice*· 3 oz. ($\frac{3}{8}$C) butter.
*Or use white wine vinegar.

To make   Put the egg yolks, seasoning and lemon juice into a basin over a pan of hot water or into the top of a double saucepan. Make sure the basin or alternative utensil is sufficiently large to be able to whisk well; a very narrow container hampers movement.
To cook   Beat with a hand or electric whisk until the mixture is light and fluffy. If using an electric whisk check that the egg mixture really is thickening well. To do this remove from the heat, if the eggs remain thick all is well. Sometimes one can whisk so vigorously that the mixture *appears* to thicken, then 'flops' as it has just been aerated, *not* cooked as it should be. When the eggs are thick, add a small piece of butter, whisk hard until well blended. Continue like this until all the butter is incorporated.
To serve   Hot or cold over vegetables or with fish. This is an excellent sauce for cauliflower or broccoli. *All recipes based on this serve 6–7.*

Rich Hollandaise Sauce

Ingredients as Blue Print recipe PLUS extra 3 oz. ($\frac{3}{8}$C) butter. Method as the Blue Print but use the larger amount of butter.

Fluffy Mayonnaise

Ingredients as Blue Print PLUS $\frac{1}{2}$ teaspoon *made* English or French mustard and $\frac{1}{2}$–1 teaspoon sugar. Method as Blue Print. Add the mustard and sugar with the other seasoning. Allow the sauce to cool, then fold 2–3 tablespoons whipped cream into the egg mixture. Taste the sauce then add extra seasoning and lemon juice if required.

To give a more pronounced flavour, add the finely grated rind of 1 lemon to the egg yolks.

Tartare Sauce

Ingredients as Blue Print PLUS 1–2 teaspoons capers, 2–3 teaspoons chopped parsley and 2–3 teaspoons chopped gherkins (or use freshly chopped cucumber).
Make as the Blue Print recipe, then add the ingredients above. This is delicious with any fish.

Zabaione

3 egg yolks; 2–3 oz. ($\frac{1}{4}$–$\frac{3}{8}$C) caster sugar; 3–4 tablespoons Marsala.
Put the egg yolks and sugar into the container, whisk as the Blue Print. When the mixture is thick, gradually whisk in the Marsala. Serve warm by itself as a dessert or over fruit. *Serves 2.*
To vary
Orange Zabaione   Add the finely grated rind of 1–2 oranges to the egg yolks and flavour with 1 tablespoon Curaçao and 2 tablespoons orange juice in place of the Marsala.

Storing and Freezing   *Although Hollandaise sauce can be stored for up to 24 hours it does lose some of its light texture. It can however be frozen very successfully, but use as soon as possible after defrosting. Zabaione is nicer served freshly made.*

seven

PUDDINGS & DESSERTS

Few forms of cooking are more interesting and rewarding than producing a delicious pudding or dessert, often with the minimum of effort, for some of the most interesting recipes are the simplest. The dessert 'rounds off' the meal and helps to turn it into something exciting and memorable.

Many people feel that the old traditional puddings are no longer as popular as they were. I think this may be true to some extent, for iced desserts have now become so popular and are simple to make with modern refrigerators or home freezers. I still find though that the majority of people also delight in a truly feather-light steamed sponge or suet pudding topped with fruit or syrup, and there is a varied selection on pages 96 and 97 with the points for successful results.

The sauces to accompany puddings are important, be original in your choice of ingredients and combination of flavourings, for example a coffee sauce is splendid with a chocolate pudding.

Fruit flans are always a delight to look at, as well as to eat. However, often a perfect fruit flan is spoiled because the cook is too impatient to put the ingredients together, the method on page 99 shows the right way to do this.

A baked or steamed custard may seem very homely fare but it is the basis of so many interesting and indeed quite exotic desserts. I have lost count of the number of people who ask me why custards curdle or why the pastry rises and the custard sinks in a tart. You will find the answers on page 105 in the BLUE PRINT and the recipe for a Custard Tart. On most pages I have given you a BLUE PRINT RECIPE,

for if you know how to make the simple basic dish, upon which so many other recipes are based, you have unlimited scope for imaginative and varied puddings.

Meringue, as well as being an essential part of Lemon Meringue Pie (page 106) is also a very useful standby for last minute desserts topped with cream and fruit. Store in air-tight tins.

With the development in freezing and excellent canning, practically every fruit can now be obtained in some form for most of the year, so fruit desserts should never be monotonous. A variety of these are on pages 101 and 102. For those of you who are watching your weight and counting calories the water ice recipes are very helpful in adding interest to a slimming diet. In fact on several pages you will find a special recipe, or adaptation of a recipe, that will enable you to eat a pudding and not 'upset' your diet.

The gâteau on page 110 may look ambitious but it is relatively easy to make and can be stored until ready to fill, or frozen complete with fillings.

The puddings on this page are light in texture. They are all based on a type of sponge mixture.

Blue Print Recipe

Vanilla Sponge Pudding

4 oz. ($\frac{1}{2}$C) butter or margarine · 4 oz. ($\frac{1}{2}$C) sugar · 2 eggs · 6 oz. (1$\frac{1}{2}$C) self-raising flour (or plain flour and 1$\frac{1}{2}$ level teaspoons baking powder) · few drops vanilla essence · 3 tablespoons milk.

To make Cream together the butter or margarine and sugar until soft and light. Whisk the eggs well and beat gradually into the butter mixture. Sieve the flour or flour and baking powder, mix the vanilla essence and milk. Fold the flour and milk alternately into the creamed mixture. Grease a 1$\frac{1}{2}$–2-pint (5C) basin, put in the mixture and cover with greased greaseproof paper or foil.

To cook Put into a steamer over boiling water or stand on an upturned patty tin (so the basin will not crack) in a pan half filled with boiling water. Cook for 1$\frac{1}{4}$–1$\frac{1}{2}$ hours, filling up with boiling water as necessary.

To serve Turn out on to a heated dish and serve with jam or hot marmalade or the fruit sauce on this page. *All recipes based on this dish serve 4–6.*

When making light sponge puddings:
● **AVOID** *Too slow cooking at the start, this can cause a heavy pudding.*
● **TO RECTIFY** *This is almost impossible if the pudding is really heavy; you can only camouflage it by serving with a super sauce.*

For Family Occasions

Lemon Pudding

Follow the Blue Print recipe but cream the finely grated rind of 1 lemon with the butter and sugar. Mix with lemon juice and milk to give 3 tablespoons. Cook as Blue Print. Serve with fruit sauce.

Fruit Sauce

Put the juice of 1 orange and 1 lemon into a saucepan, add 2 oz. ($\frac{1}{4}$C) sugar, 4 good tablespoons ($\frac{1}{2}$C) orange or lemon marmalade and 2 teaspoons cornflour or arrowroot blended with 4 tablespoons water. Stir well over a gentle heat until clear and slightly thickened.

Chocolate Pudding

Omit vanilla from Blue Print recipe and substitute 2 tablespoons chocolate powder in place of the same amount of flour. Cook as Blue Print. Serve with Rich Chocolate or Coffee Sauce below.

Coffee Sauce

Blend 1 tablespoon cornflour with $\frac{1}{4}$ pint ($\frac{2}{3}$C) *strong* coffee. Put into a saucepan with 2–3 tablespoons sugar, small knob butter and $\frac{1}{4}$ pint ($\frac{2}{3}$C) milk. Stir over a gentle heat until thickened.

For Special Occasions

Fudge Pudding

Follow the Blue Print recipe but add 1 extra oz. butter and sugar and use *brown* sugar in place of white and 1 tablespoon golden syrup. Reduce the amount of milk to 2 tablespoons. Coat the inside of the basin with a generous layer of butter and brown sugar. Cook as Blue Print. Serve with Rich Chocolate Sauce.

Rich Chocolate Sauce

Melt 4–6 oz. plain chocolate with $\frac{1}{4}$ pint ($\frac{2}{3}$C) thin cream in a basin over hot water or top of a double saucepan. Flavour with a little vanilla essence or brandy. For family occasions use milk in place of cream.

Nut and Pineapple Upside Down Cake

Follow the proportions for the Blue Print recipe but use 1 extra oz. butter and sugar. Melt 2 oz. ($\frac{1}{4}$C) butter in a 7–8-inch cake tin or oven-proof dish, top with 2 oz. ($\frac{1}{4}$C) brown sugar. Arrange a design of pineapple rings, pecan or halved walnuts and Maraschino cherries on the butter and sugar. Top with the sponge mixture. Bake in the centre of a very moderate oven, 325–350°F, Gas Mark 3–4, for about 1 hour. Turn out, serve hot or cold with cream.

Storing and Freezing Prepare—*store up to 12 hours in a refrigerator or wrap and freeze. Thaw, cook as recipe.* Cook—*store in a refrigerator from 1–2 days or wrap and freeze. Thaw and reheat.*
To use any left over *The upside down pudding is eaten cold as a cake. The other puddings should be re-steamed for 30 minutes.*

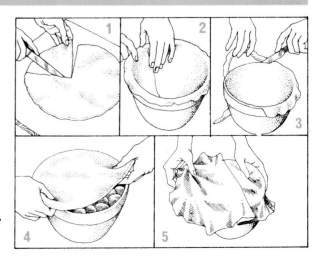

Nut and pineapple upside down cake

1. Roll out suet crust thinly to form a round large enough to fill the basin. Cut out $\frac{1}{4}$ of the round, put on one side for the lid.
2. Lower the $\frac{3}{4}$ into the greased basin, seal the joins together.
3. Trim the top of the pastry. Add these pieces to the $\frac{1}{4}$ reserved.
4. Fill the pastry with fruit. Roll out remaining crust into a neat round. Damp top edges of pastry with water. Seal firmly.
5. Cover with greased foil or greaseproof paper, with a 'pleat' in, to allow for the pudding rising during cooking.

Christmas pudding

For Family Occasions

Fruit Pudding

Roll out the suet crust pastry, made as Blue Print 1, line a 2-pint (5–6C) basin as Sketches 1–3. Fill with halved stoned plums or peeled and sliced apples or mixed berry fruits. Add sugar to taste and about 2 tablespoons water. Flavour apples with grated lemon rind or spice and a few sultanas or mix with blackberries. Cover the fruit with a 'lid' of pastry and foil or greaseproof paper as Sketches 4–5. Cook as directions in Blue Print on page 2, for about 2 hours. Turn out, sprinkle with sugar and serve hot with cream or custard sauce.

Toffee Sultana Pudding

Make the suet pudding as Blue Print 2, but add 4 oz. ($\frac{1}{2}$C) sultanas to the flour. Grease the basin, to be used for cooking the pudding, generously with butter, sprinkle with brown sugar and put 2 tablespoons golden syrup at the bottom. Add the suet pudding mixture, cover, as Sketch 5, and cook as the Blue Print recipe.

For Special Occasions

Traditional Christmas or Rich Fruit Pudding

Follow Blue Print 2, but use brown sugar, 2 eggs and $\frac{1}{4}$ pint ale or beer to mix; omit the milk. Sieve 1 teaspoon mixed spice, $\frac{1}{2}$ teaspoon powdered cinnamon and $\frac{1}{2}$ teaspoon grated nutmeg with the flour. ADD 12 oz. (1$\frac{1}{2}$C) seedless raisins, 4 oz. ($\frac{1}{2}$C) sultanas, 4 oz. ($\frac{1}{2}$C) currants, 4 oz. ($\frac{1}{2}$C) chopped candied peel, 2–4 oz. ($\frac{1}{4}$–$\frac{1}{2}$C) chopped, blanched almonds, 4 oz. ($\frac{2}{3}$C) grated cooking apple, grated rind and juice of 1 lemon and 2 tablespoons brandy or sherry.
Mix very thoroughly and divide between 2 or 3 greased basins. Cover as Sketch 5, and steam over boiling water, for a minimum of 5 hours. Remove the wet covers and put on dry foil or greaseproof paper. Store in a cool, dry place and cook for a further 2–3 hours on Christmas Day. If more convenient cook for the same length of time in a slow oven. Stand the basin in a larger container half-filled with cold water. Cover both the basin *and* the container with foil to prevent the water evaporating. Serve with Brandy Butter or Hard sauce. *Serves 8–10.*

Brandy Butter or Hard Sauce

Cream 2 oz. ($\frac{1}{4}$C) unsalted butter with 4 oz. ($\frac{3}{4}$C) sieved icing sugar. Gradually blend in 2 tablespoons brandy. Pile or pipe into a dish, decorate with blanched almonds and glacé cherries; chill thoroughly. *Serves 4–5.*

Golden Apricot Pudding

Make and cook as Christmas Pudding but use chopped apricots in place of raisins and currants and white wine in place of beer.

Steamed suet pudding

Suet Crust and Suet Puddings

Puddings made with suet crust pastry are almost more adaptable than any others, the pastry may be filled with some kind of fresh fruit during every month of the year. Suet puddings range from the simple Blue Print to a rich traditional Christmas recipe.

Blue Print Recipes

1. Suet Crust Pastry

8 oz. (2C) flour* · pinch salt · 4 oz. ($\frac{2}{3}$C loosely packed) chopped or shredded suet · water to mix.
*either self-raising to give a thicker crust, or plain flour for a thin crust.

To make Sieve the flour and salt together. Add the suet and enough water to give a soft rolling consistency.
To cook As the Blue Print on page 96 for about 2 hours.

2. Suet Pudding

4 oz. (1C) self-raising flour (or plain flour and 1 level teaspoon baking powder) · 4 oz. (1C) soft fine breadcrumbs · 4 oz. ($\frac{2}{3}$C) suet (see above) · 4 oz. ($\frac{1}{2}$C) sugar · 1 or 2 eggs · milk to mix.

To make Sieve the flour or flour and baking powder. Add the breadcrumbs, suet and sugar together with the beaten egg or eggs and enough milk to make a sticky consistency.
To cook Put into a well greased 2-pint (5–6C) basin. Cover well as Sketch 5. Steam as directions in Blue Print on page 96 for about 2 hours.
To serve Turned out, with a sauce of hot jam, marmalade, golden syrup or fruit purée.
All recipes based on these Blue Prints serve 4–6 except where stated differently.

● **AVOID** *Too slow cooking (except for Christmas puddings) and too dry a mixture. Always fill up the pan with boiling water.*
● **TO RECTIFY** *See page 96.*
Storing and Freezing *The plain puddings may be kept and frozen as those on page 96, but rich puddings mature better at room temperature.*
To use any left over *Re-steam, or cut Christmas pudding into neat slices, fry in a little butter, serve as fritters, sprinkled with sugar.*

Fruit Pies and Tarts

It is strange how confusing these two terms can be. In the past one could assume that when a British cook talked about 'making a pie' she would mean fruit (or some other food) would be put into a deep dish and topped with pastry, whereas a tart was a base of pastry with a topping of fruit or other food.

Nowadays these two words are used less rigidly as you will see from the recipes such as the Lemon Meringue Pie on page 106. A flan is similar to a tart but has a more perfect, and often deeper, shape.

The Blue Print recipe is for sweet short crust, although similar to short crust, the small quantity of sugar helps to give an added crispness to the pastry.

Blue Print Recipes

Sweet Short Crust Pastry

6 oz. (1½C) flour, preferably plain pinch salt · 3 oz. (⅜C) butter, margarine or fat · ½–1 tablespoon caster sugar · cold water to mix.

To make Sieve the flour and salt into a mixing bowl. Rub the butter, margarine or fat into the flour with your fingertips, as Sketch 1, until like fine breadcrumbs. Add the sugar, then *gradually* stir just over 1½ tablespoons water (or enough to bind the mixture) into the dough. Blend with a palette knife, gather together into a ball with the tips of your fingers but do not overhandle, see Sketch 2. Roll out the dough, use and cook as the recipes.

● **AVOID** *Over-handling the pastry: Using too much water, for this produces a dough that is over-sticky and difficult to handle, and a pastry that, when baked, is tough rather than crisp and short.*
● **TO RECTIFY** *If the pastry is damp and sticky, flour the pastry board and rolling pin generously, but this is not an ideal remedy as you alter the basic proportions.*
● **SHORT CUT** *Use frozen or packet short crust pastry. Mix sugar to packet mix before adding liquid, or sprinkle on frozen pastry as you roll it out.*

Fruit Pie

Use Blue Print recipe PLUS 1–1¼ lb. prepared fruit, a little water and sugar to taste. Make the pastry as the Blue Print. Prepare the fruit. Put into the pie dish; choose one which is small enough for the fruit to come to the top or use a pie support. Add about 4 tablespoons water with firm fruit or 1–2 tablespoons water with very ripe or soft fruit with sugar to taste. Roll out the pastry until sufficiently large to cover the pie and give an extra band round the edge of the dish. Moisten the rim of the pie dish with water, cut a long strip of pastry, and put on to the rim. Lift the rest of the pastry on to the top of the pie using the rolling pin for support, see Sketches 1 and 2 opposite. Press the edges lightly, cut away the surplus, and decorate as shown in the picture and Sketch 3. Fruit pies are left plain on top. Stand the pie dish on a baking tray,

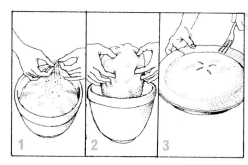

in case any juice should boil out. Bake in, or just above, the centre of a hot oven, 425°F, Gas Mark 6–7, for 15–20 minutes to set the pastry then lower the heat to very moderate to moderate, 350–375°F, Gas Mark 4–5, for a further 20–25 minutes to make sure the fruit is cooked. *Serves 4–5.*

Fruit Tarts

Use the Blue Print or the fleur pastry opposite. Roll out the pastry and line small or medium-sized individual tins. Prick the pastry with a fork and bake 'blind', see opposite, until golden brown. Cool, then either fill with fruit and glaze as for a fruit flan opposite, or put a layer of whipped cream in the bottom of the case and top with fresh fruit, such as raspberries, strawberries or blackberries.

Storing and Freezing *Fruit Flans, opposite, and tarts are better eaten fresh. They can be frozen, but the filling tends to soften the pastry as they defrost. Pies keep well when frozen; thaw before reheating.*

Fruit tarts
Simple fruit pie

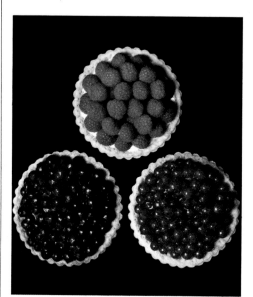

Cherry flan

There are various types of pastry you can use for the flan case but fleur pastry, often called flan or biscuit crust, combines best with the fruit and glaze.

Blue Print Recipe

Fleur Pastry

Sufficient for one 8-inch flan ring: 3 oz. ($\frac{3}{8}$C) butter or best quality margarine · 2 oz. ($\frac{1}{4}$C) caster sugar · 1 egg yolk · 6 oz. ($1\frac{1}{2}$C) flour, preferably plain · little cold water.

To make Cream the butter or margarine and sugar until soft and light. Beat in the egg yolk, add the sieved flour and blend with a palette knife. Gradually stir in enough water to bind. Roll out to a circle about 10 inches in diameter.

If using a sandwich tin grease lightly. If using a flan ring stand on an upturned baking tray or sheet.

Putting the rolling pin under the pastry to support it, lower into the tin or flan ring, see Sketch 1. Slip the rolling pin away as you do so, Sketch 2. Press the pastry into the case with your fingers.

Either cut away any surplus pastry with a sharp knife, or else take the rolling pin backwards and forwards over the pastry, as Sketch 3.

To cook To keep the flan case a perfect shape it should be weighted to prevent the pastry base rising and the sides losing their shape, this is called 'baking blind'. The two best methods to use are either to prick the base of the flan case, then put in a double thickness of foil and press firmly against the pastry. Or grease a round of greaseproof paper lightly and place greased side downwards into the flan case. Fill with dried haricot beans or crusts of bread, see Sketch 4.

Bake in the centre of a moderate to moderately hot oven, 375–400°F, Gas Mark 5–6, for 15–20 minutes, or until the pastry is just set. Remove the foil, or paper and beans or bread, then continue baking for a further 5–10 minutes until golden brown. Lift away the flan ring and if the pastry is a little pale return to the oven for a few minutes. Cool slightly, put on to a wire cooling tray. When cold fill and glaze.

To Fill the Flan

You will need about 1 lb. of fruit. If using *cooked fruit*, poach carefully (as page 101). Lift from the syrup and put in a sieve over a bowl. Retain the syrup. *Canned fruit* should be drained in the same way. *Frozen fruit* should be *almost* defrosted, then drained as above. It spoils the appearance and taste of *ripe cherries, raspberries and strawberries* if they are poached in syrup. Make a syrup from sugar and water (see page 101). Put the fruit into the syrup while it is still warm. Leave for 2–3 minutes, lift out and strain as above. Put the drained fruit into the flan case carefully.

To Make the Glaze

If the flan case is fairly shallow use $\frac{1}{4}$ pint ($\frac{2}{3}$C) syrup, but if it is fairly deep, use $\frac{1}{2}$ pint ($1\frac{1}{3}$C). Blend the syrup with 1 or 2 teaspoons arrowroot or cornflour. Put into the saucepan, stir well and cook until thickened. Add a few drops of colouring if necessary, or about 2 tablespoons red currant jelly or sieved raspberry jam for extra flavour. When thickened and clear, cool but do not allow to set. Brush or spread over the fruit, see Sketch 5. *Serves 6.*

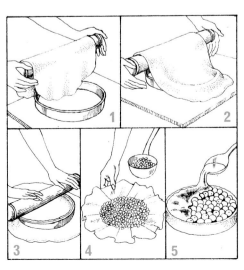

Charlottes and Crumbles

Contrasting textures in food add interest to many dishes and both Fruit Charlottes and Crumbles are excellent examples of combining ultra crisp toppings and soft fruit. They are quick and easy to make and ideal for family or special occasions.

Blue Print Recipes

1. Fruit Charlotte or Brown Betty

$1-1\frac{1}{4}$ lb. prepared fruit · little water · sugar to taste. For the charlotte mixture: 4–5 large slices bread · 3 oz. ($\frac{3}{8}$C) butter or margarine · 2 oz. ($\frac{1}{4}$C) sugar (preferably brown).

To make If using firm fruit, such as apples, plums, etc., cook in a covered saucepan with a *little* water and sugar to taste until softened. Berry fruit (such as raspberries, loganberries, etc.) may also be cooked first, but if you prefer these to remain firm then do not heat.

There are two ways of making a charlotte. The first is to remove the crusts and then cut the bread into neat fingers; the second method is to make fairly coarse crumbs from the bread. Heat the butter or margarine in a large frying pan and fry the bread in this until just golden coloured. Put one third of the bread slices or crumbs into a pie or oven-proof dish, sprinkle with some of the sugar. Add half the fruit purée. If using uncooked soft fruit sprinkle with sugar. Put a second layer of bread and a sprinkling of sugar, then the rest of the fruit purée or fruit and sugar. Top with an even layer of bread and sugar.
To cook Bake for about 35–40 minutes in the centre of a moderate oven 350–

375°F, Gas Mark 4–5.
To serve In the dish or invert this on to a hot serving plate and decorate with cooked or raw fruit.
To vary See below under Crumble.

2. Fruit Crumble

$1-1\frac{1}{4}$ lb. prepared fruit · little water · sugar to taste. For the crumble: 4 oz. (1C) flour* · 2 oz. ($\frac{1}{4}$C) butter or margarine · 2–3 oz. ($\frac{1}{4}-\frac{1}{3}$C) sugar.
*can be plain or self-raising.

To make Put the fruit into a pie or oven-proof dish. If cooking soft berry fruit use no water or about 1 tablespoon if very firm; with harder fruit use 3–4 tablespoons. Add sugar to sweeten. Cook gently in the oven for 10–15 minutes. If you prefer berry fruit to be firm, do *not* cook this before adding the crumble topping. Sieve the flour, rub in the butter or margarine, add the sugar. Sprinkle over the top of the fruit.
To cook Bake in the centre of a moderate oven 350–375°F, Gas Mark 4–5, for 25–30 minutes until crisp and golden brown.
To serve In the baking dish, with cream or custard sauce. It is nicer served hot rather than cold. *All recipes based on these Blue Prints serve 4–5.*
To vary Sieve $\frac{1}{2}$–1 teaspoon ground ginger, cinnamon or other spice with the flour, or add the grated rind of 1 or 2 oranges or lemons. Use the same flavourings in the charlotte and either mix with the crumbs and sugar or sprinkle over the fingers of bread, after frying.

● **AVOID** *Too much fat in a crumble mixture, this prevents it becoming crisp: Too much liquid when cooking the fruit, this will spoil both the appearance and texture of the topping.*
● **TO RECTIFY** *If you find the fruit is too soft strain away surplus moisture before adding the topping.*
● **SHORT CUT** *Use canned fruit or canned fruit pie filling.*

Apricot fruit crumble (above right)
Cornflake Brown Betty (left)

Cornflake Brown Betty
Use Blue Print 1, but substitute 4–5 oz. ($3-3\frac{3}{4}$C) cornflakes for the breadcrumbs. Toss the cornflakes lightly in the hot butter or margarine then mix with the sugar. Bake as Blue Print 1.

Coconut Crumble
Ingredients as Blue Print 2 PLUS 2 oz. desiccated coconut.
Make the crumble, then add the coconut. Bake as Blue Print 2.

For Special Occasions

Choose the 'luxury' fruits for either the Fruit Charlotte or Crumble.

Apple Raisin Brown Betty
Use Blue Print 1 PLUS 4 oz. ($\frac{1}{2}$C) seedless or stoned raisins, 1 good tablespoon brandy or lemon juice and 2 tablespoons blanched chopped almonds.
Follow the Blue Print, but mix the raisins and brandy or lemon juice with the cooked fruit (in this case apples) and blend the chopped almonds with the breadcrumbs, before tossing in the hot butter or margarine. Bake as Blue Print 1 and serve with Hard Sauce (see page 97).

Chocolate Chip Crumble
Ingredients as Blue Print 2 PLUS 3 oz. plain chocolate.
Prepare the crumble as the Blue Print, add the coarsely grated or chopped chocolate with the sugar. Bake as Blue Print 2, but take care not to over-cook, to avoid scorching.

Storing and Freezing *Both Charlottes and Crumbles may be made over-night, stored in a cool place and cooked as the recipe. They may be frozen, wrapped and stored for 2–3 months. Thaw out before cooking or re-heating.*

One of the simplest and most enjoyable desserts is fresh fruit. Serve it plain or with cream or ice cream, or give additional flavour with a liqueur, wine or other fruit juice (see page 102). Other fruits are better cooked and it is important that they retain colour, texture and flavour by careful cooking. In either case it is important that the fruit is well prepared and given interesting flavours.

To Prepare and Flavour Fruit

Wash in cold, not hot water and use immediately after washing.

Apples and Pears Peel thinly unless retaining peel on eating apples. Core and slice. Both these fruit discolour easily, so sprinkle with lemon juice or keep in cold water until ready to use or cook. Flavour with spices, dried fruit, lemon rind and/or juice or cook with sliced quince.

Apricots and Plums Halve or use whole. Flavour with lemon juice.

Bananas If using raw sprinkle with lemon juice to prevent discoloration.

Blackcurrants Remove from stalks singly, or as redcurrants.

Cherries Choose cooking or black cherries when possible. Flavour with almond essence or Maraschino.

Gooseberries Top and tail, i.e. remove stalk and flower ends with kitchen scissors. Flavour with finely grated orange rind, 1–2 leaves of Ivy geranium and/or a little white wine.

Grapes Split carefully, remove pips, skin if wished, use raw.

Oranges and Citrus Fruits Cut away peel with the pith. Do this over a basin to retain the juice, Sketch 1. Cut the segments of fruit

between the skin and discard any pips, Sketch 2. When all the fruit has been removed squeeze pith and skin remaining to extract any juice.

Raspberries Prepare and flavour as directions for strawberries.

Redcurrants Pull the fruit very carefully from the stalk with the prongs of a fork. A delicious dessert can be made by flavouring redcurrants with vanilla sugar and leaving for 1 hour; stir once or twice. This is particularly good as a topping on sliced fresh peaches.

Rhubarb Cut into neat lengths. Flavour with orange rind, sultanas and/or spices.

Strawberries Remove stalks i.e. 'hull' them. Flavour with wine but other additions are unnecessary.

Blue Print Recipe

Compôte of Fruit

Water (see method) · sugar (see method) · approximately 1 lb. prepared fruit.

To make Allow between $\frac{1}{4}$–$\frac{1}{2}$ pint ($\frac{2}{3}$–$1\frac{1}{3}$C) water and 2–4 oz. ($\frac{1}{4}$–$\frac{1}{2}$C) sugar to cook very firm fruit, such as hard plums, or half the quantity of water for soft fruit, such as blackcurrants.

To cook Put the water and sugar into a large pan, stir until the sugar has dissolved. Put in the prepared fruit, lower the heat,

cover the pan to prevent the liquid evaporating and simmer gently until tender. This varies a great deal, firm fruit takes 10–20 minutes, soft fruit about 5 minutes.

Another way of cooking soft fruit is to put this, and sugar to taste, in the top of a double saucepan and cook over hot water until tender. This is particularly suitable for forced rhubarb, blackcurrants and raspberries.

If preferred the fruit may be cooked in a covered casserole in a very moderate oven, 325°F, Gas Mark 2–3. It is best to make the sugar and water syrup in a pan, put this into a warm casserole and *then* add the fruit. In this way you retain more colour.

To serve Hot or cold with cream, custard or ice cream. *Serves 4–6.*

● **AVOID** *Putting the sugar, water and fruit in the pan at the same time if you wish to keep the fruit in good shape: Too rapid cooking softens the outside of the fruit before the centre is tender.*

● **TO RECTIFY** *If you find the fruit is cooking too rapidly remove the pan from the heat, cover with a tightly fitting lid, and let the fruit continue cooking in the steam retained in the pan.*

● **SHORT CUT** *By cutting fruit in smaller pieces you shorten the cooking time but run the risk of it becoming over-soft and looking less attractive.*

● **TO SLIMMERS** *Make as much use of fruit desserts as possible, particularly the citrus fruits. Use sugar substitute instead of sugar for sweetening fruit salad.*

To Cook Dried Fruit

Cover 8 oz. (1C) dried fruit with $\frac{1}{2}$ pint ($1\frac{1}{3}$C) cold water and soak overnight. If preferred give additional flavour by soaking in cider or white wine, or add lemon juice to apples, pears and apricots, weak tea to prunes and weak coffee to figs. Tenderized fruit does not need soaking. Add sugar to taste and simmer until tender. The time varies, some tenderized fruit will need only $\frac{1}{2}$–$\frac{3}{4}$ hour. Others are better given longer.

Fresh fruit salad

here is infinite variety in a fresh fruit salad depending on the time of the year. Try to have a good blending of colour and texture, i.e. add firm apple and pear slices to balance the softness of oranges and bananas. The easiest way to prepare a fruit salad is, as the picture on this page, to blend canned and fresh fruit. Choose canned pineapple or peaches with fresh oranges, apples, grapes and pears. The syrup from the can provides the liquid. If preferred sweeten with fresh orange juice, or make a sugar and water syrup as the Blue Print and flavour with pieces of orange rind or a liqueur. A fruit salad is suitable for family or special occasions.

More Fruit Desserts

Fruit is so adaptable that it can be used in a great variety of ways and pages 98-101 cover some of these.

One of the best simple fruit desserts is a Baked Apple, and since this can be varied in innumerable ways I have made it one of my Blue Prints on this page.

Blue Print Recipes

1. Baked Apples

4 medium-sized to large cooking apples · approximately 1 tablespoon brown or white sugar.

To make Core the apple, do this either with an apple corer or a pointed knife. In order to prevent the skin 'bursting' during cooking either slit this round the centre or cut as in the picture. Put the apples into an oven-proof dish, fill the centres with sugar.
To cook Bake for approximately 1 hour in the centre of a moderate oven, 350–375°F, Gas Mark 4–5, or allow 15 minutes longer in a very moderate oven, 325°F, Gas Mark 2–3.
To serve The skin may be left on the apples unless planning either of the last two variations below. Serve with custard sauce, cream or ice cream. *All recipes based on this dish serve 4.*

2. Fruit in Rum

2 oz. ($\frac{1}{4}$C) butter · 2 oz. ($\frac{1}{4}$C) brown sugar · 2–3 tablespoons orange juice · 2–3 tablespoons rum · fruit (see method).
To make and cook Heat the butter and sugar in a frying pan stirring until the sugar has dissolved. Add the orange juice and rum, stir to make a syrup. Put 4 halved bananas or skinned peaches, or 8 apricots into the syrup and simmer gently for 10 minutes.
To serve Hot with cream. *All recipes based on this dish serve 4.*
Storing and Freezing *Most of the dishes on pages 101 and 102 may be kept a day or two in a refrigerator, but do not freeze well.*

● **AVOID** *Cooking the apples too quickly, this gives an ultra-soft outside before the fruit is cooked through to the centre.*
● **TO RECTIFY** *If you find the fruit cooking too quickly lower the heat or move the dish to a cooler part of the oven.*

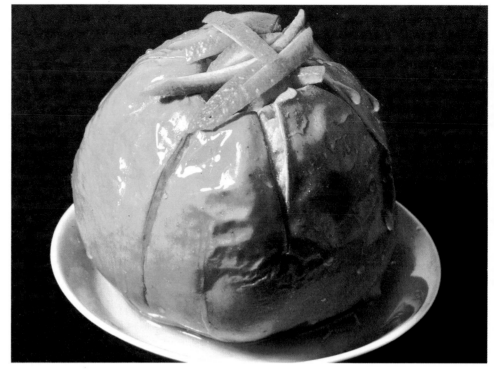
Baked apple with orange filling

For Family Occasions

Orange Filling
As Blue Print 1 MINUS the sugar. Blend 2–3 tablespoons of orange marmalade with the finely grated rind of 1–2 oranges and approximately 2 tablespoons orange juice.
Put into apples before cooking. While the apples are cooking, cut neat pieces of fresh orange (as page 101). Remove the apples from the oven a few minutes before serving, spoon the orange segments on top, return to the oven to heat, or omit orange pieces and decorate with strips of rind as in the picture.

Ginger-Apricot Filling
As Blue Print 1 MINUS sugar. Blend 2–3 tablespoons of apricot jam with 1–2 tablespoons chopped preserved ginger.
Put into apples and cook as the Blue Print. Serve with cream which may be flavoured with a little syrup from the preserved·ginger.

Coconut-Fudge Filling
As Blue Print 1 (choose brown sugar), PLUS 1 oz. butter and 2–3 tablespoons desiccated coconut.
Prepare the apples as the Blue Print but mix the sugar with the butter and coconut. Put into the centre of the apples and cook as the Blue Print.

For Special Occasions

Macaroon Apples
As Blue Print 1 PLUS 2 tablespoons ground almonds, 2 eggs, almond essence, 2 oz. ($\frac{1}{4}$C) caster sugar and 1 tablespoon chopped blanched almonds.

Prepare the apples as the Blue Print. Blend the ground almonds with the sugar in the Blue Print, egg yolks and a few drops of almond essence. Put into the centre of the apples and cook as the Blue Print. Remove the apple skins. Whisk the egg whites until very stiff, gradually whisk in the caster sugar. Spread over the apples. Top with the almonds then return to the oven for a few minutes. Serve at once.

Coconut Apples
Follow the recipe for the Coconut-Fudge filling. When the apples are cooked remove from oven, take off the skins and coat with desiccated coconut.

Baked Oranges
4 large or 8 medium-sized oranges; 1 oz. butter; 2 oz. ($\frac{1}{4}$C) brown sugar, 1–2 tablespoons sherry or rum; 4 glacé cherries.
Cut the peel and pith from the oranges. Cut into thick slices then put together again as Sketch 3, page 101, with cocktail sticks. Put into an oven-proof dish. Spread the softened butter on the top of the oranges, sprinkle with the sugar and add the sherry or rum. Bake for 30 minutes as Blue Print 1. Decorate with the cherries, serve hot.

Luxury Touches with Fresh Fruit
Prepare the fruit, put·into a dish with wine, liqueur or fruit juice, see below, and leave for about 1 hour. Do not add sugar as everyone differs in the amount of sweetening they like. Some combinations you might like to try are strawberries in white wine; sliced ripe peaches in a mixture of white wine and crème de menthe; sliced fresh pineapple sprinkled with kirsch or apricot brandy; sliced bananas in orange juice and Curaçao.

Gelatine, obtainable both in sheet and powder form, can be used to set clear liquids such as fruit juices, fruit purées, milk and/or cream mixtures. However, it is not always used as successfully as it might be, so Blue Print 1 covers the correct way to dissolve and incorporate it into other foods. Commercial jellies are favourites with all the family and make interesting dishes with the minimum expenditure of time and trouble.

Jellies of All Kinds

Blue Print Recipe

1. To use Gelatine

The instructions on the packet will give exact quantities. Generally one uses 1 envelope, which is $\frac{1}{2}$ oz. or 1 tablespoon to 1 pint ($2\frac{2}{3}$C) clear liquid or half this quantity for thickened liquids (see page 109), or the equivalent in sheet gelatine.

To dissolve Put the gelatine into a basin, add 2–3 tablespoons *cold* liquid from the 1 pint ($2\frac{2}{3}$C). Stand the basin in, or over, a pan of hot water, leave until the gelatine has dissolved. There is no need to stir *as the gelatine softens*, do this just before blending with the other ingredients. Heat the remainder of the liquid, pour over the gelatine, stir until well blended.

To set Rinse a mould or basin in cold water, leave damp. Pour in the jelly, when set invert on to a *damp* serving dish. This means you

can slide the jelly easily into the centre of the dish. *All recipes based on this serve 4.*

Blue Print Recipe

2. Fruit Filled Jelly

1 packet jelly · water and fruit juice or syrup from a can · canned, cooked or fresh fruit.

Read the instructions on the packet for the exact amount of water or liquid required; this varies slightly according to different makes. If using canned or cooked fruit strain off the syrup, dilute with water to make up to the quantity given on the packet *less* about 1 tablespoon. This is because the fruit is moist and will dilute the strength of the jelly. If using fresh fruit such as bananas or berries you can use the full quantity of water because these are firm. If you wish to use a little fresh orange or lemon juice then this counts as part of the total amount.

Dissolve the jelly according to the instruc-

tions. Pour a little into the rinsed mould (see Blue Print 1). Allow this to become nearly set and arrange the first layer of fruit on top. It is easier to do this if you dip the fruit in liquid jelly. When set pour over a little more jelly and continue filling the mould like this to give an interesting design. Allow to set and turn out as Blue Print 1.

● **AVOID** *Adding gelatine to hot liquids, soften first (see Blue Print 1).*
● **TO RECTIFY** *If gelatine does not dissolve well, due to putting it into hot liquid without softening, allow to stand until cool, stir well and reheat gently.*
● **SHORT CUT** *To speed the setting of jellies use some crushed ice instead of the same quantity of water.*
● **TO SLIMMERS** *Many jelly recipes are suitable for low calorie desserts. Use sugar substitute instead of sugar.*

Fresh Orange Jelly
2–3 large oranges; 1 small lemon; water; 2–3 oz. ($\frac{1}{4}-\frac{3}{8}$C) sugar; 1 tablespoon gelatine.
Pare the rind from the oranges and lemon, put into a saucepan with about $\frac{1}{2}$ pint ($1\frac{1}{3}$C) water. Simmer for 10 minutes, strain, add sugar while hot. Squeeze the juice from the fruit and measure. The juice *plus* fruit liquid should give 1 pint ($2\frac{2}{3}$C). Soften the gelatine in a little cold liquid as Blue Print 1. Heat the rest of the liquid, pour over the gelatine mixture. Stir until dissolved, then follow Blue Print 1 for setting and turning out the jelly.

Fresh Lemon Jelly
Recipe as above but use 2 large or 3 medium-sized lemons.
You will note I added a lemon to the orange jelly above. You may like to omit this but it does *not* conflict with the orange flavour, and it seems to give a more refreshing jelly.

Jellied Fruit Snow
$\frac{1}{2}$ pint ($1\frac{1}{3}$C) thick sweetened fruit purée*; 1 teaspoon powdered gelatine; 2 tablespoons water or fresh fruit juice; $\frac{1}{4}$ pint ($\frac{2}{3}$C) thick cream; 3 egg whites.
*in the picture apple purée was used and tinted with a little green colouring.
Warm the purée gently, soften the gelatine in the water or fruit juice as Blue Print 1. Mix with the purée, stir until dissolved. Allow to

cool, fold in half the lightly whipped cream and 2 stiffly beaten egg whites. Spoon into 4–6 serving glasses and allow to set lightly (this will never be sufficiently stiff to turn out). Whip the remainder of the cream and the third egg white in separate basins, fold together and pile on top of the dessert. Decorate with lemon slices if wished. *Serves 4–6.*

Gooseberry Sparkle
Method as Blue Print 2. Choose canned gooseberries and a lime jelly. Decorate with whipped cream, chopped glacé cherries and chopped crystallised ginger.

Gooseberry sparkle

Jellied fruit snow

Egg Custards

Eggs or egg yolks have the ability to thicken liquids (generally milk), to make either a pouring sauce, or quite a firm pudding. The higher the proportion of eggs used, the more solid the result, 2 eggs or egg yolks and 1 pint (2⅔C) milk produces a lightly set custard or a custard sauce, however, 4 eggs or 2 whole eggs and 2 egg yolks, or 5 egg yolks and 1 pint (2⅔C) liquid will give a custard sufficiently firm to turn out of the dish such as the Caramel Custard on the opposite page.

Blue Print Recipe

Baked Egg Custard

1 pint (2⅔C) milk · 2 eggs · 1 oz. sugar · nutmeg.

To make Heat the milk but do not let it boil; it should be about blood temperature. Beat the eggs and sugar together, then add the hot milk, stirring all the time.

To cook Strain into a greased pie dish, grate a little nutmeg on top. Stand the dish in a 'bain-marie', i.e. another dish containing cold water, and bake in the coolest part of a slow oven, 275–300°F, Gas Mark 1–2, for approximately 45 minutes to 1 hour until the mixture is set.

To serve In the pie dish. It is not sufficiently firm to turn out. This can be a pudding by itself or it can be served with cooked fruit. *All recipes based on this dish serve 4–5.*

● **AVOID** *Over-heating, which causes the mixture to curdle (separate). You can see when this has happened by the 'watery' liquid in the dish: Pastry rising and custard sinking in a custard tart. The recipe gives the best way of preventing this, i.e. to bake the pastry 'blind' first and then to pour in the hot custard mixture.*

● **TO RECTIFY** *Whisk sharply, this is quite often effective in a sauce. If unsuccessful emulsify in a liquidiser. This gives a thinner mixture. If time permits whisk in an extra egg or egg yolk, cook again to thicken. The only other alternative is to spoon the pudding carefully from the dish, leaving the 'watery' liquid behind.*

● **SHORT CUT** *Make a sauce with custard powder or cornflour, when thickened add an egg or egg yolk. Simmer gently for 2–3 minutes only.*

Fruit queen of puddings

For Family Occasions

Custard Sauce

Ingredients as Blue Print. Strain the custard into the top of a double saucepan, or basin balanced on a pan, over *hot* but not boiling water. Cook gently, stirring well, until the custard coats the back of a wooden spoon. If serving cold cover with damp greaseproof paper to prevent a skin forming.

Custard Tart

Sweet short crust pastry made with 6 oz. (1½C) flour, etc. (page 98). Half ingredients as Blue Print (i.e. ½ pint (1⅓C) milk, etc., but use 2 eggs for a firmer filling).

Line a 7–8 inch flan case or a sandwich tin with the pastry. Bake 'blind' (see page 99) in the centre of a hot oven, 425–450°F, Gas Mark 6–7, for 10 minutes to set the pastry and prevent it rising. Prepare the custard as the Blue Print, strain the hot custard into the hot pastry case, top with grated nutmeg. Lower the heat to very moderate, 325–350°F, Gas Mark 3–4, cook for a further 35–40 minutes until the custard is set. Serve hot or cold.

Small custard tarts are made in the same way. Set the pastry cases for 5 minutes, fill with custard, cook for 20–25 minutes.

Bread and Butter Pudding

Ingredients as Blue Print PLUS 4 large slices bread and butter, 2–4 oz. (¼–½C) dried fruit and 1 extra tablespoon sugar.

Cut the bread and butter into triangles. Put into a pie dish with the fruit. Strain over custard and top with the sugar and grated nutmeg, if wished. Bake as Blue Print.

For Special Occasions

Snow Eggs or Floating Islands

Ingredients as Blue Print PLUS 2 oz. (¼C) caster sugar and a few drops vanilla essence or a vanilla pod.

Pour the milk into a shallow pan or deep frying pan. Separate the eggs. Whisk the egg whites stiffly, cover the egg yolks to prevent them from drying. Gradually whisk the caster sugar into the egg whites. Heat the milk to about 190°F, i.e. until simmering. Drop spoonfuls of the meringue mixture on top of the hot milk, poach for 2 minutes. Turn with a perforated spoon, or fish slice, and poach for the same time on the second side. Lift the meringues from the milk, drain on a large sieve. Meanwhile strain the milk on to the beaten egg yolks and sugar. Add the vanilla essence or pod. Cook as custard sauce on this page. If using a vanilla pod remove this. Pour into a shallow dish, cool, top with meringue balls.

Fruit Queen of Puddings

2 tablespoons jam; 2 oz. (½C) soft breadcrumbs; 2 eggs; ¾ pint (2C) milk; 3 oz. (⅜C) caster sugar; 3 tablespoons fresh or canned fruit.

Spread half the jam in an oven-proof dish. Add the crumbs. Separate the egg yolks and make the custard as Blue Print using the yolks, milk and 1 oz. sugar. Pour over the crumbs and bake as the Blue Print, until firm. Spread with the jam and most of the fruit. Whip egg whites until very stiff, fold in remaining sugar. Pile on to the custard and top with the remaining fruit. Bake for 15 minutes in a moderate oven, 375°F, Gas Mark 4–5. Serve hot.

More Egg Custards

As caramel combines well with egg custards, a caramel sauce is the Blue Print on this page.

Blue Print Recipe

Caramel Sauce

3 tablespoons granulated or caster sugar (or equivalent in loaf sugar) · 3 tablespoons water.

To make Put the sugar and water into a strong saucepan.
To cook Stir over a low heat until the sugar has dissolved. If the sugar and water splash against the sides of the saucepan brush with a pastry brush dipped in cold water. This helps to prevent the mixture crystallising. Allow the sugar and water syrup to boil steadily until golden brown, then use in individual recipes.

● **AVOID** *Leaving the sugar and water until the sugar has dissolved, stir all the time. When the sugar has dissolved do not stir, or you will hinder the syrup reaching the right temperature and it could crystallise and never become brown: Too dark a coloured caramel, this tastes unpleasantly bitter: Adding milk to the very hot caramel, this could cause curdling.*
● **TO RECTIFY** *Add a little more water if mixture crystallises. Stir until a clear syrup, proceed as usual: If the caramel is going too dark, immediately add 2 tablespoons cold water or put pan into cold water to lower the temperature.*
● **SHORT CUT** *Use 3 tablespoons golden syrup instead of 3 tablespoons sugar. Do not add water. Brown the syrup for a very few minutes.*

Storing and Freezing *All the recipes on these two pages keep for 2–3 days in a refrigerator. Only the Crème Brûlée can be frozen because it contains a high percentage of cream.*

For Family Occasions

Caramel Custard or Crème Renversée
Caramel as Blue Print PLUS 1–2 tablespoons water, custard made with 4 eggs, 1 tablespoon sugar and 1 pint (2⅔C) milk.
Make the caramel as the Blue Print. When golden brown add the extra water and heat. Coat a 7–8-inch, oval or round oven-proof dish with the caramel. Make the custard as the Blue Print opposite. Strain into the dish. Bake as Blue Print but allow 1½–2 hours until firm. Cool for about 10 minutes, invert on to a serving dish. *Serves 4–6.*

For Special Occasions

Crème Brûlée
Caramel as Blue Print PLUS ½ pint (1⅓C) milk, 4 eggs, 1 tablespoon sugar, ½ pint (1⅓C) thick cream. *For the topping:* 2 tablespoons blanched almonds, 2 tablespoons sieved icing sugar.
Make the caramel as the Blue Print. Leave in the saucepan, cool slightly. Add the milk, heat gently until blended with the caramel. Beat the eggs with the sugar and cream, add the caramel and milk. Strain into an oven-proof or soufflé dish. This can either be a deep dish, as in the Caramel Custard above, or you can cook it in a shallow dish, as in the photograph, in which case you may like to use a little extra topping. Bake as Blue Print on the opposite page, allowing 1½–2 hours until firm. Top with almonds and sugar and brown for a few minutes under the grill. *Serves 4–6*

Coconut Meringue
Ingredients as Blue Print opposite PLUS 3 tablespoons desiccated coconut, 2 tablespoons glacé cherries, 2 tablespoons apricot jam and 2 tablespoons caster sugar.
Separate the egg yolks and whites. Make the custard as the Blue Print opposite with the egg yolks only. Pour on to 2 tablespoons coconut. Leave for 30 minutes. Add most of the chopped glacé cherries. Pour into a pie dish and bake as Blue Print. Spread with the jam. Whip the egg whites until very stiff, fold in the caster sugar. Pile this on the custard. Top with the rest of the coconut and glacé cherries. Return to the oven for 20–25 minutes. Serve hot with cream.

Chestnut Meringue
Substitute sliced marrons glacés for the coconut in the above recipe.

To use any left over *Eat cold, or emulsify the plain or caramel custard in a liquidiser. They make a delicious sauce to serve with fruit. Any left over egg whites can be used for meringues (see page 106).*

Crème brûlée (above left)
Caramel custard or crème renversée (below)

Meringues

A meringue topping on a dessert, as the Lemon and Lime Meringue Pies illustrated, gives a look of luxury as well as a pleasant taste. Meringues are also one of the best 'stand-by's' in a tin. Small meringues may be sandwiched together with cream or ice cream, or a large meringue case may be turned into a party gâteau.

Blue Print Recipe

Meringue

2 egg whites · 4 oz. ($\frac{1}{2}$C) caster sugar (or use half caster and half sieved icing sugar).

To make   First check that the bowl is free from grease and that the egg whites are not too cold. If you have brought them out of the refrigerator allow to stand an hour before whisking.

Separate the egg yolks from the whites, cover the yolks with a little cold water to prevent hardening, store in a cool place until they may be used. Check no yolk has gone into the whites. If there is a particle remove with the half egg shell as a scoop, or the corner of a damp, clean tea towel or damp kitchen paper.

Whisk the egg whites until very stiff. If they seem slow in whisking, after taking the precautions above, then it may be the kitchen is too hot, so move to an open window.

To test   The egg whites are sufficiently stiff when they stand up in peaks and you can turn the bowl upside down without the mixture moving.

There are several ways of incorporating the sugar. The best way is *gradually* to beat in *half* the sugar, then fold in the remainder gently and slowly. A softer meringue is given if you *gradually* fold in *all* the sugar and a very firm meringue (only successful if you have a mixer) is obtained if you *gradually* beat in *all* the sugar.

To cook   As individual recipes.

● **AVOID** *Adding the sugar until the egg whites are* really *stiff (see the Blue Print): Adding the sugar too rapidly: Baking the meringue mixture too quickly, unless serving hot.*

● **TO RECTIFY** *If egg whites are not becoming stiff consult the Blue Print: If sugar is added too rapidly you will have a softer meringue, which can be used for a dessert but is not good for small meringues or a gâteau.*

Lemon Meringue Pie

Fleur pastry (page 99); 2 lemons; water; 2$\frac{1}{2}$ tablespoons cornflour; 4–8 oz. ($\frac{1}{2}$–1C) caster sugar (see method); $\frac{1}{2}$–1 oz. butter; 2 eggs.

Make the flan case and bake 'blind' (as page 99). Grate the top rind (zest) from the lemons, squeeze out juice, measure and add water to give $\frac{1}{2}$ pint (1$\frac{1}{3}$C). Blend the cornflour with the lemon juice and water, put into a pan with the grated rind, 2–4 oz. ($\frac{1}{4}$–$\frac{1}{2}$C) sugar (depending on whether you like a sharp or sweet flavour) and the butter. Stir over a gentle heat until thickened. Remove from the heat, separate the eggs, add the beaten yolks. Cook *gently* for several minutes.

Taste, add even more sugar if wished. Spoon into the pastry case. Whisk the egg whites until very stiff, add 2 or 4 oz. ($\frac{1}{4}$ or $\frac{1}{2}$C) sugar as the method in the Blue Print. Spoon over the lemon mixture, so meringue touches the pastry rim.

To serve freshly cooked   Use the smaller quantity of sugar if desired. Brown for 20 minutes in the centre of a very moderate oven, 325–350°F, Gas Mark 3–4, or 5–8 minutes in a hot oven.

To serve cold   Use full proportions of sugar as Blue Print, bake for at least 1 hour in the centre of a very slow to slow oven, 225–250°F, Gas Mark $\frac{1}{2}$–1.

Lime Meringue Pie

Use bottled or fresh lime juice in place of lemon juice. Allow 4–5 tablespoons bottled juice and add grated lemon rind if fresh limes are not available. If liked decorate with a twist of lime.

Biscuit Crust Pie

Instead of the pastry case make the flan of biscuit crumbs. Crush 8 oz. plain graham or cream crackers or similar biscuits. Cream 4 oz. ($\frac{1}{2}$C) butter and 2 oz. ($\frac{1}{4}$C) caster sugar. Add the crumbs, form into an 8-inch flan shape, do not bake. Fill with the lemon or lime mixture, proceed as above.

Lemon meringue pie (above left)
Lime meringue pie (below)

Removing the pancake from the frying pan

For Family Occasions

Fruit Fritters

Ingredients as Blue Print PLUS 1 tablespoon flour; pan deep fat or oil for frying or 3–4 oz. ($\frac{1}{2}$C) fat for shallow frying; 4 good-sized cooking apples or bananas, 8 pineapple rings (drain canned pineapple well) or 12 plums; caster sugar to coat.

Prepare the batter as the Blue Print in a large basin (this makes it easier to coat the fruit). Put the flour on a large plate. Heat deep fat or oil—*test if correct temperature*—a cube of bread should turn golden in 30 seconds. Lower the heat so the fat does not over-heat. Peel and core apples, cut into $\frac{1}{2}$-inch rings. Halve large bananas. Coat the fruit first with flour (this makes sure the batter adheres well) and then in the batter. Lift out with a fork, hold over the basin to allow surplus to drop into the basin. Drop into the hot fat, cook steadily for 4–5 minutes, until golden brown. Lift out, drain on absorbent paper, coat in sugar and serve hot. *If frying in shallow fat* heat this *as you coat the fruit. Turn the fritters after 2–3 minutes and brown other side. Serves 4.*

Lemon Pancakes

Ingredients as Blue Print (or economical variation) PLUS $\frac{1}{4}$ pint ($\frac{2}{3}$C) milk or milk and water, oil or fat for frying, 1–2 tablespoons caster sugar, 1 or 2 lemons.

Make the batter as the Blue Print, adding the extra liquid. Put 1–2 teaspoons oil or a small knob of fat into a frying pan, heat thoroughly. Pour or spoon enough batter into the pan to give a *paper thin* layer. Cook quickly for 1–2 minutes until brown on the under side, turn

or toss, cook on the second side. Remove from the pan, see picture, put on to sugared paper, roll and keep hot on a plate over a pan of boiling water. Continue until all the batter is used. Serve with sugar and sliced lemon. *Serves 4.*

Syrup Waffles

Ingredients as Blue Print PLUS 1 teaspoon baking powder (if using plain flour), 1$\frac{1}{2}$ tablespoons melted butter or oil *and* butter, and butter, golden or maple syrup for serving.

Make the batter as the Blue Print, sieving the baking powder and flour and adding the extra butter or oil and butter. Heat the waffle iron, oil if necessary. Spoon enough batter on to the iron to give a good coating. Close the lid, cook until the steaming ceases. Lift the lid, remove the waffle and serve hot topped with butter and syrup. *Serves 4.*

For Special Occasions

Almond Cream Fritters

Stone large plums, ripe apricots or small peaches. Fill with cream cheese and chopped blanched almonds. Omit 1 tablespoon milk from the Blue Print and add 1 tablespoon brandy instead. Coat, fry and serve as Fruit Fritters.

Chocolate Ice Cream Pancakes

Make the pancakes as directed. Keep hot until ready to serve. Fill with ice cream, top with hot chocolate sauce and serve at once.

Apple fritters

Making Batters

The batter for pancakes, fritters and waffles is basically the same, it is just the consistency that varies. A batter for pancakes has a higher percentage of liquid to give a wafer thin result. When coating fruit with batter (for fritters), or for making waffles, it needs to be thicker.

Blue Print Recipe

Fritter Batter

4 oz. (1C) flour, preferably plain · pinch salt · 2 eggs · $\frac{1}{4}$ pint ($\frac{2}{3}$C) milk or milk and water · 1–2 teaspoons melted butter or olive oil.

To make Sieve the flour and salt. Gradually beat in the eggs and liquid giving a smooth thick batter. Add the butter or oil just before cooking.

To vary *For a lighter texture:* separate the eggs. Add the yolks to the flour, then the milk and oil. Fold the stiffly beaten egg whites into the mixture *just before coating* the fruit.

Economical batter: use 1 egg only.

● **AVOID** *Cooking too slowly, this makes a heavy mixture inclined to stick to the pan or waffle iron.*

● **TO RECTIFY** *If the first pancake or waffle cooks too slowly heat the pan, or iron, to a higher temperature before adding more mixture. The method of testing fat is given in the recipe for Fruit Fritters.*

● **SHORT CUT** *Emulsify ingredients in a liquidiser. Put milk and eggs in first then add flour, etc.*

Storing and Freezing *Batters may be stored for several days in a refrigerator. Wrap cooked pancakes and waffles in aluminium foil, store for several days in a refrigerator or 10–12 weeks in a home freezer. Reheat as required.*

Hot Soufflés

A hot sweet soufflé is one of the most delicious puddings. It is so light in texture that it is a perfect choice after an elaborate main dish. The secrets of success are to make a smooth sauce and to incorporate the egg whites carefully, folding them gently but thoroughly into the mixture with a metal spoon or palette knife. If you choose a large-sized saucepan, in which to prepare the mixture, it gives room to do this well.

Soufflés are economical as well as interesting; and can be varied in so many ways. If you like a firm-textured dessert use the smaller quantity of liquid. For a more delicate and moist texture use the larger amount.

Blue Print Recipe
Vanilla Soufflé

1 level tablespoon cornflour · $\frac{1}{4}$ pint—12 tablespoons ($\frac{2}{3}$–1C) milk · vanilla pod or vanilla essence · 2 oz. ($\frac{1}{4}$C) sugar · $\frac{1}{2}$ oz. butter · 4 eggs (see To vary) · little icing sugar.

To make Butter a 6–7-inch soufflé dish or prepare as the Blue Print opposite (this is not essential for a hot soufflé, unless using a very small soufflé dish). Put the cornflour into a basin and blend with 3 tablespoons cold milk. Heat the remainder of the milk, in a large saucepan, with the vanilla pod or essence. Pour over the cornflour, stirring well, then return to the pan. Remove the vanilla pod. Bring to the boil, add the sugar and butter, stir well and cook steadily until a thickened smooth mixture. Remove from the heat. Separate the eggs and gradually beat in the egg yolks. Whisk the egg whites stiffly and fold into the mixture, see photograph. Spoon into the greased soufflé dish, smooth flat on top.

To cook Bake in the centre of a moderate oven, 350–375°F, Gas Mark 4–5, for approximately 25 minutes, until well risen. Have the icing sugar ready.

To serve Take the dish from the oven, shake the icing sugar through a sieve as quickly as possible, remove the paper (if you have used this) and serve at once. To give a pleasant caramellised top to the soufflé pull the oven shelf out gently and carefully about 6 minutes before the end of the cooking time. Dredge the soufflé with the icing sugar and push the shelf back into the oven. *All recipes based on this dish serve 4–5.*

To vary You make a lighter soufflé if you use 3 egg yolks and 4 egg whites. If you care to omit the yolks completely and use just the egg whites, the soufflé has less flavour but sinks far less rapidly.

● **AVOID** *Too slow cooking: Keeping the cooked dish waiting—this means that you should time the cooking carefully, so the soufflé can be served as soon as it is cooked.*

● **TO RECTIFY** *A 'fallen' soufflé (and it will fall if kept waiting) never rises again. The flavour is still very pleasant though, providing the mixture is still hot.*

● **SHORT CUT** *Cook in individual dishes for 10–12 minutes only.*

Chocolate Soufflé

Although one can make a chocolate soufflé as the Blue Print, adding 2 oz. melted plain chocolate or $\frac{1}{2}$ oz. sieved cocoa to the sauce *before* the egg yolks, the following variation gives a light and very moist soufflé.

Melt 3 oz. plain chocolate in $\frac{1}{2}$ pint ($1\frac{1}{3}$C) milk. Heat 3 oz. ($\frac{3}{8}$C) butter in a large pan. Stir in 1 oz. cornflour or 2 oz. ($\frac{1}{2}$C) flour and cook for several minutes. Gradually blend in chocolate liquid. Bring to boil and cook until thickened. Beat in 2 oz. ($\frac{1}{4}$C) sugar and 4 egg yolks. Fold in the 4 whisked egg whites. Proceed as Blue Print but bake for 40 minutes. Dust with sieved icing sugar if wished, and serve with cream.

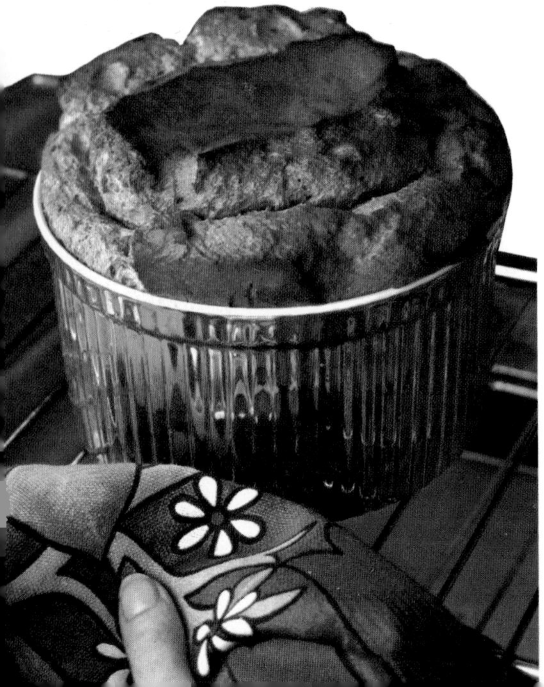

Coffee Soufflé

Recipe as Blue Print, but use either *all* strong coffee instead of milk, or half coffee and half milk. Make and cook the soufflé as the Blue Print.

Liqueur Souffle

Follow the Blue Print recipe but reduce the amount of milk by 2–3 tablespoons and use

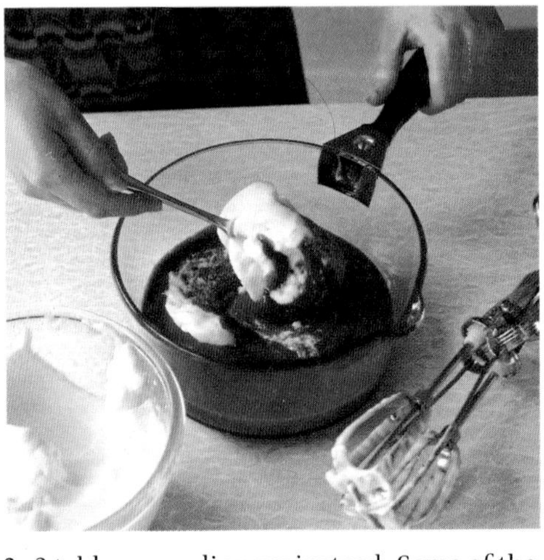

2–3 tablespoons liqueur instead. Some of the most suitable are Apricot Brandy, Cherry Brandy, Curaçao, Crème de Menthe, Tia Maria (which can be used with milk, as in the Blue Print, or with coffee). Bake as Blue Print.

Fruit Soufflé

There are several ways of incorporating fruit flavours into hot soufflés.

If using citrus fruits, i.e. orange, tangerine, lemon or lime. Follow the Blue Print recipe but use fruit juice (or fruit jùice PLUS fruit liqueurs such as Curaçao or Apricot Brandy) instead of milk PLUS 2–3 teaspoons very finely grated fruit rind.

With most other fruits, particularly apricots, blackcurrants and gooseberries, use the Blue Print recipe but substitute thin smooth fruit purée for milk.

Cooked or canned cherries and canned pineapple make excellent soufflés. Follow the Blue Print recipe but use $\frac{1}{4}$ pint ($\frac{2}{3}$C) of the syrup instead of the milk, reduce the amount of sugar if wished. When the sauce has been prepared add 3–4 tablespoons well drained diced fruit *before* the egg yolks and whites. Bake as Blue Print.

Folding in the egg whites (left)
Chocolate soufflé (far left)

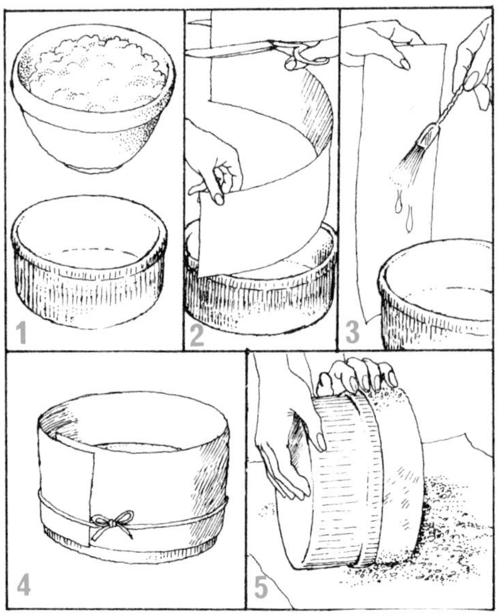

Put together beaten eggs, thick cream, flavouring (this can be fruit, rich chocolate or coffee) and bind them with gelatine and you have the ingredients to produce one of the most elegant of desserts—a cold soufflé. Naturally any soufflé is a fairly expensive dish, which is why I have included a simple 'family' adaptation: Orange Soufflé.

Blue Print Recipe

Five Stages to a Perfect Soufflé

Stage 1 Separate the egg yolks from the whites, put the yolks, sugar, flavouring and liquid (where used) into a basin over a pan of very hot water. Whisk until thick and creamy.

Stage 2 Soften the gelatine in some cold liquid. Add to the mixture above, stir over the heat until the gelatine has dissolved. Cool and allow to stiffen slightly.

Stage 3 Whip the cream lightly, fold into the jellied mixture.

Stage 4 Whisk the egg whites until stiff, but not too dry, fold into the mixture. Spoon into the prepared soufflé dish.

Stage 5 Allow to set and remove the paper slowly and carefully. Decorate the top and sides with whipped cream, finely chopped nuts, ratafia biscuits or mimosa balls.

Preparing the Soufflé Dish

It is traditional that a cold soufflé should look as if it has 'risen' in the dish, as the hot soufflé opposite. In order to achieve this result choose a soufflé dish with a smaller capacity than the amount of mixture produced, see Sketch 1. A 6-inch dish is ideal for all the recipes on this page.

Cut a band of greaseproof paper three times the depth of the dish, see Sketch 2.

Fold the paper to give a double thickness and brush the part that will stand above the dish with a very light coating of melted butter, see Sketch 3.

Tie or pin the band of paper *very securely* round the outside of the soufflé dish, see Sketch 4.

● **AVOID** *Over-whipping the cream, this makes it difficult to incorporate: Beating the egg whites until too stiff: Adding the cream and egg whites too early; wait until the jellied mixture is lightly set.*

● **TO RECTIFY** *If the cream or egg whites have been beaten too stiffly then soften with a few drops of water. Fold this in gently and carefully.*

● **SHORT CUT** *Use the mixer to whisk the egg whites, do not over-whip: Make a smooth fruit purée in the liquidiser.*

Storing and Freezing *Keep in a cool place immediately before serving. The cold soufflé, with the high percentage of cream may be frozen, but tends to lose some of its light texture. The hot soufflé cannot be stored or frozen.*

To Use Any Leftover *Put spoonfuls of the soufflé into glasses and top with a whirl of whipped cream.*

Lemon Soufflé

Finely grated rind of 2 lemons; 4 tablespoons lemon juice; 3 eggs; 4–6 oz. ($\frac{1}{2}$–$\frac{3}{4}$C) caster sugar; $\frac{3}{4}$ tablespoon powdered gelatine; 4 tablespoons water; $\frac{1}{2}$ pint (1$\frac{1}{3}$C) thick cream. *To decorate*: small ratafia biscuits.

Put the lemon rind, juice, egg yolks and sugar into a basin. Whisk as Stage 1 in Blue Print. Soften the gelatine in the cold water, add to the egg yolk mixture and continue as Blue Print. Press some finely crushed ratafia biscuits on to the sides, see Sketch 5, and decorate the top with ratafias. *Serves 5–6.*

Fruit Soufflé

If using dessert fruit, such as raspberries and strawberries, sieve the raw fruit and measure. If using firm fruit, such as apricots, blackcurrants and gooseberries, cook in the minimum of water until soft, sieve and measure. If sugar has been used in cooking the fruit omit a little in the recipe below.

$\frac{1}{4}$ pint ($\frac{2}{3}$C) thick fruit purée; 3 eggs; 4 oz. ($\frac{1}{2}$C) caster sugar; $\frac{1}{2}$ tablespoon powdered gelatine; 2 tablespoons water; $\frac{1}{2}$ pint (1$\frac{1}{3}$C) thick cream. *To decorate*: nuts and cream.

Put the fruit purée, egg yolks and sugar into a basin. Whisk as Stage 1 in Blue Print. Soften gelatine in the cold water, add to egg yolk mixture and continue as Blue Print. Chop a few nuts very finely, press against the sides of the soufflé, see Sketch 5. Decorate the top of the soufflé with cream.

Chocolate Soufflé

4 oz. plain chocolate; 2 tablespoons milk; 3 eggs; 3 oz. ($\frac{3}{8}$C) caster sugar; $\frac{1}{2}$ tablespoon powdered gelatine; 2 tablespoons water; $\frac{1}{2}$ pint (1$\frac{1}{3}$C) thick cream. *To decorate*: grated chocolate and cream.

Break the chocolate into pieces, put into a basin with the milk, egg yolks and sugar. Whisk as Stage 1 in Blue Print. Soften the gelatine in the cold water, add to the egg yolk mixture, continue as Blue Print. Decorate with coarsely grated chocolate and whipped cream. *Serves 5–6.*

Orange Soufflé

Dissolve an orange flavoured jelly in $\frac{3}{4}$ pint (2C) very hot water. Add grated rind of 1 orange and 2 tablespoons orange juice. Cool slightly. Whisk 1 egg yolk and pour on the warm orange jelly. Allow to cool and stiffen slightly then fold in 2 tablespoons cream or evaporated milk (lightly whipped) and 1 beaten egg white. Put into a 5-inch soufflé dish. Decorate with cream. *Serves 4–5.*

Lemon soufflé

Cream and Cold Desserts

So many desserts are improved by topping or decorating with cream, or incorporating cream among the ingredients, but often the piping or dessert itself can be less than perfect because the cream has been over-whipped.

Blue Print Recipe

To Whip Fresh Cream

Put thick cream into a basin. Use an electric or hand whisk or a fork to whip the cream. The latter is slow, but safer if the cream is very rich. Whip slowly and steadily until the cream *begins* to stand in peaks. This consistency is ideal when adding cream to desserts. If using the cream for piping the cream should be stiffer and stand in peaks.

To make a lighter cream
1. Whip as Blue Print and then fold in an equal quantity of thin cream. Whip again until it stiffens. This will be rarely firm enough to use for piping.
2. To each $\frac{1}{4}$ pint ($\frac{2}{3}$C) thick cream add one egg white. Whip the cream and egg white in separate basins and fold together *just before* serving. You can pipe this, although it tends to be much softer than thick cream alone.

● **AVOID** *Over-whipping cream because if you do it will separate, giving you a solid butter-like substance and watery liquid.*
● **TO RECTIFY** *If the cream begins to separate add a little milk or water and fold gently into the mixture.*
● **SHORT CUT** *Use an electric mixer for whisking but choose a very low speed and watch the cream as it thickens to avoid over-beating.*

For Special Occasions

Banana Cream Syllabub

3 ripe firm bananas; 2 tablespoons lemon juice; 2 tablespoons white wine; 2 tablespoons caster sugar; $\frac{1}{2}$ pint ($1\frac{1}{3}$C) thick cream.
Peel the bananas and mash with the lemon juice, wine and sugar. Whip the cream as the Blue Print. Fold into the banana mixture. Spoon into serving dishes and chill before serving. *Serves 4–6.*

Creamy Apple Crunch

This recipe, somewhat similar in texture to a Charlotte (page 100) uses soured cream to give additional interest to the apple mixture. 4 oz. ($\frac{1}{2}$C) caster sugar; $\frac{1}{4}$ pint ($\frac{2}{3}$C) water; 4 or 5 medium-sized cooking apples; 10 fl. oz. ($1\frac{1}{4}$C) soured cream; $2\frac{1}{2}$ tablespoons soft brown sugar; 4–6 gingernut biscuits; 2 tablespoons chopped blanched almonds.
Make a syrup with the caster sugar and water in a large pan. Peel, core and slice the apples and poach in the syrup until just tender, but unbroken. Lift the apple segments into a basin, blend with the soured cream and 2 tablespoons brown sugar. Spoon into a heat proof dish. Crush the biscuits with a rolling pin; do this between 2 sheets of greaseproof paper or put the biscuits into a large bag. Blend with the almonds and remaining brown sugar. Sprinkle over the fruit and brown for 2–3 minutes only under a hot grill. Serve cold. (Illustrated on page 95). *Serves 4–6.*

Apple Surprise Pie

One of the old fashioned farmhouse traditions, when making a fruit pie, was to cover the fruit with thick cream before baking. This has been done in the pie shown on page 95. Apples or plums are the most suitable fruit for this purpose.

Either put the prepared fruit into the pie dish with sugar and water as page 98, or, to give a firmer fruit layer, poach the fruit for about 10 minutes with the sugar and water in a saucepan. Lift out the fruit only, (serve the liquid with the pie if wished,) and put this into the pie dish. Whichever method is used, top the fruit with $\frac{1}{4}$–$\frac{1}{2}$ pint ($\frac{2}{3}$–$1\frac{1}{3}$C) whipped cream, then with the pastry. Bake as the fruit pie on page 98.

Storing and Freezing *Dairy cream, and any desserts using cream, must be used when fresh unless stored in a home freezer.*

Banana cream syllabub

Special Gâteau

This delicious recipe for gâteau would make either a dinner party dessert or a special treat for the family. All the techniques can be found in the Blue Prints.

Fruit Cream Bande

This recipe, is based on puff pastry (see page 92). The excellent frozen pastry enables you to make a seemingly elaborate dessert very easily.
12–13 oz. packet frozen puff pastry or puff pastry made with 6 oz. ($1\frac{1}{2}$C) flour etc.; 2 tablespoons custard powder or cornflour; $\frac{1}{2}$ pint ($1\frac{1}{3}$C) milk; 2 tablespoons sugar; $\frac{1}{4}$ pint ($\frac{2}{3}$C) thick cream; 6–8 dessert plums; 1 red-skinned dessert apple; 1 dessert pear; 3–4 tablespoons apricot jam.
Roll out about $\frac{2}{3}$ of the pastry into a rectangle about 11 inches × 8 inches. Put on to a baking sheet or tray. Roll out the rest of the pastry into a long strip, cut 2 pieces 11 inches × $\frac{1}{2}$–$\frac{3}{4}$ inch wide and 2 pieces $6\frac{1}{2}$–7 inches × $\frac{1}{2}$–$\frac{3}{4}$ inch wide. Damp the edges of the pastry rectangle and press the bands into position. The pastry case should look like a 'picture frame'. Bake just above the centre of a very hot oven, 450–475°F, Gas Mark 8–9 for about 5 minutes, then lower the heat to moderately hot, 400°F, Gas Mark 5–6 for a further 15 minutes or until the pastry is golden brown. Allow to cool. Blend the custard powder or cornflour with the milk. Put into a saucepan with the sugar, cook gently, stirring all the time until thickened. Allow to cool, stirring from time to time to prevent a skin forming. Blend with the whipped cream, spread over the pastry. Halve the plums, remove the stones, slice the apple and peeled pear. Arrange on the cream layer and top with the warmed and sieved jam at once to keep the fruit a good colour. (Illustrated on page 95.) *Serves 5–6.*

Variations

The recipe above uses plums, an apple and a pear, but any combination of fruits, such as blackberries, raspberries and apple would be just as delicious.

eight
HOME BAKING

There is a great sense of achievement in producing a perfect cake, home-made bread or a selection of biscuits. The secrets of perfection can be summed up as follows:

1. To use (and follow) a well balanced recipe, by this I mean a recipe that gives the right proportions of fat, sugar, etc. For example, if you have too much fat in proportion to flour the cake will be heavy and greasy, the biscuits will spread in cooking and will not crisp. Too little fat, on the other hand, will make most cakes dry and unappetising unless eaten when very fresh. If you 'cut down' too much on the sugar in a recipe the cake will not only be lacking in flavour, but much heavier, for sugar lightens sponges and cakes. One must have a good proportion of eggs in relation to the fat and flour used, otherwise the mixture will not 'bind together'.

2. To select the best method of blending the ingredients together for that particular type of cake and to follow the recommended method of handling the ingredients, i.e. 'folding gently' when advised

to do this. Rubbing-in is an ideal method for family type cakes, for it is quick and easy, but the cakes are generally less light and smooth in texture than those produced by creaming the fat and sugar or by whisking eggs and sugar. The whisking method on the other hand gives such an ultra-light texture that it is quite unsuitable for fruit cakes. There is more about these methods in the various Blue Prints.

3. To bake the cake, loaf or biscuits correctly. It is essential to appreciate that individual ovens vary a great deal and that suggested temperatures in recipes can be based on the 'average' oven only.

Always consult your own manufacturer's instruction card or book the first time you bake a particular type of cake.

Baking too quickly will set the outside of a cake in too short a period, make it over-brown and prevent the heat penetrating to the centre, so you may well have an over-cooked cake or loaf on the outside and a nearly 'raw' mixture in the centre.

Baking too slowly can prevent a cake or loaf from rising properly and gives a heavy texture.

4. Take care when turning cakes out of the tins. Many a perfect cake is spoiled by a little part 'breaking-away' as it is turned out; this could probably be avoided. Allow all cakes to stand for 2–3 minutes in the tin before turning out, this allows the mixture to contract slightly. Certain cakes and biscuits should be cooled completely before being handled and this information is given in the recipes.

Perhaps you have never made your own bread, please try it once in a while as the Blue Print on page 121 gives very detailed instructions.

I have chosen some of the cakes and buns made by rubbing the fat into the flour as 'family' cakes, for these are quickly made and most of them are reasonably economical.

● **AVOID** *Making the mixture too soft, for since the fat is rubbed into the flour, it often looks deceptively stiff. Sketch 2 shows the consistency for small cakes, Sketch 4 the slow dropping consistency ideal for most large cakes: Using too much fat for this type of mixture, unless in a specific recipe: Baking too slowly.*
● **TO RECTIFY** *If you feel you have made the mixture for small cakes too soft either work in extra flour (which will slightly spoil the proportions and flavour) or put the mixture into patty tins or paper cases so it does not spread too badly.*
● **SHORT CUT** *There are many cake mixes on the market which will enable you to follow most of the recipes on these pages.*

Blue Print Recipe

Vanilla Buns

8 oz. (2C) self-raising flour (or plain flour with 2 teaspoons baking powder) · 4 oz. ($\frac{1}{2}$C) fat (choose margarine, butter or cooking fat) · 4–6 oz. ($\frac{1}{2}$–$\frac{3}{4}$C) caster sugar · $\frac{1}{4}$ teaspoon vanilla essence · 2 eggs* · little milk. To decorate: few lumps sugar. *If wished use 1 egg only.

To make Sieve the flour or flour and baking powder into a mixing bowl. Add the fat then rub this into the flour with the tips of your fingers until like fine breadcrumbs. Lift the mixture as Sketch 1 to incorporate air. Add the sugar. Beat the vanilla essence with the eggs and stir into the fat mixture, blend well. Add a very little milk, if necessary, to make a sticky mixture.
To cook Grease and flour 2 flat baking trays or sheets. Lift out teaspoons of the mixture and put on the trays. Shape into rounds with the help of a second teaspoon, see Sketch 3. Leave room for the cakes to spread in cooking. Crush the lumps of sugar lightly and sprinkle over the cakes. Bake for 12–15 minutes above the centre of a moderately hot to hot oven, 400–425°F, Gas Mark 5–6.
To serve With coffee or tea. *All recipes based on this make 12–14 buns.*

Rich Vanilla Buns

Ingredients as Blue Print but use nearly 6 oz. (nearly $\frac{3}{4}$C) fat, 2 eggs and no milk. These are very brittle when cooked so cool for a few minutes before removing from the trays.

Jam Buns

Ingredients as Blue Print MINUS crushed sugar topping and PLUS a little jam and caster sugar.
Prepare the buns as the Blue Print, put the mixture on to the trays. Make an indentation in each bun with a floured finger. Put in some jam and bring the mixture up round the jam. Sprinkle with a little caster sugar. Bake as the Blue Print.

Rock Buns

Ingredients as Blue Print MINUS vanilla essence and sugar topping and PLUS 4–6 oz. ($\frac{1}{2}$–$\frac{3}{4}$C) dried fruit.
Add the fruit with the sugar. Bake as the Blue Print. (Illustrated on page 111).

Orange Buns

Ingredients as Blue Print MINUS vanilla essence and sugar topping and PLUS grated rind of 2 oranges and a little chopped candied orange peel. Add the orange rind and peel with the sugar. Bake as the Blue Print, allow to cool and then dust with sieved icing sugar or decorate as the recipe below.

Orange Jamaican Buns

Orange buns above; 6–8 oz. (1$\frac{1}{4}$C) icing sugar; little orange juice; 2–3 tablespoons candied orange peel; 2–3 tablespoons chopped plain chocolate or chocolate 'dots'.
Allow the orange buns to cool. Blend the icing sugar with enough orange juice to give a stiff spreading consistency. Spread in the centre of each bun and top with the candied peel and chocolate.

From the top: Orange Jamaican buns, Orange buns, Rock buns, Vanilla buns and Jam buns

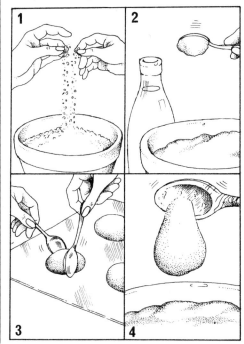

Orange Raisin Cake

Ingredients as Blue Print using all raisins, MINUS the spice and PLUS the grated rind of 2 oranges, which should be added with the sugar.

Bake as the Blue Print or bake in a loaf tin as illustrated for barely 1 hour.

To vary Top the cake with warmed marmalade and cover with a thick layer of coconut.

Coat the top of the cake with orange flavoured icing (see Orange Jamaican Buns opposite). Sprinkle a neat band of coconut round the top edge of the cake and decorate with glacé cherries.

Cherry Coconut Cake

6 oz. (1½C) self-raising flour (or plain flour and 2 *level* teaspoons baking powder); 4 oz. (½C) fat (see Blue Print opposite); 6 oz. (¾C) caster sugar; 2 oz. (generous ¾C) desiccated coconut; 3 oz. (⅜C) glacé cherries; 2 eggs.

Sieve the flour or flour and baking powder. Rub in the fat as the Blue Print opposite. Add the sugar and coconut. Halve the cherries, add ⅔ to the cake mixture then bind with the beaten eggs. Grease and flour an 8-inch cake tin or baking dish as shown in the picture. Put in the mixture and press the remaining halved cherries on top. Bake in the centre of a moderate oven, 350–375°F, Gas Mark 4–5, for approximately 1 hour. Test by pressing firmly on top.

Although this is delicious cold with tea or coffee it is equally good served hot as a dessert.

Oslo Apple Cake

For the apple layer: 3 large cooking apples; 2 oz. (¼C) sugar; 1 teaspoon finely grated lemon rind; 1 tablespoon lemon juice.

For the cake layer: 8 oz. (2C) self-raising flour (or plain flour and 2 *level* teaspoons baking powder); 4 oz. (½C) fat (see Blue Print opposite); 4 oz. (½C) caster sugar; 1 small egg.

Peel, core and slice the apples and cook with the sugar, lemon rind and juice. If necessary add a little water but keep a very firm mixture. When soft, strain to remove any surplus moisture and cool thoroughly. Sieve the flour or flour and baking powder. Rub in the fat. Add half the sugar and the egg. Knead together well then add the rest of the sugar. Roll or press out ⅔ of the dough to make an 8-inch round. Put into a well greased 8-inch cake or deep sandwich tin (preferably with a loose base). Top with the apple mixture. Roll out the remaining dough, cut into strips and make a lattice design over the top of the apples. Bake in the centre of a moderate oven, 350–375°F, Gas Mark 4–5, for about 40 minutes. Either eat hot with coffee or tea or allow to cool, but serve when fresh – delicious with fresh cream.

Empress Cake

Ingredients for the cake layer as Oslo Apple Cake but MINUS the apple layer and PLUS 3 oz. (⅜C) caster sugar, 3 oz. (¾C) finely chopped blanched almonds, ½ egg white and little water.

Prepare the base of the cake as recipe above. Mix the sugar, almonds, egg white and water together. Spread over the base, top with the lattice and bake as the Oslo Apple Cake.

To vary Blend 1 small boiled, sieved potato and a few drops almond essence with the ingredients for the almond layer above. This gives a soft moist texture which is very pleasant.

Storing and Freezing *Keep in an airtight tin for a very limited period. The uncooked cake dough may be stored overnight before baking. The cakes on these two pages freeze well, particularly the Empress Cake and Oslo Apple Cake and these may be heated gently from the frozen state. The other cakes are better thawed out slowly.*

To use any left over *Use these cakes as quickly as you can as they 'dry-out' easily.*

Granny's spice cake

You will often find that large cakes made by the rubbing-in method have a tendency to crack slightly on top as the cake on this page. This is not a fault in rather 'short' crumbly cakes that have a pleasantly crisp textured crust. All spoon measures throughout this book are level, but where I insert the word it is of particular importance.

Blue Print Recipe

Granny's Spice Cake

12 oz. (3C) self-raising flour (or plain flour and 3 *level* teaspoons baking powder) · 1–2 teaspoons allspice · 6–8 oz. (¾–1C) fat (see Blue Print opposite) · 6–8 oz. (¾–1C) caster or light brown sugar · 6–8 oz. (about 1C) mixed dried fruit · 2 eggs · milk to mix.

To make Sieve the flour or flour and baking powder and spice together. Rub in the fat as described in the Blue Print opposite, add the sugar, fruit, the beaten eggs and enough milk to make a sticky consistency, see Sketch 4. Put into a greased and floured 7–8-inch round cake tin, smooth flat on top.

To cook Bake in the centre of a moderate oven, 350–375°F, Gas Mark 4–5, for approximately 1 hour for an 8-inch tin, 1¼ hours for a 7-inch tin. Reduce the heat to very moderate, 325–350°F, Gas Mark 3–4, after 45 minutes. Test by pressing quite hard on top, and the cake is cooked when quite firm to the touch.

To serve When fresh, this type of cake is delicious with cheese.

To vary Omit the spice or use ground ginger or cinnamon.

Use all one kind of fruit such as currants or sultanas.

Cherry coconut cake and Orange raisin cake

The biscuits and cookies on this particular page are based on several methods of mixing the ingredients and reference will be made to relevant Blue Prints. The points listed below, however, apply to all biscuits and biscuit-type cookies.

● **AVOID** *Making any biscuit dough too soft and sticky by adding excess liquid. You cannot over-handle most biscuit doughs, the more you knead the better the texture and if the dough seems too dry, knead very well before adding extra liquid. You will probably find that handling produces the right texture. Baking too quickly, most biscuit doughs need steady baking.*

● **TO RECTIFY** *If you have made a somewhat soft biscuit dough, chill for several hours and then try to handle it: If the biscuits seem to be baking too rapidly, lower the oven temperature immediately.*

● **SHORT CUTS** *Use the quick creaming fats which save time in blending: See the short cuts suggested in the sketches.*

Blue Print Recipe
Orange Biscuits

These are made by the rubbing-in method.
8 oz. (2C) flour, preferably plain · 5 oz. (⅝C) margarine or butter · 4–6 oz. (½–¾C) caster sugar · very finely grated rind of 1 or 2 oranges.
To make Put the flour into a mixing bowl. Rub in the margarine or butter as the Blue

Biscuits and Cookies

Print on page 112. Add half the sugar and orange rind. Knead firmly and work in the rest of the sugar. This dough should need *no* liquid but if necessary add a *few* drops orange juice.

Put the dough on to a very lightly floured pastry board. Roll out very firmly until about ⅛-inch in thickness. Cut into rounds about 2–2½-inches in diameter. This is quicker than using a pastry cutter. Put on to ungreased baking trays. These biscuits should not spread (with self-raising flour they may spread a little). Prick lightly with a fork.
To cook Put as near the centre of the oven as possible and bake for about 10–12 minutes in a very moderate oven, 325–350°F, Gas Mark 3–4. Cool on the baking trays.
To serve With tea or coffee or as an accompaniment to ice cream. *Makes 14–18.*

Orange Laurel Rings
Ingredients as Blue Print PLUS angelica and a little sieved jam or marmalade (optional).
Prepare the dough as the Blue Print but cut into rings instead of rounds. Bake as the Blue Print. Decorate with pieces of angelica. These can be brushed first with a little jam

or marmalade to make sure they stick on to the biscuit. *Makes 18–20.*

Orange Cream Cookies
Ingredients as Blue Print PLUS 2 oz. (¼C) butter, 4 oz. (nearly 1C) sieved icing sugar and finely grated rind of 1 orange.
Make the dough as the Blue Print. Roll out and cut an equal number of rounds and rings (the size to fit on top). Bake as the Blue Print, allow to cool. Do not decorate until the day you intend to serve these as the butter icing can soften the biscuits. Cream the butter, nearly all the icing sugar and grated orange rind together. Spread the rounds with a thin layer of the butter icing. Place the rings on top, dust with the remaining icing sugar. Use the remaining butter cream to pipe rosettes to fill the centre 'hole'. *Makes 8–9.*

Sugar Rings
Ingredients as Blue Print but MINUS grated orange rind and PLUS 1 egg white, 2 oz. (¼C) caster sugar and few drops vanilla essence. Make the dough as the Blue Print but cut into rings. Bake as the Blue Print for about 8–9 minutes until well set and nearly cooked. Remove from the oven. Whisk the egg white until it begins to hold its shape. It must not be as stiff as a meringue. Fold in nearly all the sugar and the vanilla essence and spread over the nearly cooked biscuits. Dredge with the remaining sugar. Return to the oven, but lower the heat to very cool, 250–275°F, Gas Mark ½–1, and leave for about 40 minutes until the topping is very crisp but still white. *Makes 18–20.*

Left to right: Orange laurel rings, Cherry ginger cookies, Chocolate shortbreads, Sugar rings, Zebra biscuits and Orange cream cookies

Macaroons and Meringues

These are delicious to serve not only with tea or coffee, but also as a dessert. They can be varied in many ways to give interest to meals and are suitable for both family and special occasions.

Macaroons may be topped with ice cream for a special occasion and meringues can be filled with cream, cream and fruit or ice cream.

Blue Print Recipe

Coconut Macaroons

2 egg whites · 5–6 oz. ($\frac{5}{8}$–$\frac{3}{4}$C) caster sugar · approximately 6 oz. (nearly 2C) desiccated coconut · rice flour or cornflour (optional, see method) · rice paper (see method). To decorate: glacé cherries.

To make Put the egg whites into a mixing bowl and whisk lightly; do not over-whip, the whites should just be 'frothy' not stiff. Add the sugar (the amount given above is on the generous side and if wished you can use as little as 4 oz. ($\frac{1}{2}$C)). Stir in the coconut steadily, as since egg whites vary in size you may need a little less than the amount given. The mixture should just roll into balls. If you wish a firmer texture then use a little less coconut and add 1–2 teaspoons rice flour or cornflour. When blended roll into about 10–12 balls. Either put on rice paper on baking trays or sheets, or grease these lightly and put on the balls. Allow room for the mixture to flatten out during cooking. Press half a glacé cherry on top of each biscuit.

To cook Bake in the centre of a very moderate to moderate oven, 350–375°F, Gas Mark 4–5, for about 18–20 minutes. If you like a slightly sticky macaroon then put a dish of water in the oven while cooking.

To serve Remove from the baking trays or sheets when nearly cold, cut or tear round the rice paper and serve with tea or coffee or top with a scoop of ice cream. I like to put the ice cream on about 5 minutes early so it softens the macaroon slightly. *All recipes based on this make 10–12.*

● **AVOID** *Cooking macaroons too slowly otherwise they become too hard: Cooking meringues too quickly or they brown on the outside before becoming crisp.*

● **TO RECTIFY** *As you cannot rectify mistakes check the baking carefully.*

Storing and Freezing *Macaroons become dry after 1 or 2 days if stored in a tin. Meringues keep well for weeks. Macaroons can be wrapped and frozen and they store for some weeks without losing their soft texture inside. Meringues contain such a high percentage of sugar that they never become frozen.*

To use any left over *Macaroons can be crumbled and added to trifles. Meringues can be put back into the tin, unless they are filled with cream, etc., when they will soften very quickly. You can therefore freeze left over filled meringues.*

Put the egg whites into a bowl, free from any specks of dust or particles of egg yolk. Whisk until very stiff. Gradually whisk in half the sugar and fold in the remainder (alternative ways of adding the sugar are given on page 106). Brush the baking trays with a very little oil or butter, or brush greaseproof paper on the trays with oil. Either spoon or pipe the meringues on to the trays as Sketches 1 and 2. Bake in the coolest part of a very slow oven, 225–250°F, Gas Mark 0–$\frac{1}{2}$, for about 2 hours until crisp, but still white. Lift from the tin with a warm, but dry, palette knife. Store in an airtight tin until ready to fill.

Coconut macaroons

The meringues may either be filled with whipped cream or with butter icing, to which grated rind can be added for flavour. You can flavour with vanilla instead of orange or other essences or a little sieved cocoa (as in the picture) or instant coffee. They are delicious if filled with fruit or ice cream. To incorporate more filling press the base of each meringue gently so you break this slightly and make a 'hollow', then sandwich two together with the filling. A 'nest' shape also enables you to use a generous amont of cream and other filling.

To tint meringues add a few drops of colouring essence to the egg whites before they are quite stiff.

To flavour meringues add a few drops essence to the egg whites before they are quite stiff. If you wish to add cocoa or instant coffee powder, blend either of these with the sugar.

Almond Macaroons
Flavour with almond essence, use ground almonds in place of coconut. Top with blanched almonds.

Oatmeal Macaroons
Use all rolled oats or half rolled oats and half coconut or ground almonds. Top with almonds or glacé cherries.

Crumb Macaroons
Use all crisp fine breadcrumbs or half crumbs and half coconut or ground almonds. Flavour breadcrumbs version well with essence, i.e. almond, rum or vanilla.

Meringues
The Blue Print on page 106 gives details about making the meringue mixture but some of the most important points are repeated below.
2 egg whites; 4 oz. ($\frac{1}{2}$C) caster sugar (or use half caster and half sieved icing sugar).

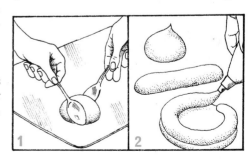

1. Take a spoonful of meringue mixture. Hold over the baking tray and form into a neat shape with a second spoon.

2. Put the mixture into a piping bag with a $\frac{1}{4}$-inch pipe. Pipe into rounds, fingers or nest shapes.

This method of blending ingredients is often used for cakes containing a high percentage of syrup, treacle or honey. The cakes are generally moist in texture, such as a gingerbread.

treacle, or a mixture of these, in place of honey. The amount of ground ginger may be increased to 2 teaspoons as the Blue Print has a very mild flavour.

● **AVOID** *Having the mixture too dry, most recipes produce a very soft texture before baking which gives a pleasantly moist cake: Baking too quickly, otherwise you will burn or over-cook the outside before the cake is set: Turning the cake out of the tin when freshly baked, or it could break due to the weight of the syrup, honey or treacle.*

● **TO RECTIFY** *If the cake should appear dry, store for a week with an apple in the cake tin and this should produce the right texture.*

Blue Print Recipe

Golden Ginger Loaf

10 oz. (2½C) plain flour · 1 level teaspoon bicarbonate of soda · ½ teaspoon ground ginger · 6 oz. (⅜C) clear honey · 4 oz. (½C) fat · 6 oz. (¾C) sugar · 2 tablespoons syrup from jar preserved ginger · 1½ tablespoons milk · 2 eggs · To decorate: 1 tablespoon honey · few leaves angelica · 2–3 tablespoons preserved ginger (cut in neat pieces).

To make Sieve the dry ingredients into the mixing bowl. To weigh the honey, put an empty saucepan on the scales, note the weight, then add 6 oz. honey. If the measuring cup is floured the honey (syrup or treacle) pours out easily into the saucepan. Add the fat and sugar. Heat gently until the fat melts, pour over the flour and beat well. Warm the syrup and milk in the pan, add to the flour mixture with the eggs and beat until smooth. Line a 2½–3-lb. loaf tin with greased greaseproof paper. Pour in the mixture.

To cook Bake in the centre of a slow to very moderate oven, 300–325°F, Gas Mark 2–3, for 1–1¼ hours until *just firm* to the touch, do not over-cook. Remove from the oven, cool in the tin for about 15 minutes. Remove from the tin, take off the paper, then brush the top with the honey and press the pieces of angelica and ginger into position.

To serve As a cake with coffee or tea, or spread with butter as a tea-bread. This is also delicious sliced and topped with apple purée.

To vary To make a darker, stronger flavoured loaf use golden syrup or black

Iced Ginger Loaf

Make the variation of the Blue Print with all black treacle and 2 teaspoons ground ginger. When the loaf is cooked and cold, top with icing made by blending 6–8 oz. (1¼C) icing sugar with enough warm water to give a flowing consistency. Pour on top of the loaf and allow to 'trickle' down the sides. Leave until nearly set then top with pieces of preserved or crystallised ginger. (Illustrated on page 111).

Golden ginger loaf

The true gingerbread was served, as the name suggests, as a rich tea-bread. It is excellent with cheese or topped with fruit, especially apple sauce, and ice cream as a dessert. A rich gingerbread matures and improves in texture and taste if kept for at least a week before cutting.

Gas Mark 3–4. It is advisable to put in one tray at a time so you do not have too many biscuits ready to roll at once. Remove from the oven, cool for 2–3 minutes, roll round the greased handle of a wooden spoon. Hold until biscuit begins to harden, remove care-

Almond sultana gingerbread

Brandy snaps

Old Fashioned Gingerbread
8 oz. (2C) plain flour; $\frac{3}{4}$ teaspoon bicarbonate of soda; $\frac{1}{2}$–1 teaspoon ground cinnamon; $1\frac{1}{2}$–2 teaspoons ground ginger; 4 oz. ($\frac{1}{2}$C) butter or cooking fat; 4 oz. (nearly $\frac{3}{4}$C) moist brown sugar; 5 oz. (just over $\frac{1}{4}$C) black treacle; 2 eggs; 4 tablespoons milk.
Sieve the dry ingredients. Put the butter or fat, sugar and treacle into a pan and melt carefully. Add to the dry ingredients, beat well, then add the eggs and milk. Beat again. Put into a 7–8-inch square tin, lined with well-greased greaseproof paper and bake in the centre of a slow to very moderate oven, 300–325°F, Gas Mark 2–3, for about $1\frac{1}{4}$ hours. A 7-inch square cake takes rather longer than an 8-inch cake because of the greater depth of the mixture. Cut into squares to serve. (Illustrated on page 111).

Almond Sultana Gingerbread
Ingredients as the Old Fashioned Ginger-bread PLUS 4–5 oz. (generous $\frac{1}{2}$C) sultanas and 2 tablespoons finely chopped blanched almonds and 2–3 tablespoons flaked blanch-ed almonds.

Make the gingerbread as the recipe above then add the sultanas and chopped almonds. Put the mixture into the prepared tin, top with the flaked almonds and bake as the Old Fashioned Gingerbread.

Brandy Snaps
These classic biscuits are ideal to store in a 100% airtight tin and to fill with whipped cream as a dessert, or to serve with ice cream instead of wafers. They are also a perfect choice for tea or coffee.
2 oz. ($\frac{1}{4}$C) butter or cooking fat; 2 oz. ($\frac{1}{4}$C) caster sugar; 2 oz. ($\frac{1}{8}$C) golden syrup; 2 oz. ($\frac{1}{2}$C) plain flour; $\frac{1}{4}$–$\frac{1}{2}$ teaspoon ground ginger; 1 teaspoon brandy or lemon juice (optional). If not using the brandy or lemon juice I always take away about 1 teaspoon of flour so the mixture is not too thick.
Melt the butter or fat with the sugar and golden syrup in a pan. Sieve the flour and ginger, stir into the syrup mixture and blend well, adding the brandy or lemon juice. Grease 2–3 baking trays or sheets. Put teaspoons of the mixture on these, allowing room for them to spread out into rounds of 3–4 inches. Bake for approximately 8–10 minutes near the centre of a very moderate to moderate oven, 325–350°F,

fully, cool on a wire cooling tray. Continue until all the biscuits are rolled. If some have hardened on the trays, warm for 1–2 minutes in the oven. *Makes 14–16.*

Yorkshire Parkin
Ingredients as the Old Fashioned Gingerbread PLUS 4 oz. ($\frac{2}{3}$C) coarse oatmeal and $\frac{1}{4}$ pint ($\frac{2}{3}$C) milk instead of 4 tablespoons, but MINUS half the bicarbonate of soda as this does not rise as well as a true Gingerbread.
Prepare as the Old Fashioned Gingerbread mixing the oatmeal with the flour. Bake as the Old Fashioned Gingerbread in an 8-inch tin. This is delicious covered with warmed golden syrup, after baking, then topped with a thick layer of chopped nuts and chopped preserved ginger and finally dusted with sieved icing sugar.

Storing and Freezing *The gingerbreads keep well in tins for several weeks, but can be wrapped and frozen if wished. Do not freeze the brandy snaps.*
To use any left over *If the gingerbread has become stale, steam gently until soft and serve hot with fruit or syrup sauce.*

117

The Creaming Method for Making Cakes

This method is used for making the largest selection of cakes, from a light Victoria sandwich to a Christmas cake.

Blue Print Recipe

Victoria Sandwich or Butter Sponge

4 oz. ($\frac{1}{2}$C) margarine, butter or cooking fat · 4 oz. ($\frac{1}{2}$C) caster sugar · 2 large eggs · 4 oz. (1C) self-raising flour (with plain flour use 1 teaspoon baking powder).

To make Cream the margarine, butter or fat with the sugar until soft and light in colour, use a wooden spoon for this. If using the mixer warm the bowl *but not the fat* to ease mixing. Gradually beat in the eggs, then fold in the sieved flour or flour and baking powder with a metal spoon. Divide the mixture between two 6–7-inch greased and floured sandwich tins.

To cook Bake above the centre of a moderate oven, 350–375°F, Gas Mark 4–5, for 15–20 minutes until just firm to the touch. Cool for 2–3 minutes in the tins, turn out carefully.

To serve Fill with jam or jam and whipped cream and top with sieved icing sugar or caster sugar and serve with coffee, or for tea, or fill with fruit and cream.

● **AVOID** *Melting the fat, for the secret of success is to incorporate as much air as possible into the mixture by beating well: Adding the eggs too quickly, for this could curdle the mixture: Over-beating the flour, as this spoils the texture.*

● **TO RECTIFY** *If the fat has been melted, allow to cool and solidify again before trying to cream the mixture: If the eggs have been added too quickly and the mixture shows signs of curdling, blend in a little sieved flour.*

● **SHORT CUTS** *Use the quick creaming margarines and fats and put all the ingredients into the basin and beat for about 2 minutes. As less air has been beaten into the mixture it is advisable to sieve an extra level teaspoon baking powder with each 4 oz. (1C) flour. This means however that the cakes tend to dry out more easily.*

Orange Layer Cake

Ingredients as Blue Print PLUS 2 tablespoons orange juice and an extra 1 oz. flour. Use 2 small eggs. *For the filling:* 4 oz. ($\frac{1}{2}$C) butter or margarine; 8 oz. (1$\frac{3}{4}$C) sieved icing sugar; grated rind 1 orange; little orange juice. *For the icing:* 6 oz. (1$\frac{1}{4}$C) icing sugar; little orange juice; pink colouring; few crystallised orange slices; little pieces of angelica.

Make the sponge as the Blue Print, but mix the orange juice with the beaten eggs and bake in 7-inch tins. When the cakes are cool, split to give 4 layers. Cream the butter or margarine and icing sugar, add the orange rind and enough juice to make the consistency of a thick whipped cream. Sandwich the cakes together with most of this, top with the icing made by blending the sugar with enough orange juice to give a soft spreading consistency and 2 or 3 drops of colouring. When firm, pipe rosettes of the remaining butter icing and decorate with portions of crystallised orange slices and little pieces of angelica.

Walnut Layer Cake

Method of mixing cake as Blue Print, but use 6 oz. ($\frac{3}{4}$C) margarine or cooking fat; 6 oz. ($\frac{3}{4}$C) caster sugar; 3 large eggs; 6 oz. (1$\frac{1}{2}$C) self-raising flour (or plain flour and 1$\frac{1}{2}$ teaspoons baking powder).

Make the cake as the Blue Print, but bake in two 7–8-inch sandwich tins for about 20–25 minutes. Make vanilla butter icing with 8 oz. (1C) butter, etc. (see page 124). Use two-thirds of this to sandwich the cake and coat the sides, then roll the sides in chopped walnuts. Spread the rest of the butter icing on top of the cake and mark neatly with a skewer,

Butterfly cake

then decorate with glacé cherries. (Illustrated on page 41.)

Butterfly Cakes

The basis of these cakes is a small plain sponge cake, which can be made exactly as the Blue Print but as you wish the little cakes to rise into peaks it is better to use only 3 oz. ($\frac{3}{8}$C) margarine to give a firmer texture. The sugar can be reduced to 3 oz. ($\frac{3}{8}$C) if wished or left as the Blue Print. Put the mixture into about 12–15 well greased and floured patty tins or into paper cake cases. Bake for about 10–12 minutes towards the top of a moderately hot to hot oven, 400–425°F, Gas Mark 5–6. When cold cut off the tops, pipe or spread a little butter icing (see page 124) or whipped cream on top of the cakes. Halve the slices removed, press into the icing or cream to form 'wings'. Dust with sieved icing sugar if wished. *Makes 12–15.*

Orange layer cake

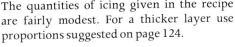

More Cakes by the Creaming Method

The cakes shown in the picture on this page were made with soft table margarine and by the speedy, one stage method described on page 118 and in the Blue Print. To compensate for the very short creaming period extra baking powder is added. In both the Mocha Torte and Lemon and Honey cake the extra amount is slightly less than the usual 1 teaspoon to each 4 oz. (1C) flour, this is to ensure that the cake rises with an *even flat* surface for perfect icing.

Blue Print Recipe

One Stage Mixes

Choose quick creaming margarine or fat.

Choose a large mixing bowl for easy beating.

Put in *all* the ingredients (or ingredients as specified in the recipe).

If creaming by hand use a wooden spoon, beat gently for about ½ minute so the flour etc. does not 'fly' out of the bowl, when blended increase the beating action. If using an electric mixer switch to the lowest speed until the ingredients are blended, then use medium speed.

Honey and Lemon Cake

For the cake: 6 oz. (¾C) quick creaming margarine or fat; 5–6 oz. (⅝–¾C) caster sugar; 3 large eggs; 1 tablespoon clear honey; 6 oz. (1½C) self-raising flour and 1 level teaspoon baking powder (with plain flour use 2½ level teaspoons baking powder); few drops almond essence. *For the icing:* 4 oz. (½C) quick creaming margarine; 8 oz. (nearly 2C) sieved icing sugar; generous tablespoon lemon juice. *To decorate:* few blanched almonds; angelica; violet petals or mimosa balls.

Put the margarine, sugar, eggs and honey into the mixing bowl. Sieve the flour and baking powder into the bowl, add the essence. Beat until smooth. Grease and flour, or line two 7–8-inch sandwich tins with greased greaseproof paper. Divide the mixture between the two tins, bake just above the centre of a very moderate to moderate oven 325–350°F. Gas Mark 3–4 for approximately 30–35 minutes until firm. Turn out and allow to cool.

Note: Choose a lower temperature than for Victoria Sandwich because of the honey content.

Beat the ingredients for the icing together and use half to sandwich the cakes together. Spread the remaining icing on top of the cake. Decorate as in the photograph, forming flower petals with the almonds, leaves and stalks with the angelica and flower centres with pieces of violet petals or mimosa balls.

To vary Omit the almond essence from the cake and add the finely grated rind of 2 lemons or 2 oranges.

Omit a little icing sugar and add 1–2 teaspoons honey in the icing.

Use orange juice to flavour the icing instead of lemon juice.

The quantities of icing given in the recipe are fairly modest. For a thicker layer use proportions suggested on page 124.

Mocha Torte

For the cake: 3 oz. (⅜C) quick creaming margarine or fat; 3 oz. (½C) soft brown sugar; 3 large eggs; 2 tablespoons sweetened coffee essence; 3 oz. (¾C) self-raising flour and 1 level teaspoon baking powder (with plain flour use 1¾ level teaspoons baking powder); 3 oz. digestive biscuits. *For the icing:* 4 oz. (½C) quick creaming margarine; 12 oz. (nearly 3C) sieved icing sugar; 3 oz. (¾C) sieved cocoa; 5 tablespoons hot water. *To decorate:* few digestive biscuits.

Put the margarine or fat, sugar, eggs and coffee essence into the mixing bowl. Sieve the flour and baking powder into the bowl, add the coarsly crushed biscuits, beat together until smooth. Line the bottoms of three 7-inch sandwich tins with greaseproof paper, grease and flour the tins. Divide the mixture between the tins, bake in, or near, the centre of a very moderate oven, 325°F, Gas Mark 3 for about 20–25 minutes until firm. Cool for 5 minutes, turn out carefully, allow to cool.

To make the icing beat all the ingredients together. Sandwich the cakes together with about ⅓ of the mixture. Spread another ⅓ round the sides of the cake and roll in finely crushed digestive biscuit crumbs. Spread the top of the cake with most of the remaining icing. Pipe a design, as shown in the picture, with a star pipe and decorate with the biscuit crumbs.

Primrose Cakes

For the cakes: 6 oz. (¾C) quick creaming margarine or fat; 6 oz. (¾C) caster sugar; 3 large eggs; 6 oz. (1½C) self-raising flour and 1½ level teaspoons baking powder (with plain flour use 3 level teaspoons baking powder). *For the icing:* 3 oz. (⅜C) quick creaming margarine; 8 oz. (nearly 2C) sieved icing sugar; 1 tablespoon milk. *To decorate:* 2 oz. (¾C) desiccated coconut; few drops green colouring; 18 mimosa balls or silver balls.

Mix the ingredients for the cake together, then put into an oblong tin approximately 11 × 7-inches lined with greased greaseproof paper and bake as the Honey and Lemon cake, on this page, for about 25 minutes until firm. Turn out and cool then cut into 18 rounds with a 2-inch cutter (any pieces left may be used in a trifle). Beat the ingredients for the icing together. Colour the coconut by blending the green colouring into this. Allow to dry for an hour before using. Coat the sides of the cakes in some of the icing, then in the coconut.

Pipe a design on top of the cakes with the rest of the icing, as shown in the picture, and decorate with the mimosa balls. *Makes 18.*

Honey and lemon cake, Mocha torte and Primrose cakes

Whisking Method of Making Cakes

The sponges made by this method are often considered the only 'true' sponges.

Blue Print Recipe

Sponge Sandwich

3 large eggs · 3–4 oz. ($\frac{3}{8}$–$\frac{1}{2}$C) caster sugar · 3 oz. ($\frac{3}{4}$C) flour*.

*So much air has been beaten into the eggs and sugar that raising agent is really unnecessary, but you can use self-raising flour if wished.

To make Put the eggs and sugar (the larger quantity produces a lighter sponge) into a basin and whisk hard until a thick mixture. You should see the mark of the whisk. Sieve the flour very well, then fold into the whisked eggs with a metal spoon or palette knife. The mixture should flow readily, so if it seems a little stiff add up to a tablespoon hot water or flavouring (see below). Divide between two 7–8-inch well-greased and floured sandwich tins or tins lined with greased greaseproof paper. If preferred coat the tins with fat then with an equal amount of caster sugar and flour.

To cook Bake above the centre of a moderately hot oven, 400°F, Gas Mark 5–6, for approximately 15 minutes. If preferred bake in one prepared cake tin for 30–35 minutes in the centre of a very moderate to moderate oven, 325–350°F, Gas Mark 3–4. Cool for 2–3 minutes before turning out of the tins or tin. When cold sandwich the sponges with jam or jam and cream, or split the one cake if wished and fill.

To serve With tea or coffee or as a dessert, particularly suitable when filled with cream and fruit.

● **AVOID** *Overhandling the flour when blending the ingredients. It must be folded carefully into the eggs and sugar.*

● **TO RECTIFY** *There is no remedy for a sponge where the flour has been over-beaten. You are sure to have a rather heavy 'tight' texture, instead of a light one.*

● **SHORT CUT** *Make use of the packet sponges which do produce very acceptable results.*

Orange Sponge

Ingredients as Blue Print PLUS finely grated rind of 1–2 oranges and 1 tablespoon hot orange juice. *To fill and decorate:* orange marmalade or orange curd; $\frac{1}{2}$ pint (1$\frac{1}{3}$C) thick cream; little sugar; Curaçao (optional); crystallised orange slices.

Make the sponge as the Blue Print, but add the orange rind to the eggs and sugar, and fold the hot orange juice in after the flour. Bake as the Blue Print. When cold, fill with marmalade or orange curd and a little whipped cream. Sweeten the remainder of the cream and flavour with a few drops of Curaçao if liked. Pipe round the edge of the sponge as shown in the picture. Decorate with the orange slices.

Lemon Sponge

As the Orange Sponge, but use lemon rind and juice, fill with lemon curd and cream and decorate with fresh lemon slices. If wishing to flavour the cream use an apricot brandy.

Chocolate Sponge

Ingredients as Blue Print MINUS 1 tablespoon flour and PLUS 1 tablespoon cocoa sieved

Orange and lemon sponges

with the flour. Fill with chocolate butter icing or cream.

Coffee Sponge

Ingredients as Blue Print but use 1 tablespoon very strong hot coffee instead of the hot water in the Blue Print.

Sponge Flan

Use the same method of making as the Blue Print, but use only 1 egg etc., for a 6–7-inch flan tin or 2 eggs etc., for an 8–9-inch flan tin. Bake as the sandwich in the Blue Print, allowing about 10–12 minutes. Turn out, allow to cool, then fill with fruit and glaze as a fruit flan made with pastry (see page 99).

Storing and Freezing *The sponge should be cooked as soon as possible after mixing. The cooked sponge tends to dry if kept more than 1 or 2 days, but freezes well.*

To use any left over *Any stale sponge is excellent for making trifles.*

Cooking with yeast is most rewarding, for it produces delicious buns and bread with the minimum of expenditure. Many people feel it takes a very long time to prepare, but for most of the time the yeast mixture is rising or 'proving' and you have nothing to do but leave it until it is ready.

Cooking with Yeast

Blue Print Recipe

White Bread

3 lb. strong PLAIN white flour*· 3–7 teaspoons salt**· 1 oz. fresh yeast · 1 teaspoon sugar · approximately 1½ pints (4C) tepid water.

*It is possible to buy strong flour now and this is worth using, since it gives a better texture to bread.

**The first time you make bread use the smaller quantity of salt until you are sure how much you like. Remember refined table salt is less strong than cooking salt.

To make Sieve the flour and salt into a warm bowl. Cream the yeast with the sugar, add *most of the liquid*. Make a well in the centre of the bowl of flour, pour in the yeast liquid and sprinkle flour on top. Cover the bowl with a clean cloth and leave for about 20 minutes, until the surface is covered with bubbles. Mix the liquid with the flour, if too dry then add sufficient tepid liquid to give an elastic dough. Turn out of the bowl on to a floured board and knead until smooth (see below for method of testing this). Either put back into the bowl and cover with a cloth or put into a large greased polythene bag. Leave to rise until almost double the original size. Turn on to the board again and knead. Form into the shaped loaves you like, for the tin loaf illustrated grease, flour and warm the tins. Form the dough into an oblong shape, fold into three to fit the tin and lower into the tin. The dough should come just over half-way up the tins. If you brush the loaves

with a little melted fat or oil it produces an excellent crust. Covers the tins with a cloth or polythene, allow to rise for 20 minutes.

To cook Bake for about 20–25 minutes in the centre of a hot oven, 425–450°F, Gas Mark 6–7, after this lower the heat to very moderate and complete cooking. A 1 lb. tin loaf takes a total of about 35–40 minutes.

To test Turn the loaves out of the tins; knock firmly on the base, the bread should sound hollow. If it does not, return to the oven for a little longer. *Makes 3 loaves.*

To vary

Richer bread Use half milk and half water and rub 1–2 oz. fat into the flour.

Milk loaf Use all milk for mixing, plus an egg if wished and rub 2 oz. butter or margarine into the flour.

Brown bread Use half white and half wholemeal flour.

Wholemeal bread Use all wholemeal flour but this absorbs more liquid.

● **AVOID** *Putting the yeast mixture in too warm a position, room temperature is generally ideal: Over-kneading the dough.*

● **TO RECTIFY** *If you have put the dough in too hot a place you have 'killed' the yeast too early and the dough will not rise. Test to see if you have kneaded sufficiently, then* stop. *The way to test is to press with a lightly floured finger; if the impression comes out the dough is ready for the next stage.*

● **SHORT CUT** *One can buy risen, partially cooked bread doughs.*

● **TO USE DRIED YEAST** *Allow half the quantity of fresh yeast (½ oz. dried yeast = 1 oz. fresh yeast). Mix the sugar with the tepid liquid. Sprinkle the yeast on top, wait for about 10 minutes, stir well then proceed as fresh yeast.*

Lardy Bread

Ingredients as the Blue Print using 1 lb. flour, etc. PLUS a little lard, sugar and dried fruit. Roll the risen dough out to an oblong shape. Spread with a very thin layer of softened lard, about 1 oz., the same amount of sugar

and some dried fruit. Fold just as in puff pastry then repeat this once or twice more adding the lard, sugar and fruit. Form into required loaf shape and score the top. Bake as the Blue Print, but allow a little longer cooking time. (Illustrated on page 111.)

Bun Dough

Most small buns are made as the Blue Print, but to each 1 lb. flour rub in about 2 oz. (¼C) fat, add about 2 oz. (¼C) sugar and mix with an egg and enough tepid liquid to bind.

Soft Topped Baps

Ingredients as the Blue Print PLUS a little milk and flour for topping.

Make the dough as the Blue Print; be quite sure it is a soft consistency. Allow it to 'prove' in bulk as the Blue Print but form into small rounds instead of a loaf. Put on to warmed, lightly greased baking trays. Press these slightly with your hand to flatten, brush with milk and sprinkle with flour. Allow to 'prove' for about 15 minutes. Bake for about 12 minutes towards the top of a hot oven.

Fruit Loaf

Ingredients and method as Blue Print but add 2–4 oz. (¼–½C—good measure) dried fruit to the flour.

Fruit Malt Loaf

Ingredients and method as Blue Print PLUS 1–2 tablespoons powdered malt and 2–4 oz. (¼–½C—good measure) added to the flour. (Illustrated on page 111.)

Storing and Freezing *This is a somewhat complex subject so consult your freezer book but you can store the unproven dough overnight in the refrigerator where it will begin to rise slowly or you can freeze both unbaked and baked yeast breads.*

To use any left over *Stale bread can be freshened by heating in the oven or by dipping quickly in a little liquid if very stale and heating in the oven.*

Scones and Muffins

There are few things more delicious than a feather-light, freshly baked scone, topped with plenty of butter.

Blue Print Recipe

Plain Scones

8 oz. (2C) flour* · good pich salt · 1 oz. margarine or cooking fat · milk to mix.**

*Either use self-raising flour or plain flour with 3–4 level teaspoons baking powder or plain flour with $\frac{1}{2}$ teaspoon bicarbonate of soda and 1 teaspoon cream of tartar. The amounts of baking powder added to plain flour are more than the raising agent in self-raising flour, so you *can* add 1–2 teaspoons baking powder to self-raising flour for a lighter scone. Remember that the greater amount of baking powder gives a very well risen scone, but I find it crisps less, so you can choose the type you wish.

**If you have buttermilk or sour milk, use plain flour and only the cream of tartar.

To make Sieve the flour or flour and raising agent with the salt. Rub in the margarine or fat, then blend with milk to a soft rolling consistency. The dough will make your fingers slightly sticky as you handle it. Turn out of the bowl on to a lightly floured pastry board and roll out to about $\frac{1}{2}$–$\frac{3}{4}$-inch in thickness. Cut into triangles or rounds, or make one round as

the picture on page 111. Lift the small scones or round on to an ungreased baking tray or sheet. Mark the round into 8 sections.

To cook Bake small scones towards the top of a hot to very hot oven, 450–475°F, Gas Mark 7–8, for about 10–12 minutes until firm to the touch. The scone round should be baked in the centre of the oven for about 20 minutes. Reduce the heat to moderately hot after 10–12 minutes.

To serve When fresh, with butter or whipped cream and jam. *All recipes based on this make 8–12 scones.*

To vary

Sweet Scones Add 1–2 oz. ($\frac{1}{8}$–$\frac{1}{4}$C) sugar. This not only gives flavour, but helps crisp the scones.

Fruit Scones Add sugar as above, plus 2–3 tablespoons dried fruit.

Flavoured Scones Add a little spice, grated lemon rind, etc. to the flour to flavour the mixture.

Cream Scones Mix with 1 egg and thin cream instead of milk.

Cheese Scones Add a generous amount of seasoning to the flour and 3–4 tablespoons finely grated cheese.

● **AVOID** *Making the mixture, or any tea-breads based on a scone dough, too dry; the mixture should be slightly sticky (see Blue Print): Baking too slowly.*

● **TO RECTIFY** *If the mixture is too dry be sure to add a little extra liquid: See baking instructions in Blue Print.*

● **SHORT CUT** *The scone round shown on page 111 is very speedy to prepare, although it takes longer to cook than small scones.*

Fruit Loaf

Ingredients as the Blue Print PLUS 1 teaspoon mixed spice, 2 oz. ($\frac{1}{4}$C) sugar, 1 tablespoon golden syrup and about 4 oz. ($\frac{1}{2}$C) dried fruit.

Method as Blue Print, the spice should be sieved with the flour and the sugar, golden syrup and fruit added after rubbing-in the fat. Add enough milk to make a slightly stickier dough than for the scones. Put into a well greased and floured 1$\frac{1}{2}$-lb. loaf tin and bake in the centre of a moderate oven, 350–375°F, Gas Mark 4–5, for approximately 40 minutes. Lower the heat to very moderate after about 25 minutes. Use while fresh, spread with butter.

Popovers

Although these do not resemble a scone, they are delicious served hot with butter or butter and jam or syrup or topped with savoury ingredients.

Ingredients as Blue Print opposite, PLUS 1 extra egg, and use $\frac{3}{8}$ pint (1C) milk in place of $\frac{1}{4}$ pint ($\frac{2}{3}$C), and 2 teaspoons oil or melted butter.

Make the batter as the Blue Print opposite. Add the oil just before cooking. Grease really deep patty tins, custard cups or proper Popover tins and heat them for a few minutes in a hot oven, 425–450°F, Gas Mark 6–7. Half fill with the batter and bake in a hot oven for about 20 minutes, then lower the heat to very moderate and cook for a further 15–20 minutes until really crisp and brown. Serve hot immediately. *Makes 8–12.*

Bran and Nut Muffins

3 oz.—poor weight (1C) bran; 1 large egg; $\frac{3}{8}$ pint (1C) milk; 4 oz. (1C) plain flour with 2 teaspoons baking powder (or use self-raising flour with 1 teaspoon baking powder); pinch salt; 2 oz. ($\frac{1}{4}$C) sugar; 1 oz. melted butter; 2–3 tablespoons chopped pecans or walnuts. Make a batter with the bran, egg and milk. Allow to stand for 15 minutes. Beat in the sieved flour, baking powder and salt, then add the rest of the ingredients. Grease deep patty tins or muffin tins. Bake in the centre of a moderate to moderately hot oven, 375–400°F, Gas Mark 5–6, for about 20 minutes until firm. Serve hot or cold with butter. *Makes about 12–16.*

Storing and Freezing *The batter for the Scotch pancakes and the uncooked scones on this page may be stored in a refrigerator overnight before baking. All the scones freeze well when cooked. The popovers and muffins do not freeze quite as well.*

To use any left over *Left over scones, as on this page, can be freshened if you dip them in a little milk then heat in the oven for a few minutes. Otherwise split and toast. The Scotch pancakes on the opposite page should be eaten when fresh.*

Popovers

There are many kinds of scones and all of them are delicious to serve with tea or coffee, or to take on picnics or packed meals.

The Blue Print is for one of the oldest types of scone, i.e. a Scotch Pancake or Drop or Dropped scone (often called a Flapjack or Griddle pancake).

Blue Print Recipe

Scotch Pancakes

4 oz. (1C) flour* · pinch salt · 1 egg · $\frac{1}{4}$ pint ($\frac{2}{3}$C) milk or milk and water · very little fat.

*Use either self-raising flour or plain flour with 1 level teaspoon baking powder or plain flour with $\frac{1}{4}$ level teaspoon bicarbonate of soda and $\frac{1}{2}$ level teaspoon cream of tartar.

To make Sieve the flour or flour and raising agent well with the salt. Add the egg and beat, then gradually whisk in the milk until a smooth batter.

To cook The old-fashioned griddle (sometimes called a girdle or bakestone) has become difficult to find, but modern versions are being made. The alternatives are to use a solid hotplate on an electric cooker (again becoming less plentiful with modern type cookers) or a frying pan. If the frying pan is heavy then use in the normal way, but if light-weight the scones are inclined to burn and I find the best thing is to turn the frying pan upside-down and cook the scones on the base. Grease the griddle or substitute and

Scotch pancakes

warm. Test by dropping a teaspoon of the batter mixture on to the warm plate and the batter should set almost at once and begin to bubble within 1 minute. If this does not happen then heat a little longer before cooking the scones.

Drop from the tablespoon on to the griddle and cook for 1–2 minutes until the top surface is covered with bubbles (as shown in the picture). Put a palette knife under the scone and turn carefully and cook for the same time on the second side. To test if cooked, press gently with the edge of the knife and if no batter 'oozes out' then the scones are cooked. Lift on to a clean teacloth on a wire cooling tray and wrap in the cloth until ready to serve.

To serve Either cold with butter or warm topped with butter and jam, or cooked, well

drained, fruit or syrup, as a quick and easy dessert. They are also excellent if served with cooked sausages and beans as a supper snack. *All recipes based on this make 10–12.*

To vary Add 1 tablespoon cooled, melted butter or other fat to the batter just before cooking.

● **AVOID** *Making the batter too wet, otherwise the mixture spreads too much: Cooking too slowly.*
● **TO RECTIFY** *Add a little more flour if you have been generous with the liquid: Test heat of griddle, or pan, as described above.*

Buttermilk Pancakes

Ingredients as Blue Print using plain flour and bicarbonate of soda but MINUS the cream of tartar and using buttermilk or sour milk in place of milk or milk and water. Make and cook as the Blue Print.

Oatmeal Griddle Pancakes

Method as Blue Print but use half flour and half quick-cooking rolled oats. Allow the batter to stand for several hours before cooking as the Blue Print. A tablespoon sugar can be added if wished.

The recipes on this page can turn a simple Victoria sandwich (page 118) or light sponge (page 120) into a special gâteau. The Royal icing opposite is ideal for rich fruit cakes.

● **AVOID** *Using too heavy or stiff an icing on these delicate cakes, for they would break the sponge and make it difficult to cut.*
● **TO RECTIFY** *While one cannot change a firm icing, such as Royal icing, it is possible to make other icings softer in texture so they do not break the cake.*
● **SHORT CUT** *Do not bother to sieve the icing sugar for simple glacé or water icings (unless in very hard lumps), if mixed with the liquid and allowed to stand for a while the icing will be quite smooth. The icing sugar must be sieved for other icings though.*

Choice for Fillings and Toppings

Use whipped cream, flavoured with a little vanilla and sweetened, as either a filling or topping.
Another excellent filling for light cakes (as well as pastries) is the Vanilla Cream, below. This is rarely used as a topping.
Butter icing is not only ideal to pipe on light cakes, but is excellent for fillings too.
American frosting, below, is equally good as a filling and topping for sponges as for fruit cakes.
Glacé or water icing is one of the best toppings for light cakes, but is rarely chosen for a filling.

Blue Print Recipes

1. Water or Glacé Icing

In this simple icing, the icing sugar is blended with liquid (often just water) and colouring and flavouring, if desired. The consistency varies slightly, the icing shown in the picture on page 111 was sufficiently soft to 'trickle' down the sides, but generally it should be slightly stiffer.

To 8 oz. (1¾C) icing sugar use about ¾–1 tablespoon liquid for a firm mixture, or 1½–2 tablespoons for a very soft consistency. Blend the icing sugar with cold liquid or

Coating the sides of the cake.

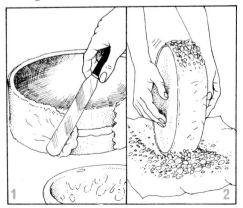

Icings & Fillings

Mocha hazel-nut gâteau

heat the liquid and sugar in a pan over a gentle heat for a better gloss.
Flavourings can be given by using orange, or other fruit juice, or coffee instead of water or adding a little cocoa, chocolate or essences.
The quantity given above would coat the top of an 8-inch cake.

2. Butter Icing

This is made by creaming butter, margarine or fat with *sieved* icing sugar and flavouring. To 4 oz. (½C) butter or other fat allow 4 oz. (nearly 1C) icing sugar and flavouring for a soft butter icing, or up to 8 oz. (1¾C) icing sugar for a firmer texture.
Flavouring is given by adding very finely grated fruit rind (with a very little juice if wished), or instant coffee powder, or strong coffee or coffee essence, or chocolate or cocoa. Always add liquids gradually to prevent curdling.
The quantity above is enough to give a good layer of filling *or* topping for an 8-inch cake. If making butter icing for coating and filling you may like to be less generous with the amounts. The Mocha Gâteau pictured on this page uses coffee butter icing for filling and topping.

Mocha Hazel-nut Gâteau

6 oz. (¾C) butter or margarine; 6 oz. (¾C) caster sugar; 3 large eggs; 5 oz. (1¼C) self-raising flour (with plain flour use 1¼ tea-spoons baking powder); ½ oz. cocoa; 1½ oz. very finely chopped hazel-nuts; 1 tablespoon strong coffee. *For the filling:* 10–12 oz. (1¼–1½C) butter or margarine; 1–1¼ lb. (3½–4½C) sieved icing sugar; 1–1½ tablespoons coffee essence or very strong coffee; 3–4 table-spoons chopped hazel-nuts; whole hazel-nuts to decorate.

Cream the butter or margarine and sugar, gradually add the beaten eggs, then fold in the sieved flour or flour and baking powder and cocoa. Add the chopped hazel-nuts and coffee. (For details of the creaming method see page 118.) Divide between two 8–8½-inch greased and floured sandwich tins and bake for 20–25 minutes above the centre of a moderate oven, 350–375°F, Gas Mark 4–5, until firm to the touch. Turn out carefully. Allow to cool. Make the butter icing as Blue Print 2 (the variation in amounts depends on the thickness and firmness preferred). Use about ¼ of the mixture to sandwich the cakes together and another ¼ to coat the sides, see Sketch 1. Roll the cake in the chopped nuts, see Sketch 2, then cover the cake with some of the remaining icing sugar and pipe rosettes on top with the last of the icing. Decorate with whole hazel-nuts.

Vanilla Cream

¾ oz. flour; ½ oz. cornflour; ½ pint (1⅓C) milk; vanilla pod or ½–1 teaspoon vanilla essence; 2 oz. (¼C) caster sugar; 1 oz. butter; 1 whole egg or 2 egg yolks; 1 tablespoon thick cream or milk.
Blend the flour and cornflour with the cold milk, put into a saucepan with the vanilla pod or essence and cook gently, stirring well, until thickened. Add the sugar and butter as the mixture begins to stiffen. Remove the pan from the heat, take out the vanilla pod (rinse in cold water and dry). Blend the egg or yolks with the cream or milk, add to the mixture in the pan and cook gently for several minutes without boiling. Stir from time to time as the mixture cools to prevent a skin forming. If wished, blend in ¼ pint (⅔C) lightly whipped cream when the filling is cold. This is also known as Confectioners Custard or Crême Patissière.
The quantity above fills about 12 good-size pastries or would provide 2 thick or 3 thinner layers in a layer cake.

American Frosting

In this icing it is essential to heat to the correct temperature. If you have a sugar thermometer then use that, otherwise have a basin of cold water for testing.
Stir 8 oz. (1C) granulated sugar and 4 tablespoons water over a low heat until the sugar has dissolved. Add a pinch cream of tartar then boil steadily until the mixture reaches 238–240°F. Choose the lower temperature for a smooth coating icing and the higher temperature when you wish the icing to stand in peaks, or if the weather is very damp. To test without the thermometer drop a little of the icing into cold water; when ready it should form a soft ball. Beat the syrup in the pan until slightly cloudy, then pour on to 1 stiffly beaten egg white and beat well. Pile the icing over the top of the cake, either smooth flat or sweep up in peaks. The quantity above is enough to give a good topping on a 6–7-inch cake.

Blue Print Recipes
1. Marzipan

Although there are many variations of this recipe (you can increase the amount of sugar and decrease the quantity of ground almonds), the recipe I prefer is to blend 8 oz. (2C) ground almonds with 4 oz. (½C) caster sugar, 4 oz. (nearly 1C) sieved icing sugar, a few drops almond essence and 2 egg yolks or 1 large whole egg to bind. You can use a little less egg and some sherry. The marzipan is then rolled out on a sugared board and put on to the cake as shown in the sketches. The secret is *not* to over handle the marzipan; if you do the natural oils from the almonds 'seep through' the icing and spoil the colour. If you handle the marzipan lightly you may ice the cake at once; if you feel it has been kneaded and rolled rather firmly then allow it to 'dry out' for 48 hours before putting on the icing.

The quantity above is sufficient to coat the top and sides of a 7½–8-inch round cake (about 2½-inches in depth).

The easiest way to calculate the amount of marzipan required is to take the *total* weight of the cake, then allow *half* this weight in marzipan.

Marzipan trimmings left from coating the cake may be coloured and used to decorate the top of the cake.

2. Royal Icing

This is the icing used on the wedding cake pictured on this page. It is essential to sieve the icing sugar. Do not over-beat, particularly in a mixer, for if you do you have large 'air bubbles' which spoil the smoothness of

Traditional two-tiered wedding cake

the icing. Beat only until the mixture stands in soft peaks (for coating) and firm peaks (for piping).

Blend 1 lb. (good 3½C) sieved icing sugar with 2 lightly beaten egg whites and ½–1 tablespoon lemon juice. To give a less hard icing add up to 1 teaspoon glycerine or use only 1 egg white and a little water to blend. If using water do not try and pipe the icing. The quantity above is sufficient to give one coating only on a 7–7½-inch round cake—with none left for piping.

The cake shown on this page would need Royal icing made with 5 lb. icing sugar, etc. This would allow for two coats of icing and the piping as shown.

Storing and Freezing *Icings harden with storage, and this makes them difficult to spread or pipe. Always cover bowls of icing with damp paper and keep surplus marzipan in a polythene bag or foil. Butter icings freeze well and many people find it an excellent idea to store small containers of different flavoured butter icings. Cakes coated with glacé icing and American frosting can be frozen, but Royal icing keeps well without freezing.*

To use any left over *Any icing left can be used at a later date, if well covered, see above. Frosting tends to lose its fluffy texture if handled again so it is better to use all of this after making.*

2. Brush the sides of the cake with sieved apricot jam or egg white.

. Roll out the marzipan. Cut a round the size of the top of the cake and band the depth and circumference of the cake.

3. Roll the cake along the strip of marzipan.

4. Brush the top of the cake and put on the round of marzipan.

5. Roll the top of the cake lightly. Roll the sides of the cake with a jam jar.

6. Brush the marzipan with egg white to form a 'seal'.

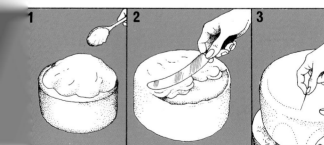

To coat the cake with icing, put the total amount for the first coating i.e. about ⅓ on the cake.

2. Spread out until evenly coated with a palette knife or icing spatula.

3. Let the first coat dry before putting on the second coat and when this is dry 'prick out' the design with a fine needle.

4. Pipe the design with a fine rose or star pipe.

5. When dry pipe the borders, you could use the same pipe. Hold the bag at an angle as shown in the sketch.

6. To make flowers, put a piece of waxed paper on an icing nail. Pipe out the petals.

7. Place the flowers in position and stand the

top tier on the pillars. Complete the cake with a spray of real flowers and ribbon on top.

Complete Index